Clyde Shipwrecks

PETER MOIR AND IAN CRAWFORD

First published by **Moir Crawford** 1988
Second edition: April 1997
Third edition: May 2004

Moir Crawford
1 Cedar Walk
Wemyss Bay
Inverclyde
PA18 6BP

Tel: 01475-520141
Mobile: 07786 077935
email enquiries: moir.crawford1@btinternet.com

ISBN: 0 9513366 2 2

Printed by Cordfall Ltd Tel: 0141 572 0878

Disclaimer: This book is a catalogue of shipwrecks within the Firth of Clyde, and is intended for research and reference only. While there are details about the wrecks current condition and location, they are not an invitation to members of the public or other interested parties to dive on any of the sites mentioned. Any individual or group intending to dive on any of the sites included within this book should undertake adequate training, planning and give due consideration to appropriate safety precautions before undertaking any dive.

Cover photographs:

Front cover: The Cypriot coaster ***Craigantlet***. Photograph by Keith Allardyce, courtesy of the Keith Alladyce Collection, Scotland's Lighthouse Museum, Fraserburgh.

Rear cover: Top L/H: The SS ***Kathleen*** and SS ***Stromboli*** reproduced by kind permission of McLean Museum and Art Gallery, Inverclyde Council

Top Mid: *A sunny day in Gourock!* - reproduced with kind permission of McLean Museum and Art Gallery, Invercylde Council

Top R/H: The SS ***Princess Patricia*** ashore Arran.

Lower: The MV ***Captayannis*** off Helensburgh, 2003 - Peter Moir.

Contents

Author's Notes

Clyde Shipwrecks was first published in 1988 after an intensive 4 year period of detailed research and was our first attempt at writing and publishing books. In 1997 we revised and extended the book as a second edition and the book has continued to prove popular with our readers.

Since 1997 we have continued to research and locate new shipwrecks throughout the area, and have pleasure in releasing our third edition which includes a number of new shipwrecks as well as providing additional details of vessels which have been located since the book was first published.

We continue to provide locations for wrecks both with GPS location and where relevant small chartlet's, which give more focused information for divers and fishermen. Please note that all positions provided in the book, suffixed with (GPS), denotes that the position has been derived using a GPS receiver.

Books such as ***Clyde Shipwrecks*** and its companion ***Argyll Shipwrecks*** are essentially work in progress, and new finds both above and below the water will always provide further impetus to update and add to the current edition. New diving technologies and techniques are now allowing the suitably trained amateur diver to go to depths previously unattainable by the amateur diver breathing compressed air. These advances have opened up a whole new field of wrecks within the Clyde area, most notably in the Lower Firth. In recent years wrecks such as HMS *Dasher*, HMS *Sealion*, HMS *Vandal* and *U 33* have all been visited by experienced teams of divers wishing to explore these wrecks in challenging diving conditions.

Clyde Shipwrecks has proved extremely popular, with a wide and varied readership. The book has helped to publicise and develop the Clyde into one of the more popular dive destinations in Scotland, if not the UK. We will continue to research and explore shipwrecks in the area and welcome any additional information which the reader can provide to build a more complete record of shipwrecks within the region.

for
Philip and Craig

Photo Acknowledgements

Author's Collection - all uncredited photographs.

George W. Burrows - Puffer Ahoy, published by Brown, Son & Ferguson, Ltd - 74.
Dumfries & Galloway Regional Library Service - 163, 164, 177, 189, 190, 194, 195.
Glasgow Herald - 20, 76, 144, 145, 171, 197, 198.
Imperial War Museum - 39, 45, 96, 202.
South Ayrshire Council Library Services - 128.
McLean Museum and Art Gallery, Greenock - 30, 65, 66, 69, 81, 105, 191.
Mitchell Library, Glasgow City Libraries - 93, 107, 108, 109, 130, 204.
National Maritime Museum, London - 25, 69, 70, 80, 139, 140, 146, 152, 154,161, 165, 174, 203.
Noordelijk Scheepvaartmuseum, Groningen - 147
Scottish Maritime Museum, Irvine - 24 (2), 35, 57, 167.
Strathclyde Regional Archives, Glasgow - 34, 100.
Wigtown Free Press - 168.
World Ship Society - 14, 95, 111, 134, 205.
Mr. Colin Campbell - 142
Mr. John Clarkson - 106.
Mr. Mike Hughes - 59.
Mr. Tom Lang - 15.
Mr. Graham Langmuir - 60, 61, 67, 175, 182, 183, 185.
Dr. William Lind - 22, 37, 43, 99, 101, 102, 104, 112, 118, 121, 125, 137, 138, 149, 169.
Sir William Lithgow Bt. - 18.
Mr. Ian McCrorie - 26, 92, 110, 160.
Mrs. M. Mitchell, Portpatrick - 173.
Mr. Donnie Nelson - 153, 179, 187.
Mr. Philip Thomas - 46.

During research for this book, the authors have sought to trace and credit the source or ownership of all photographs included within the book. However, it is clear that many old photographs are duplicated among a number of collections, and it is often impossible to trace the original source. We would like to extend apologies to any person or persons, living or dead, whose work has been reproduced without their own or their estate's permission. No breach of copyright, if in existence at the time of publication was intended.

Acknowledgements

Many people have helped with the preparation and research for this book and we would like to thank those listed below for their particular contribution.

For their detailed knowledge on various aspects of Clyde shipping history: David Burrell, the late Graham Langmuir, Philip Thomas and Dr. William Lind of the Ballast Trust.

For their assistance in research through archive material: Mrs. Valerie Boa (McLean Museum, Greenock), Mrs. Lesley Couperwhite (Watt Library, Greenock), Mrs. Alma Topen (Glasgow City Archives), Mr. Bill Walker (Scottish Maritime Museum) and the staff of the Glasgow Room and Social Sciences Department, the Mitchell Library, Glasgow.

For their information, assistance and patience while researching, locating and diving on the wrecks mentioned in this book: Ian Campbell, John Crowther, Willie Dunlop, Peter Ingram, Donald Johnston, Glyn Jones, Tom Lang, Danny McEntee, John McWhirter, Donnie Nelson, Jimmy Pinkerton, Stuart Tamblin and Ian Whittaker.

A special mention must go to the members of Irvine Branch Scottish Sub-Aqua Club who have helped out on many of our diving expeditions.

For their patience and assistance: Joyce and Sheila.

Symbols and Abbreviations

Tonnage

dt	Displacement tonnage
nt	Net tonnage
gt	Gross tonnage
bn	Burden

Hull Material

I	Iron
S	Steel
W	Wood

Type of Vessel

SS	Steamship
PS	Paddlesteamer
S. Tr	Steam trawler
A. Tr	Admiralty trawler

Type of Vessel (contd)

A. Dr	Admiralty drifter
S. Tug	Steam tug
P. Tug	Paddle tug
Syt	Steam yacht
LCV	Landing craft
Drg	Dredger
A/c	Aircraft
S	Sailing ship, fully rigged
Bk	Barque
Bkn	Barquentine
Bg	Brig
Bn	Brigantine
K	Ketch
Sk	Smack
Sl	Sloop
Sr	Schooner
Yt	Yacht

Cause of Loss

A/c	Aircraft
S	Stranding
F	Foundering
C	Collision
T	Torpedo
M	Mine
Ex	Explosion (mechanical)
S/f	Stranded on fire

CHAPTER KEY

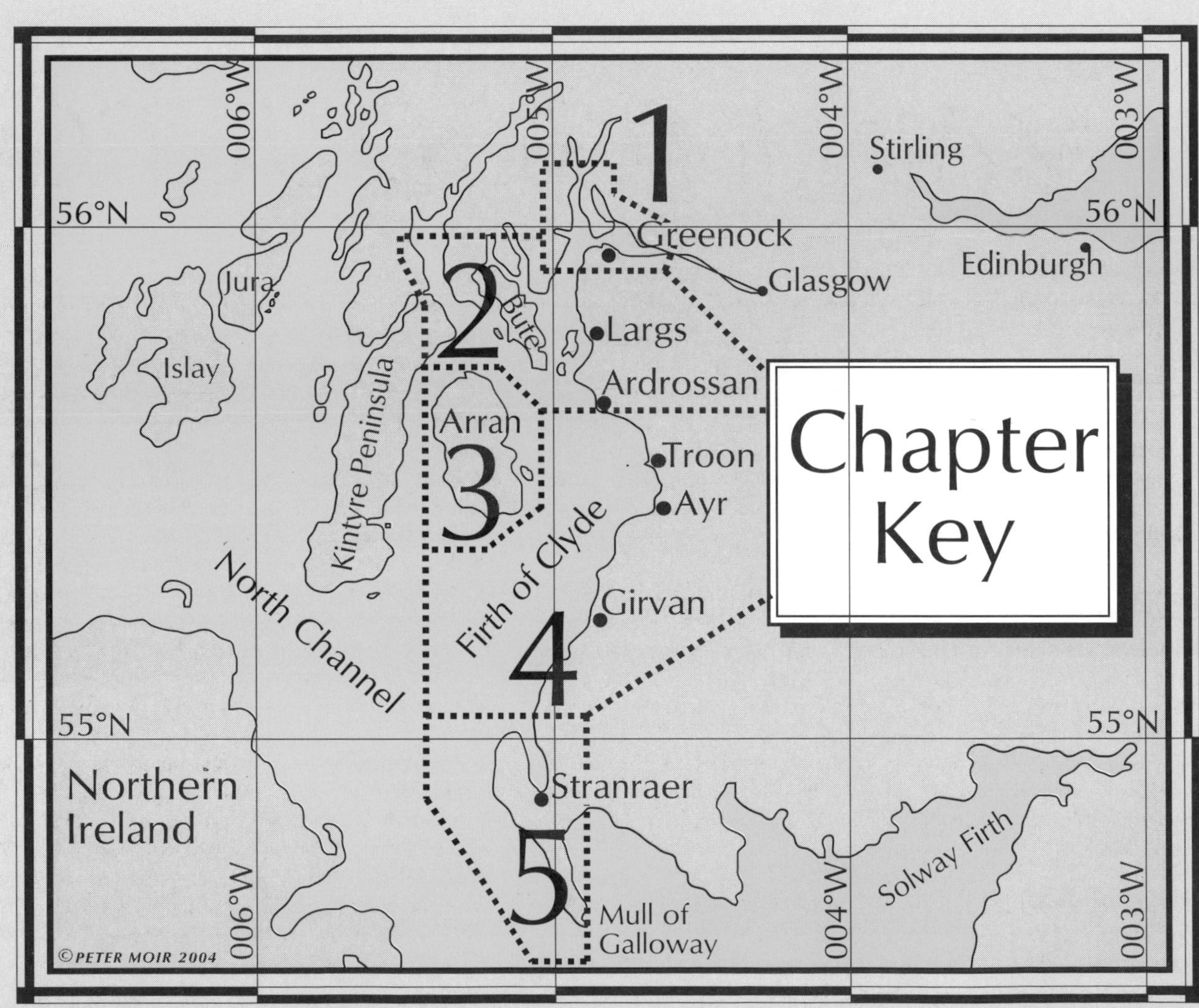

Chapter Key
1
2
3
4
5
56°N
55°N
006°W
005°W
004°W
003°W
Stirling
Greenock
Glasgow
Edinburgh
Jura
Islay
Bute
Largs
Ardrossan
Arran
Troon
Ayr
Kintyre Peninsula
Firth of Clyde
Girvan
North Channel
Northern Ireland
Stranraer
Mull of Galloway
Solway Firth
©PETER MOIR 2004

MAIN INTRODUCTION

For over a hundred years from the early nineteenth century to the middle of the twentieth century, the history of world shipping and the history of the River Clyde have been inextricably linked. The dozens of shipyards between Glasgow and Greenock saw many of the world's most famous ships launched from their slipways. Names such as *Lusitania*, *Empress of Britain*, *Queen Mary* and *Queen Elizabeth* are synonymous with Clyde shipbuilding, craftsmanship and quality. Sadly few yards remain today, and those that do, work in an extremely competitive world market.

The world's first commercial steamship service was inaugurated on the river in 1812 by Henry Bell in the *Comet* and interestingly, the world's last ocean going paddle steamer service, the *Waverley*, has plied the river's waters for many years. The Tail of the Bank, off Greenock, provided the Allies with one of their most important anchorages during the Second World War and saw the departure of thousands of troops and millions of tons of supplies for the battle fronts of Europe and Africa. Sadly the river, although still busy with pleasure craft and the odd tanker or cargo ship, is no longer the major commercial artery it was and most of the shipyards have closed. This illustrious river has, however, provided a fascinating, if tragic legacy - shipwrecks.

The small water triangle of the Firth of Clyde between Greenock, the Mull of Kintyre and the Mull of Galloway has seen hundreds of tragic incidents involving the loss of many vessels. The causes of loss range from war action to simple error. This book provides the history, details and locations of over three hundred of those wrecks. While written primarily for sub-aqua divers, the stories and locations are hoped to provide interesting reading for fishermen, steamer enthusiasts, shipping historians and anyone interested in the sea, shipping or the river itself. The many stories of courage and rescue by lifeboatmen, coastguards and the ordinary local people provide a fascinating insight into seafaring life over the last two hundred years.

The book is seperated into five chapters, each covering a geographical area from Greenock, south to the Mull of Galloway. While the Mull of Galloway is not strictly part of the Firth of Clyde, its strong links with the river and the many Clyde based ships which have foundered there justify its inclusion in this book. Each chapter is prefaced by a map showing the approximate location of each major wreck and ends with a list of smaller and older wrecks which could form the basis for further research by the interested reader. Many of the wrecks included were removed or have been heavily salvaged but have been included for completeness with details, where known, of their salvage.

While every effort has been made to establish the exact details of each ship and incident, it is impossible to guarantee the exact accuracy of every detail as the records of many are vague or misleading. The authors have visited the sites of all of the major wrecks included making this the most complete and accurate record of the dive sites in this area ever written. Where possible the positions given have been established using the GPS satellite location system and are indicated as such. We hope you enjoy the book as much as we have enjoyed researching it!

Peter Moir & Ian Crawford
May 2004.

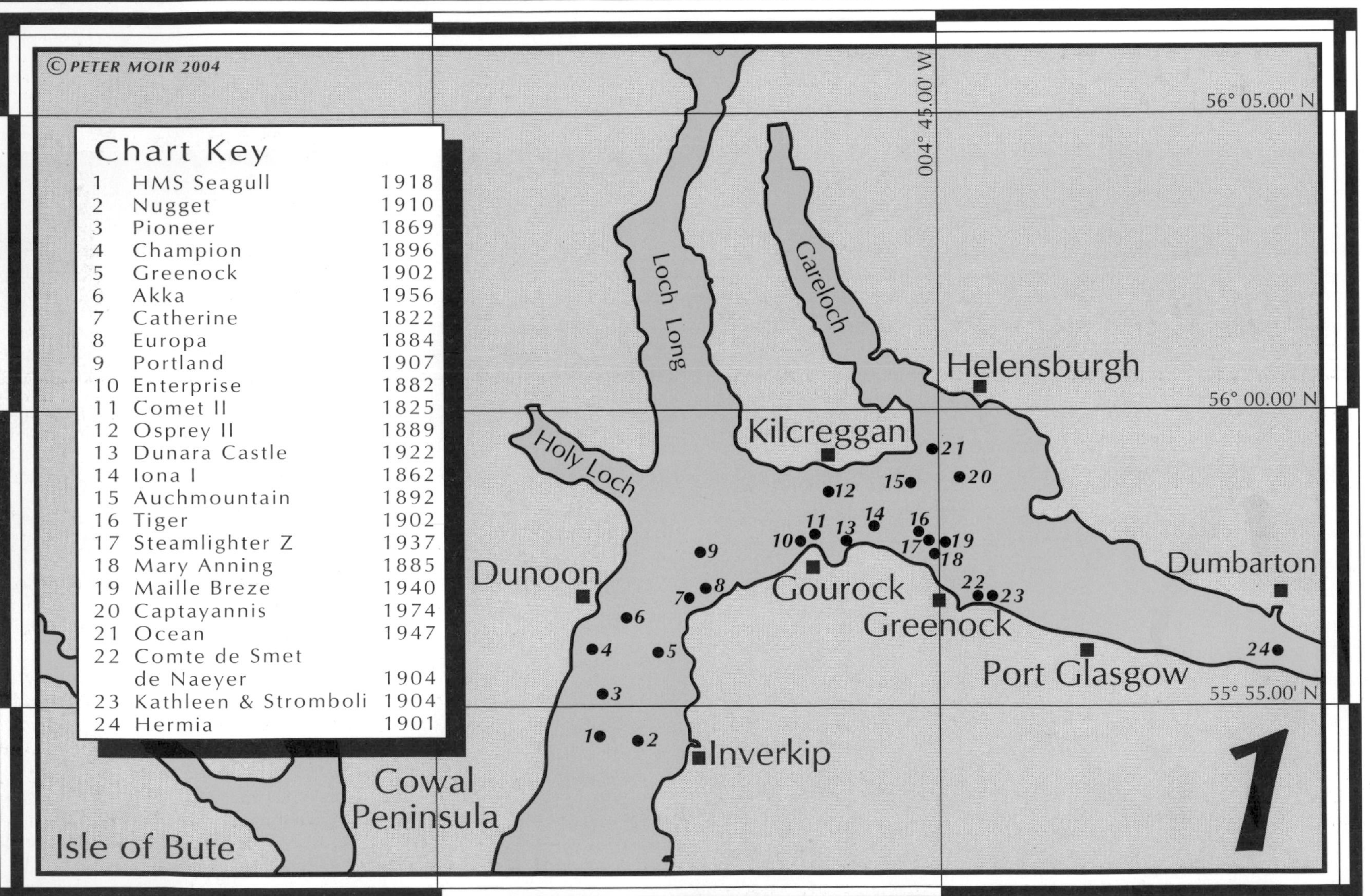
© PETER MOIR 2004
Chart Key
1 HMS Seagull 1918
2 Nugget 1910
3 Pioneer 1869
4 Champion 1896
5 Greenock 1902
6 Akka 1956
7 Catherine 1822
8 Europa 1884
9 Portland 1907
10 Enterprise 1882
11 Comet II 1825
12 Osprey II 1889
13 Dunara Castle 1922
14 Iona I 1862
15 Auchmountain 1892
16 Tiger 1902
17 Steamlighter Z 1937
18 Mary Anning 1885
19 Maille Breze 1940
20 Captayannis 1974
21 Ocean 1947
22 Comte de Smet de Naeyer 1904
23 Kathleen & Stromboli 1904
24 Hermia 1901
004° 45.00' W
56° 05.00' N
56° 00.00' N
55° 55.00' N
Loch Long
Gareloch
Helensburgh
Holy Loch
Kilcreggan
Dunoon
Gourock
Greenock
Dumbarton
Port Glasgow
Inverkip
Cowal Peninsula
Isle of Bute
1

UPPER FIRTH

Chapter 1

BOWLING TO INVERKIP

The narrow navigable channel of the Upper Clyde passes close to the townships of Port Glasgow and Greenock to reach the Tail of the Bank where the river opens into a wide, sheltered anchorage. From here the river flows west, past Greenock and Gourock to the Cloch Lighthouse and then south towards Inverkip. In this short, six mile stretch of water and the adjoining sea lochs - Gareloch, Loch Long, Loch Goil and the Holy Loch - dozens of ships of varying sizes, from the 5000 ton *Captayannis* to small lighters and steam yachts, have met with disaster.

The causes of their loss vary from bad weather, through enemy action to simple human error, but by far the most common cause of loss was collision. In its heyday, this small area of enclosed water was alive with passenger steamers, cargo ships and sailing ships of all shapes and sizes. The volume of traffic, and often the attendant cavalier actions of some of the river's captains and owners, inevitably resulted in many collisions. Often the damage was slight and only served to foster the romantic tales of the steamer trade on the Clyde but, tragically, a number of these incidents resulted in the loss of the ships and often the lives of many of the passengers and crew.

This section of the Clyde has become one of the most popular dive destinations in Scotland. While it does not have the density of shipwrecks or underwater visibility of say Scapa Flow or the Sound of Mull, it is still able to offer an excellent days diving on large, substantially intact wrecks close to the central belt of Scotland.

The depth of water and the shelter provided by the hills surrounding the anchorage, plus the fact that many of the sinkings have resulted from these collisions, mean that a substantial number of the wrecks are still relatively intact and therefore, very interesting for the sub aqua diver. Also, a good number have landed on an even keel leaving the wrecks shiplike and easy to explore. They also attract many fish and are therefore popular with local sea anglers.

In general, diving is relatively straightforward as the shelter of the surrounding land masses protect the area from all but the most severe weather and tidal flows are fairly weak. The major dangers for the diver are the depth and the darkness of many of the wrecks. Most lie in around thirty metres and, even if visibility is good, it is almost always dark. Safe use of decompression tables or dive computer and a powerful torch are essential elements of diving here. Good boat cover and use of the 'A' flag are also vital as, although the Clyde is not as busy as it used to be, there is still a lot of river traffic. Boat access is surprisingly limited with best slip facilities at Largs, Inverkip and Gourock.

MV ***Akka*** in wartime livery.

AKKA

5409gt. Steel motor vessel.
Built by Gotaverken, Sweden.
Launched September 1942.

Dimensions 442.8' x 56.5' x 25.8'

The thirty three members of the crew of the *MV Akka* could not have anticipated the tragic end to their voyage as they left Oxelsund on the 4th April, 1956 with a cargo of iron ore, bound for Glasgow. She had made many similar trips for her owners, Grangesberg Oxelsund Trafik AB. Even as she entered the Clyde on the 9th April everything was normal and by 9pm that evening she was abeam of the Cumbraes. As she passed Innellan and slowed to prepare to take on board the pilot, Captain Sundin could see the light on the Gantock Rocks and the Cloch Lighthouse.

It was at this point that things began to go wrong, as the *Akka* appeared to respond very slowly to her rudder. Captain Sundin immediately ordered the engines stopped but, despite this attempt to avoid disaster, the *Akka* ran onto the Gantock Rocks. The horrendous tearing and scraping noises as the rocks tore at the port side of the ship were heard by many ashore in Dunoon and Gourock and they rushed out of their houses to see what had happened. The *Akka* had been severely holed along almost half her length from the second hold and was filling fast. Captain Sundin attempted to reverse his ship into shallower water but this manoeuvre only served to increase the flow of water into the holds and engine room. All engines were stopped and the order was given to abandon ship. Within three of four minutes of running aground the *Akka* heeled over on her port side and sank in deep water. The resulting swell sank a number of lifeboats which had managed to get away, spilling their unfortunate occupants into the dark, cold river. As she sank, spouts of water rose twenty feet into the air and there was a large explosion. A number of rescue vessels were quickly on the scene and most of the survivors were picked up. Three of the crew went down with their ship and a further three died on the way to the hospital. The next morning the only sign of the disaster was twelve feet of the *Akka's* mast sticking out of the water, marking her position on the Dunoon Bank.

Three months later, while salvage was being considered, the wreck was hit by a passing fishing vessel. This prompted a decision to send down a demolition crew to remove the top two levels of her bridge and her funnel and masts, making the wreck safe for passing vessels. As she was lying on Dunoon Bank and, as such, did not really constitute a hazard to navigation for larger vessels, total dispersal was unnecessary.

The Wreck Today

The *Akka* is the largest, submerged, diveable wreck in the Clyde. She lies upright on the north side of Dunoon Bank in position 55°56.707'N, 004°54.397'W (GPS), which is only 25 metres north of the port hand yellow marker buoy. The seabed at the bow, which points approximately south eastwards, is about 30 metres and at the stern, about 40 metres. The deck slopes from 16 to 24 metres from bow to stern.

There are many interesting aspects to this large wreck apart from her size, the most memorable being the incredible and varied sealife which covers almost every square inch of the vessel's superstructure. She is a mass of orange and white plumose anemone and, of course, the ever present dead men's fingers. Many other species of anemone together with hydroids, nudibranch and sea squirts make the wreck a living reef inhabited by many species of fish. Some divers have been lucky enough to swim along the underwater companionways accompanied by inquisitive seals which can often be seen on the surface.

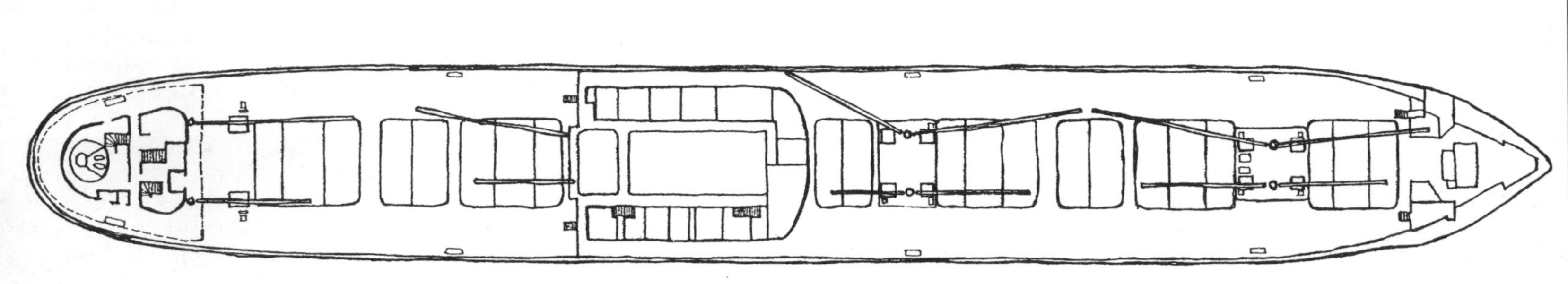

Grangesberg Oxelosund Trafik A.B.

AKKA

Apart from the sealife, the *Akka* is a very interesting wreck which remains mainly intact allowing a swim along companionways, through doors still swinging on their rusting hinges, up and down stairways and along the steeply sloping decks past the gaping dark holes that are the holds.

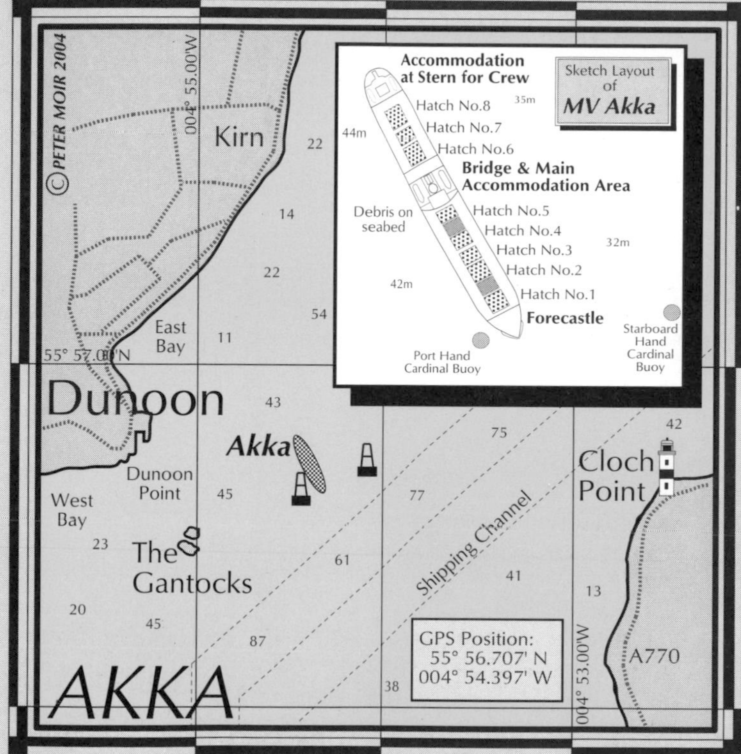

From the raised forecastle, as the diver swims aft, the first area of interest is the superstructure between the holds on the foredeck but the main interest is provided by the bridge and engine room in the middle of the wreck. Originally the bridge rose four deck levels from the foredeck but the top two levels plus the funnel and masts were removed by Metal Industries of Gareloch. The remains of the bridge area are still very impressive, appearing through the gloom as the diver approaches.

The activities of the demolition team have made access to the lower decks and engine room fairly easy, but care is essential as it is possible to penetrate deep inside the wreck. An unwary diver could become lost in rapidly decreasing visibility as the mud and silt, which covers the decks, is stirred by passing fins. Dropping onto the rear deck and a further two holds, the diver approaches the stern castle, impressively large above the deck level, with a companionway passing completely round the stern of the ship. Descending into most of the holds is unrewarding as the cargo was iron ore. However it is possible to drop into the hold forward of the bridge and swim through the gaping hole torn in the port side of the ship by the Gantock Rocks in the fateful grounding in 1956. Diving the *Akka* is relatively easy with the usual potential problems of any wreck in this part of the Clyde - darkness, possible current and fishing lines providing the major hazards.

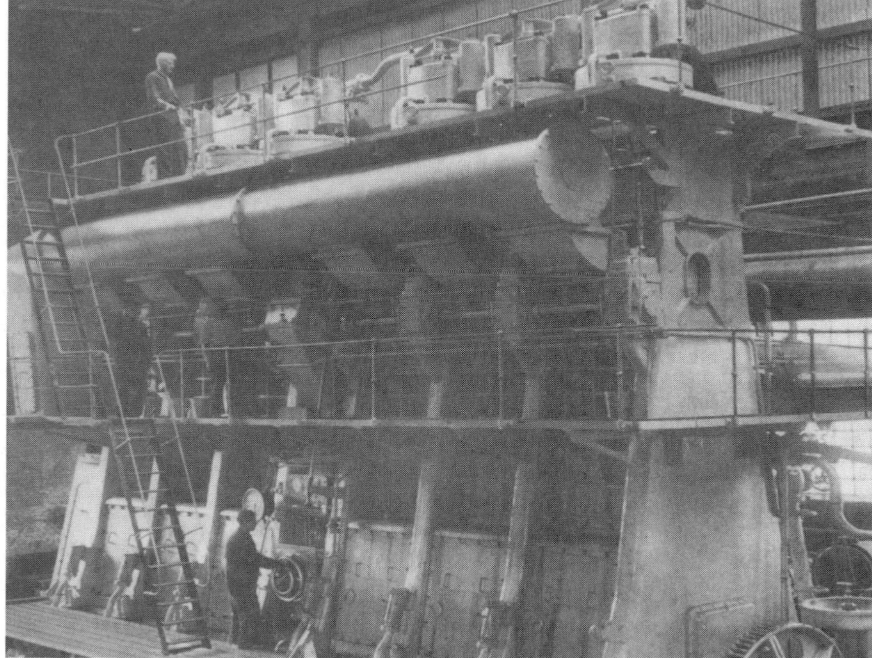

The main engine installed in the *Akka*, a Gotaverken 6 cylinder single acting type 680/1500VG diesel.

AUCHMOUNTAIN

1456gt. Steel barque.
Built by Russell & Co, Port Glasgow.
Launched July 1892.

Dimensions 235.5' x 36.0' x 21.6'

On 30th August, 1892 the *Auchmountain* left Glasgow for her maiden voyage to Sydney, Australia, with a general cargo of iron pipes, pig iron, beer and whisky for her owners, the Auchmountain Shipping Company of Greenock. The next day, after setting her compasses off Gourock, she was moored to the powder buoy, which lay near the entrance to Gareloch, to take on the final part of her cargo, twenty tons of gunpowder. This was stored in the rear hold that same day leaving her ready to set sail early the next morning.

However, Captain Jones was frustrated from setting sail in his new vessel as strong winds kept him at anchor off Greenock for the whole of Friday, 2nd September. As night fell, Chief Officer John Borland took over the watch and Captain Jones retired below, intent on an early start next day. Shortly before 10pm Borland discovered a fire in the forecastle and immediately raised the alarm.

The Captain and his crew valiantly fought the blaze for the next two hours but, as the strong winds fanned the flames, the fire gradually spread along the length of the ship towards the deadly cargo in the rear hold. At this stage Captain Jones recognised that an explosion was inevitable and ordered his crew and a startled stowaway, who had been disturbed by the smell of the smoke, into the lifeboat. He returned briefly with some of his crew to attempt to jettison the gunpowder but it was immediately obvious that the task was hopeless and that they were in great danger of being blown up along with the ship and so they abandoned the *Auchmountain* to her fate.

The fire relentlessly spread along the length of the ship with the foremast, mainmast and finally mizzen mast toppling in turn into the flames until, shortly before 5am, the fire reached the rear hold. The *Auchmountain* was torn apart by a huge explosion which shattered windows in Greenock and Gourock and even in Dumbarton. The explosion was felt as far away as Pollokshaws in Glasgow, which is over twenty miles from the scene of the incident. The residents of that area thought that a small earthquake had occurred. Papers from the ship were discovered in a garden in Kilmacolm which is six miles away. Back on the river, as the thick pall of smoke cleared, the *Auchmountain* had vanished without trace. After some initial salvage the wreck lay undisturbed for the next few years although, at intervals, pieces of the ship were washed ashore or found floating in the river after a storm.

In September 1896 the wreck was declared a hazard to shipping and an attempt was made to disperse her by agents of the liquidators of the Auchmountain Shipping Company. This operation was not carried out to the satisfaction of the Clyde Lighthouse Trust who had the responsibility for the seaways of the Clyde during this period. A few weeks later the wreckage was finally covered by the dumping of dredgings from the excavation of Cessnock dock.

CAPTAYANNIS

2620nt. Steel motor vessel.
Built by Nakskov Skibs A S Denmark.
Launched 1946.
(ex NORDEN)

Dimensions 396.7' x 56.3' x 25.0′

January 1974 saw the *Captayannis* arriving in the Clyde with a cargo of sugar from Lourenco Marques in Portuguese East Africa. She dropped anchor off the Tail of the Bank prior to offloading her cargo in Greenock. On Monday 28th January, a severe gale hit the west coast of Scotland, whipping up the sea in the normally calm anchorage with winds in excess of 60mph. In this severe weather the *Captayannis* began to drag her anchor, prompting Captain Theodorakis Ionnis to order the engines started to head towards the Gareloch for shelter.

However, before he could get sufficient power to get under way, the *Captayannis* was blown across the anchor chain of the 36,754 ton BP tanker *British Light* which had recently arrived off Greenock from Elderslie Dry Dock. The anchor chain ripped a long gaping hole in the port side of the *Captayannis*. The pumps could not cope with the torrents of water which quickly flooded the lower levels of the ship and she soon began to list substantially to port. Shortly afterwards she was plunged into darkness as the inrush of water caused a total power failure. As a number of small boats arrived on the scene to render assistance, the *Captayannis* grounded on a sandbank in the middle of the river directly between Greenock and Helensburgh. The crew of twenty five, including the captain, were taken off without injury.

The *Captayannis* subsequently became the centre of a major insurance wrangle between the parties involved. As a result, salvage was not attempted despite the fact that she is lying with a substantial portion of her bulk above sea level in fairly shallow water. She lies on her port side with her starboard side rising like a small island some three or four metres above sea level in position 55°58.566'N, 004°44.516'W. The wreck is substantially intact with superstructure and most large deck fittings still in place. She lies in 8 to 9 metres of murky water on a muddy seabed.

MV ***Captayannis*** - Summer 2003.

MV ***Captayannis*** shortly after her sinking.

CATHERINE

Wooden sloop.

Shortly after 11pm on the night of Saturday 10th August, 1822 the *Catherine* crept past the Cloch Lighthouse, sails hanging limply on the mast and the crew at the oars to give her some steerage way. The night was calm and clear and the party of reapers from Iona, who were on their way to Greenock to work on the forthcoming harvest, had retired to their bunks for the night. As she approached Levan Castle she was run down by the steam tug *Hercules* which was on an excursion to Ailsa Craig and Campbeltown. The collision sheered off the stern of the *Catherine*, instantly killing several of the passengers and the sloop sank almost immediately in deep water.

The *Hercules* picked up only four survivors leaving forty two dead, including all of the crew. The stern portion of the stricken ship was washed ashore the next morning close to Roseneath Point. A few days later relatives of the dead succeeded in raising the wreck and recovering nine bodies.

CHAMPION

26nt. Iron paddle tug.
Built by J & T Eltringham, South Shields.
Launched 1882.
(ex FLYING JAVELIN)

Dimensions 108.4' x 18.6' x 9.7'

The *Flying Javelin* was powered by a one eighty horse power surface condensing engine and was sold by her original owners, the Clyde Shipping Company, in 1887 to Alexander McKinnon of Greenock who renamed her *Champion*. She was employed on the Clyde delivering early morning mail and newspapers from Greenock to the various towns and villages of the Clyde estuary.

It was on this duty that she left Greenock at 6:20am on Wednesday 12th December, 1896 under the command of her captain, Quintin Carsell, with a crew of six. She called at Gourock, Kirn and Dunoon. There had been a dense fog on the river that morning as she left Greenock and as her voyage progressed the fog steadily thickened. By the time she pulled away from Dunoon Pier at 7:45am for Innellan, visibility had reduced to less than thirty yards.

A few minutes earlier the Caledonian Steam Packet Company paddlesteamer *Caledonia* had left Innellan Pier for the twelve minute run north to her next stop at Dunoon. Although Captain Bell positioned one of his crew on the bow as lookout, he steamed blindly into the fog at his normal speed of fifteen knots. Captain Carsell on the *Champion* steamed south at a more tentative speed of three or four knots, feeling his way through the thickening fog. He frequently sounded his steam whistle and had positioned deckhand Neil Millan forward as lookout. Within yards of Dunoon Pier he was alerted by the whistle of a steamer passing his port side. This first steamer was closely followed by the South Western Railway Company's *Minerva*, also heading for Dunoon with its whistle sounding. Captain Carsell turned to starboard to move his little vessel inshore and give a wider berth to any other steamers heading north to Dunoon.

Immediately, he heard yet another whistle off his port bow and, as required by the Regulations for Preventing Collisions at Sea, he ordered a turn to starboard and his engines stopped. The engineer had no time to carry out this order before the *Caledonia* appeared out of the fog, thirty yards from the *Champion's* bow. Captain Carsell could see all three navigation lights indicating that the *Caledonia* was bearing directly down on them. He ordered engines full astern but it was too late. The *Caledonia* ripped into the port sponson and cut six or seven feet into the hull of the steam tug, penetrating her engineroom bulkhead. She immediately began to fill with water and it was obvious that she was going to sink. The two ships held together allowing the crew of the *Champion* to jump aboard the *Caledonia*. Captain Carsell then risked his life to return to his stricken vessel to retrieve the mail. As the *Caledonia* backed away the *Champion* sank - only five minutes had passed since the collision.

The subsequent Board of Trade enquiry heard how the *Caledonia* left Innellan Pier and headed north at her usual speed, despite the thick weather and, although Captain Bell had posted a lookout, he had little time from seeing the masthead of the *Champion* appear through the murk until the bow of the *Caledonia*

The Paddle Tug ***Champion.***

cleaved into the unfortunate steam tug. Despite the evidence, Captain Bell declared that the *Champion* had in fact run into his path, the enquiry found that the collision was caused by the excessive and improper speed of the *Caledonia*. It also held that Captain Bell did not order his engines stopped or reversed on hearing the *Champion's* warning whistle as required by the Regulations for Preventing Collisions at Sea, until the *Champion* was visible through the fog. The enquiry suspended Captain Bell's Master Certificate for three months.

The wreck of the *Champion* lies where she sank in position 55°56.077'N, 004°55.616'W(GPS), about a quarter of a mile south of the Gantock Rocks and about three hundred metres from the shore. She lies upright on a sloping, sandy seabed in a general depth of 36 metres with her stern at 38 metres and the bow in 34 metres. Her bow points inshore and at an angle of about forty five degrees to the shoreline. The small wooden platform which was the bridge has long since vanished as has the single funnel, although the base of the stack is still clearly visible. Otherwise the stern section is intact. Over the years since the wreck's discovery in the late 1980's the condition of the wreck has deteriorated markedly. Forward of the engineroom bulkhead the wreck is well broken, particularly on the port side where the collision occurred. The damage to this section could indicate that the bows hit the seabed first as the tug sank.

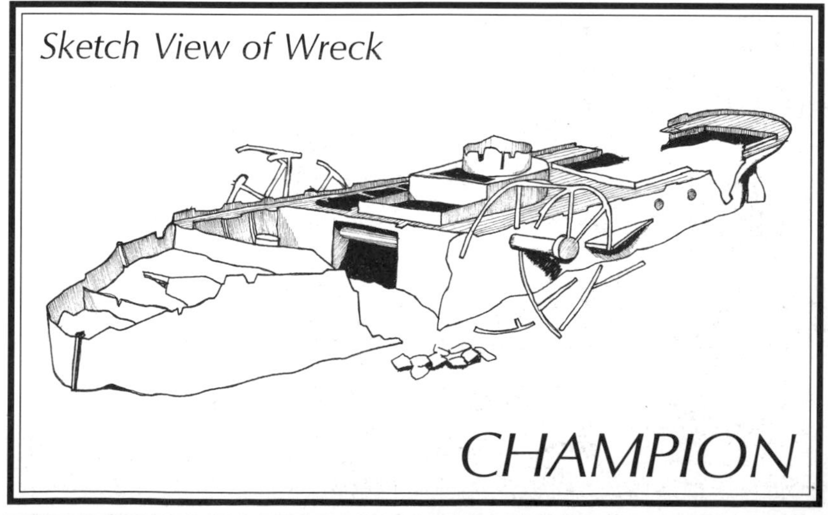

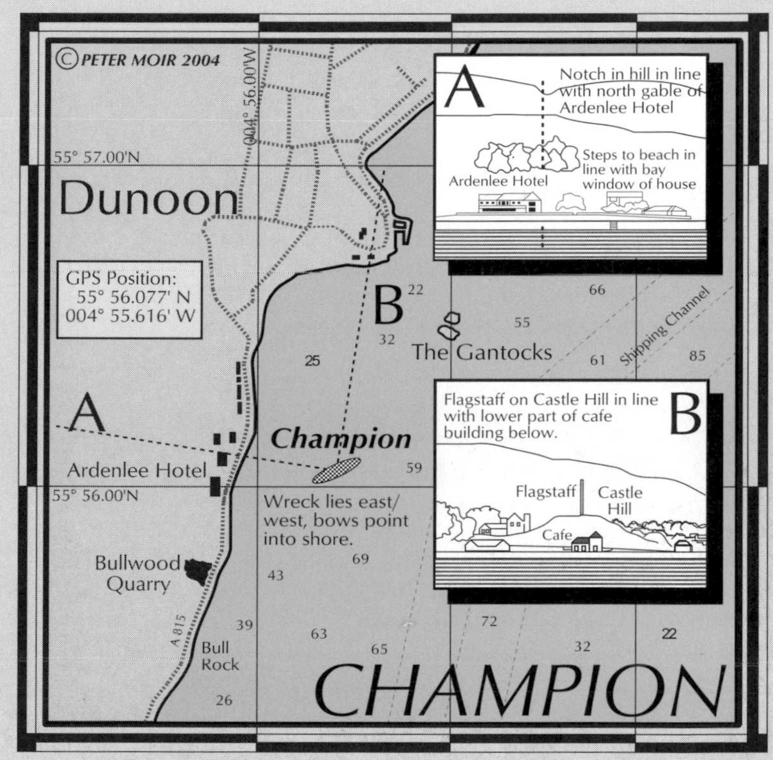

The two huge paddlewheels, which appear totally out of proportion to the rest of the vessel, are the most impressive aspect of the wreck. The starboard paddlewheel is almost completely intact and stands from the seabed well above the height of the deck of the ship. Diving the wreck provides few difficulties although its size and its deteriorating condition make it more difficult to locate and snag than the other wrecks in this area. The depth and hence the inevitable darkness also deserve respect. There are a number of old prawn creels, ropes and fishing lines so a sharp lookout is required.

COMET II

94nt. Wooden paddlesteamer.
Built by James Lang, Dumbarton.
Launched 1821.

The wreck of the ***Comet II*** ashore at Gourock.

One of the earliest and most catastrophic of all steamship disasters to take place on the Clyde was the loss of the *Comet II*. She had been built to replace the *Comet I*, the pioneer of commercial steamship navigation, which was wrecked off Craignish Point, Argyll in 1821.

In the early hours of Friday 21st October, 1825 the *Comet II*, inward bound on her regular run from Inverness to Glasgow, sank after colliding with the paddlesteamer *Ayr*. The collision occurred off Kempock Point, Gourock, the *Comet II* sinking in three minutes, taking with her around seventy three passengers and crew. The final death toll was never fully established, as the check of passengers leaving or joining the vessel at intermediate ports was not kept. However, thirteen people managed to struggle ashore including her master, Duncan McInnes. Meanwhile, the *Ayr* had put back to Greenock without making any attempt to save those struggling in the water.

The sinking of the ***Comet II.***

Much was made of this in the newspapers of the day although, as the *Ayr* was badly damaged and presumed to be in a sinking condition, the master of the *Ayr* decided to return to Greenock immediately to avoid further loss of life.

An attempt to raise the *Comet II* was made during December 1825, but was hampered by various problems, not least by the weather. The wreck lay off Kempock Point in seventeen fathoms until the following summer, when a further attempt was made. The salvage contract was let to a Mr Brown of Aberdeen, who submitted the lowest tender. Salvage works took almost two weeks, the wreck finally being beached on 21st July, 1826.

The cause of the collision was attributed to the lack of navigation lights and bow lookout aboard the *Comet*. Captain Duncan McInnes was later charged with culpable homicide, culpable neglect and reckless command in steering the vessel. He received a three month jail sentence.

COMTE de SMET de NAEYER

1863nt. Iron sailing ship.
Built by Grangemouth & Greenock Dockyard Co.
Launched December 1904.

Dimensions 267.0' x 41.1' x 23.6'

The *Comte de Smet de Naeyer* was built as a cadet training ship for her owners, the Association Maritime Belge S A. During her fitting out in James Watt Dock, Greenock, she slipped over on her beam end and sank, barely giving time for the many workers aboard to escape with their lives.

It took two weeks to raise her but fitting out was completed and she was handed over to her owners on schedule. This was not the end of the story for the *Comte de Smet de Naeyer*. Belgian experts were concerned about her seaworthiness even before she left Greenock. Their doubts were tragically confirmed when, two years later, on 19th April, 1906 she sprang a leak and sank off Ushant, drowning thirty two of the fifty four crew on board, including eighteen cadets on their first voyage.

Salvage work underway.

DUNARA CASTLE

197nt. Iron steamship.
Built by Blackwood & Gordon, Port Glasgow.
Launched 1875.

Dimensions 180.4' x 24.5' x 12.5'

The *Dunara Castle* was a very reliable steamship and served her owners, Martin Orme and Company, without incident on many routes from the Clyde to the Western Isles for a number of years.

In the early hours of the morning of 29th August, 1922 she was returning to the Clyde with one hundred passengers on board and a cargo of sheep. As she passed Gourock Pierhead the captain had to veer to starboard to avoid colliding with an unidentified tug which appeared without warning out of the dark, foggy night. Unfortunately this resulted in the *Dunara Castle* running aground at Battery Park. The grounding caused considerable damage to her hull and propeller and as the tide receded she was left high and dry on the shore. Thankfully none of the passengers, crew or even her live cargo were injured in the incident. She was refloated after nearly a week ashore and taken to James Watt Dock for repairs. She returned later to a long and successful career which included the sad evacuation of the last inhabitants of St Kilda. She was finally scrapped in 1948.

ENTERPRISE

30nt. Wooden steamlighter.
Built in Glasgow.
Launched 1865.

The steamlighter *Enterprise* was owned by Messrs Logan and Son, Paisley and skippered by Captain Dugald Carmichael. She was typical of many of these small vessels that plied the rivers and sea lochs of the west coast of Scotland taking supplies to the communities of the islands. On 19th November, 1882 she was en route from Greenock to Tarbert, Loch Fyne with empty herring boxes with a crew of seven aboard. That same evening the steamship *Strathendrick* was inbound from Limerick to Glasgow.

It was around 6pm and darkness had fallen some time earlier making both skippers alert but not concerned as the night was clear. Both vessels approached Kempock Point, Gourock and seemed to be well positioned to pass port to port when the *Enterprise* suddenly veered across the bows of the *Strathendrick*. There was no time for the skipper of the other ship to take avoiding action and the *Strathendrick's* bow tore into the starboard side midships of the *Enterprise* cutting her to the water line. She was doomed. Five of her crew managed to clamber aboard the *Strathendrick* before she sank taking her mate and fireman with her. Although the *Strathendrick* and some other vessels which had come out from shore to assist searched the area for some time, there was no sign of the two men amid the hundreds of floating herring boxes from the *Enterprise's* cargo.

The wreck of the *Enterprise* has almost completely disappeared but her boiler still stands upright in 32 metres about one hundred yards off shore at Kempock Point in position 55°57.833'N, 004°49.282'W (GPS). Around the boiler there are a few bits and pieces of wreckage including some of the copper sheathing from the ship's hull. The site lies very close to the route of the Gourock to Dunoon ferry and, as such, boat cover and the clear display of an 'A' flag are essential. Better still, time your dive between the ferry times. The site is also subject to some tidal flow at certain states of the tide and visibility is rarely more than two or three metres.

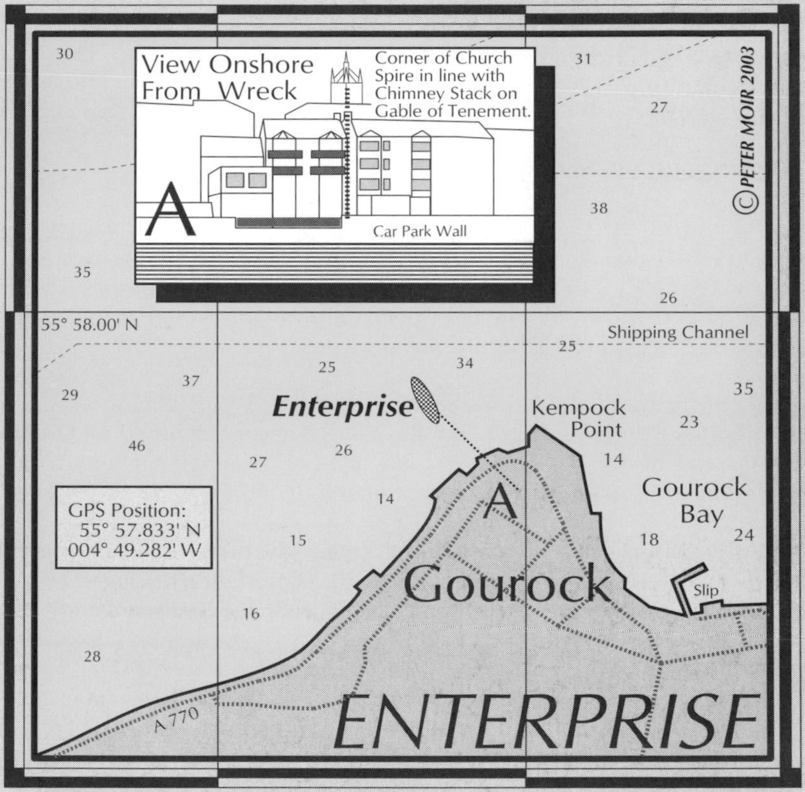

EUROPA

424nt. Iron steamship.
Built by Palmers S B and Co, Jarrow.
Launched March 1862.

Dimensions 206.5' x 26.1' x 17.2'

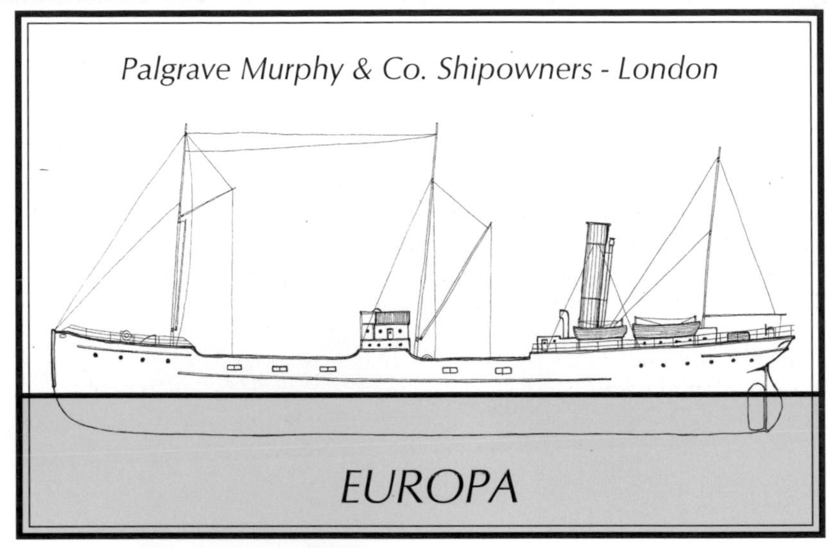

Fate played a hand in the collision between the steamships *Europa* and *Roseville* on Saturday 11th October, 1884, for if the carpenter of the *Europa* had signed on as arranged, she would not have been delayed and would have passed the tragic spot off Levan Castle hours earlier.

The *Europa* had left Glasgow for Malaga the previous afternoon with 850 tons of general cargo. Around 7pm the same day she anchored off Greenock while Captain Bushell went ashore to hire another carpenter. He returned to his vessel around 11pm, and the *Europa* proceeded on her voyage soon after.

On passing McInroy's Point shortly after midnight, the bow lookouts reported the lights of an incoming vessel dead ahead. These lights belonged to the SS *Roseville*, en route from Taganrog to Glasgow with 1850 tons of barley. As the two vessels closed the *Europa* started to cut across the track of the *Roseville*. The cries of alarm from the lookouts were too late for any evasive action to be taken. The vessels, both travelling at full speed, collided almost head on. The *Europa* was struck about her starboard hawespipe and cut through to the front of her main foredeck hatch.

Panic and confusion ensued on both vessels, as the *Europa* began to fill and settle down. Some of her crew were in their bunks at the time and they rushed on deck, half naked. They, and several others on duty, scrambled aboard the *Roseville*. Unhappily, not everyone on board the *Europa* was so fortunate as she sank quickly, some three minutes after the collision, carrying with her Captain Bushell and four of her crew. Boats were immediately launched from the *Roseville* to search for survivors, but nothing was found except large quantities of floating debris.

The *Roseville* had been seriously damaged in the collision and she too soon began to fill and settle down. Having no other option her master, Captain Dove, headed for the shore and beached the *Roseville* opposite Levan Castle, where all the survivors were safely landed. The *Europa* was buoyed for some time after the incident until her masts, which nearly reached the surface, could be removed. The *Roseville* was successfully patched up and refloated by Messrs Ross & Marshall on 25th October, 1884 and taken to Greenock for repair, which eventually cost £12,000.

The Wreck Today

The *Europa* lies approximately a mile north east of Cloch Point, in position 55°57.083'N, 004°52.112'W (GPS). Sitting upright on a gently sloping mud seabed with bow pointing south, the wreck is oriented about 005/185 degrees. Seabed depths vary from 40 metres at the stern to 34 metres at the bow. Depths on the wreck average 32 metres, however, this will increase below deck level in such areas as the engine room or stern accommodation.

Virtually all that remains of the *Europa* is the bare hull. The lack of any deck structures is possibly due to the wreck having been wire swept at some stage although, given the depth she lies in, this is unlikely, or that all the deck structures were timber and have subsequently disintegrated.

The bow section has collapsed onto the seabed forward of the main foredeck hatch. Much of this could be attributed to the damage received during the collision. Debris lies all around the wreck on the seabed, the greater proportion on the port side. Little projects above the deck level except the steering tripod, the base of her main steam vent and a locomotive boiler which was part of her cargo. Areas below deck level are heavily silted and any disturbance reduces visibility to 'groping around in the dark' within seconds. The most scenic part of the wreck is the impressive stern, which overhangs the rudder and propeller and rises some 4-5 metres above the seabed. Here the tide is most noticeable as it spills round the stern on both flood and ebb. The greater movement of water has attracted a profusion of soft corals and anemones, large transparent prawns with crimson edging to their shell are also a common site.

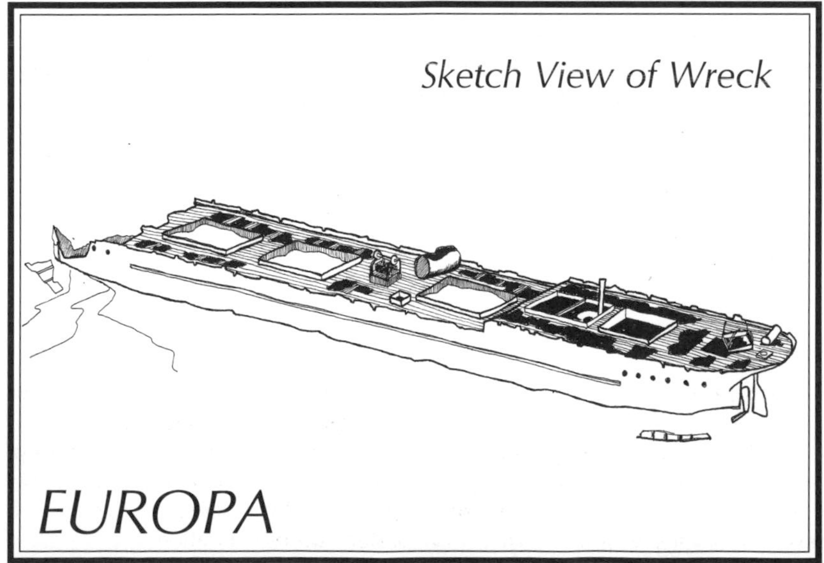

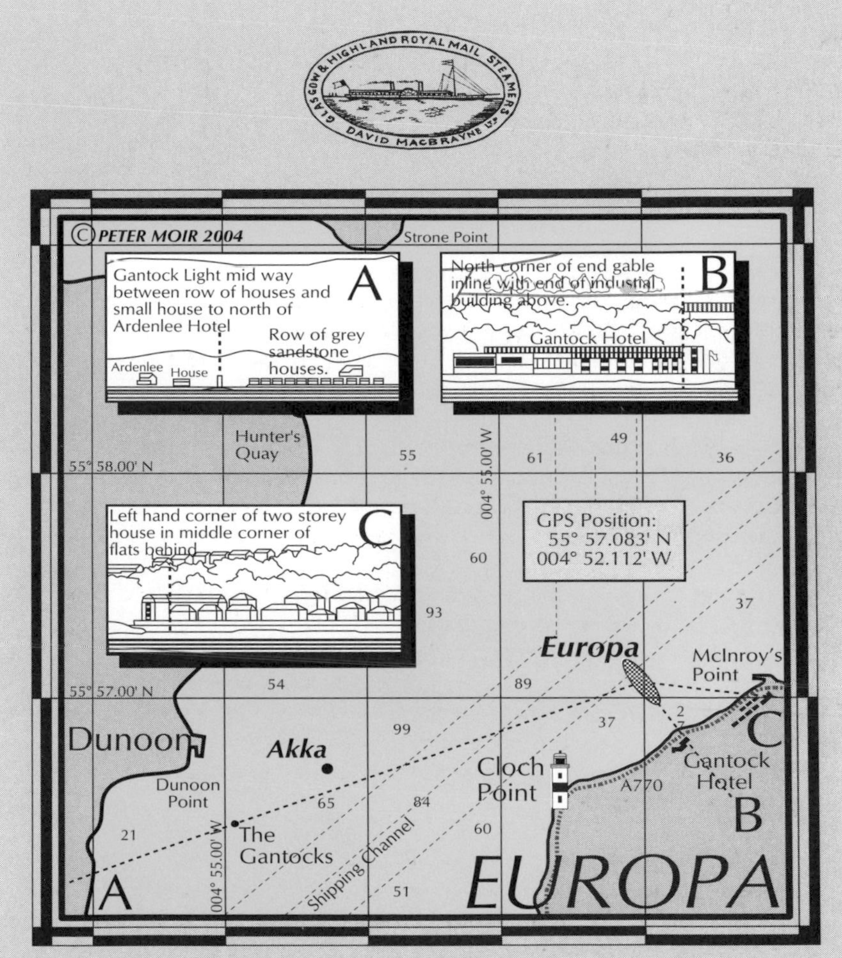

Diving the *Europa* presents no major problems other than the depth, however, bear in mind its proximity to the shipping lane and adjacent ferry traffic from McInroy's Point. Visibility on the wreck is variable, normally two or three metres and usually dark.

GREENOCK

461nt. Iron steam dredger.
Built by Wm Simons & Co, Renfrew.
Launched 1876.

Dimensions 181.5' x 38.6' x 14.2'

Built for the Greenock Harbour Trust at a cost of £25,000 the *Greenock*, a twin screw steam hopper dredger, was launched on 4th November, 1876. Designed specifically for use in the harbours of Gourock, Greenock and the surrounding estuary, she spent most of her working life around her home port, occasionally being contracted out to other harbour authorities.

On Tuesday 18th November, 1902 the dredger left Gourock Bay around mid afternoon, bound for Garroch Head, where she was to deposit her day's dredgings. The return voyage was uneventful for her master, Thomas Scott, and the sixteen crew until they were about a mile south of the Cloch Lighthouse. The bow lookout reported a steamer's lights coming around the Cloch, outward bound and taking a course inshore of the dredger.

The two vessels kept their respective courses for three of four minutes until, when almost abreast, the other vessel abruptly altered course to starboard and headed straight for the dredger. The engines of the *Greenock* were immediately reversed to try and prevent the imminent collision, but to no avail. The unknown steamer crashed into the dredger on her starboard side midships, cutting her through to the bucket well. The dredger then drew alongside the other vessel, which turned out to be the Burn's steamer *Ape*, and most of the crew were able to scramble aboard.

The *Greenock* meanwhile was turning over on her starboard side, with the stern lifting and her propellers racing in the air. The master and engineer were last to leave and, seeing that the dredger was about to sink, jumped overboard, eventually being picked up by the *Ape*. All the crew of the *Greenock* were saved except for William Rodger, the sixteen year old son of the engineer, who could not be found after a prolonged search. The *Ape* sustained some damage to her bow plating but was able to return to Victoria Harbour, Greenock with the survivors.

The wreck was located three days later by the Clyde Lighthouse Trust, lying three quaters of a mile south west of the Cloch Lighthouse in sixteen and a half fathoms. No attempt to raise or part salvage the wreck was made and insurance monies of £10,000 were later paid to her owners by the vessel's underwriters.

On Thursday 4th July, 1996 the Navy destroyed two unexploded mines which had lain on the wreck for many years. The mines had been laid during the war as part of the defenses for the Clyde anchorage which included an anti-submarine boom from the Cloch across to Dunoon and an extensive minefield to deter prowling U-boats. In fact, it is likely that the wreck of the *Greenock* received special attention from the minelayers as a wreck would provide ideal cover for a lurking submarine waiting to pounce on ships entering or leaving the anchorage.

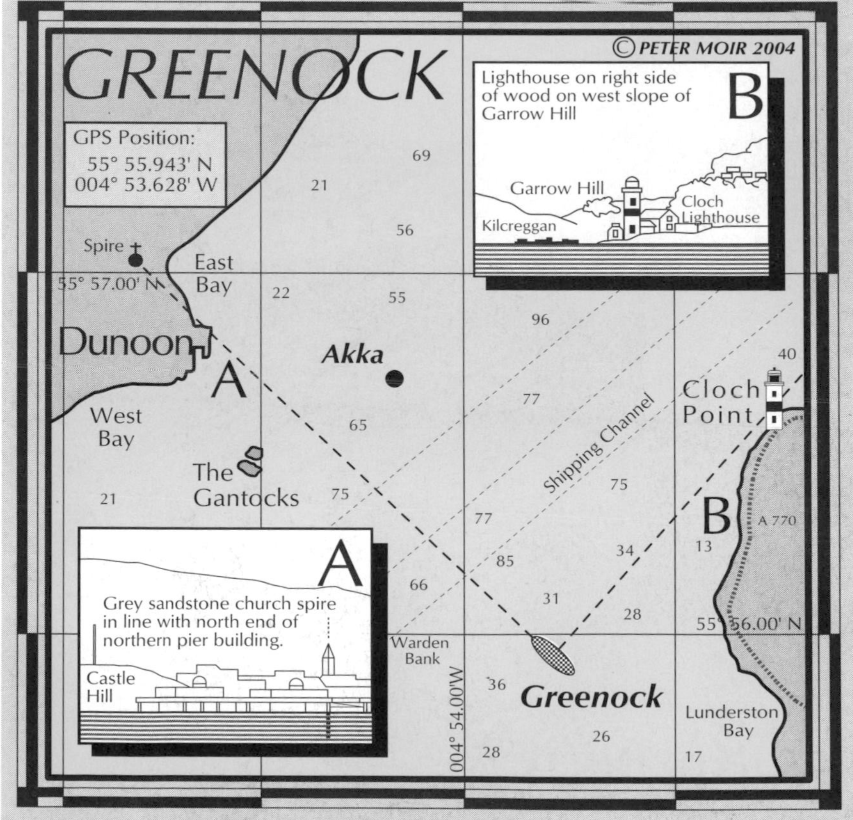

However the wreck is still substantially intact and sits upright on a flat sand/ mud seabed, in position 55°55.943'N, 004°53.628'W (GPS), 30 metres below the surface and oriented approximately 140/320 degrees with stern pointing towards Dunoon. The shallowest part of the wreck, 16 - 17 metres, is on top of the bucket gantry, which, even before the demolition team moved in, could only be described as a confused tangle of metal leaning over the starboard rail. Even in its original state the ship had virtually no deck structures other than the dredging gear.

The open area located aft of the gantry, around the engine room where the decking has fallen away to expose the two 99hp engines and forward of these the two boilers, is the only area of interest below deck level. Just aft of the port engine lies the four bladed spare propeller, originally located at deck level, which has subsequently fallen below. Beyond the engine room below deck are the heavily silted stores and on deck the main stern winch. In recent years the stern section including the engine room have become much more open and accessible, helped in no short measure by the clearance operations.

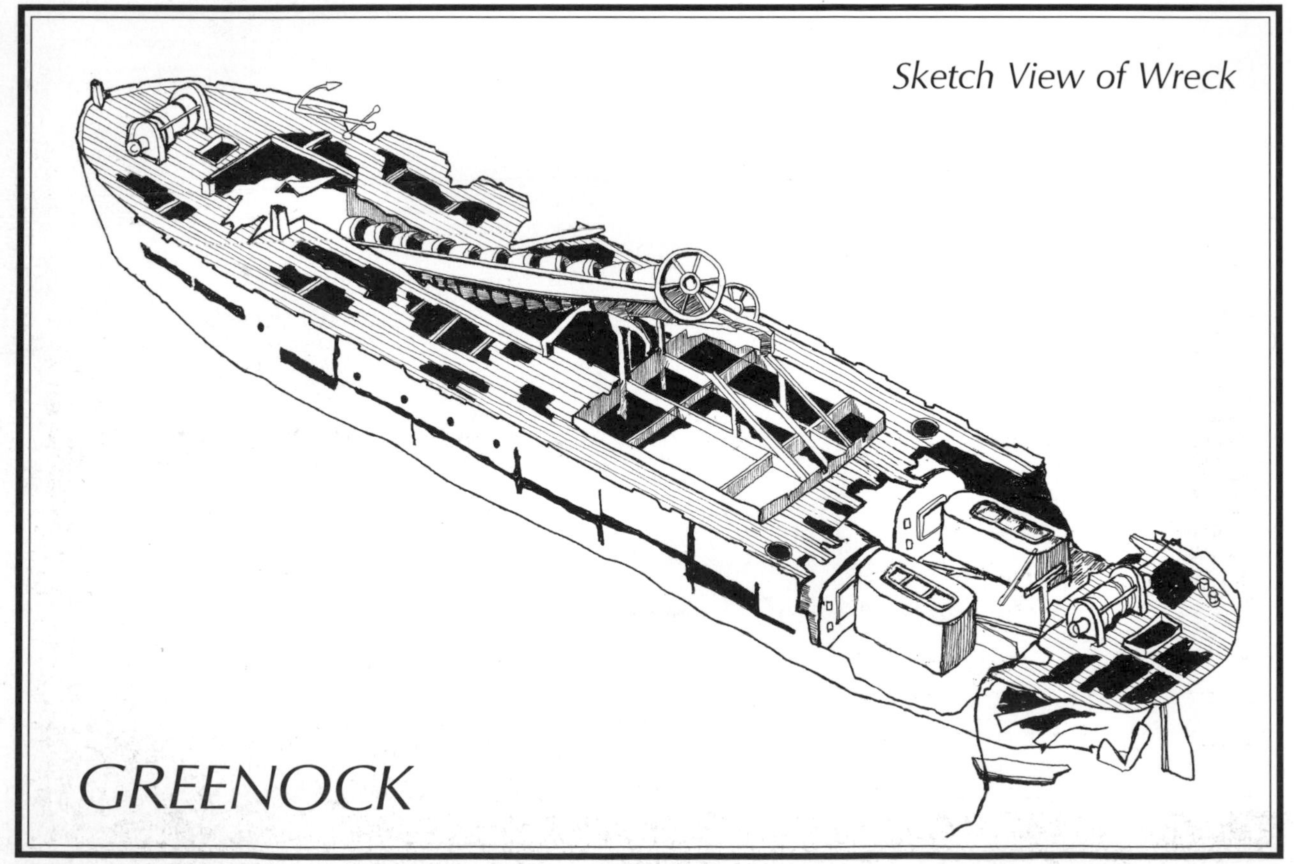

The remains of items from the raised pilot bridge orinially lay on the deck behind the aft rail of the hopper. These included the steering gear and wheel hub and two telegraphs. Also located there were the two smoke stack bases, coal chute gratings and bunkering deck plates. The hopper is partially silted up, but it is still possible, with care, to descend below, through the remains of the gantry. Moving forward, the diver passes either side of the ruined gantry where again it is possible to investigate the below deck accommodation either side of the bucket well, by dropping through the many openings in the deck. The bow section is somewhat similar to the stern, with prominent steam winch and stores below deck. Around the bow, items such as anchors, remains of a deck house and lifting tackle can still be seen.

The *Greenock* can be dived at all states of the tide, though diving on or shortly after slack water on most occasions gives better visibility.

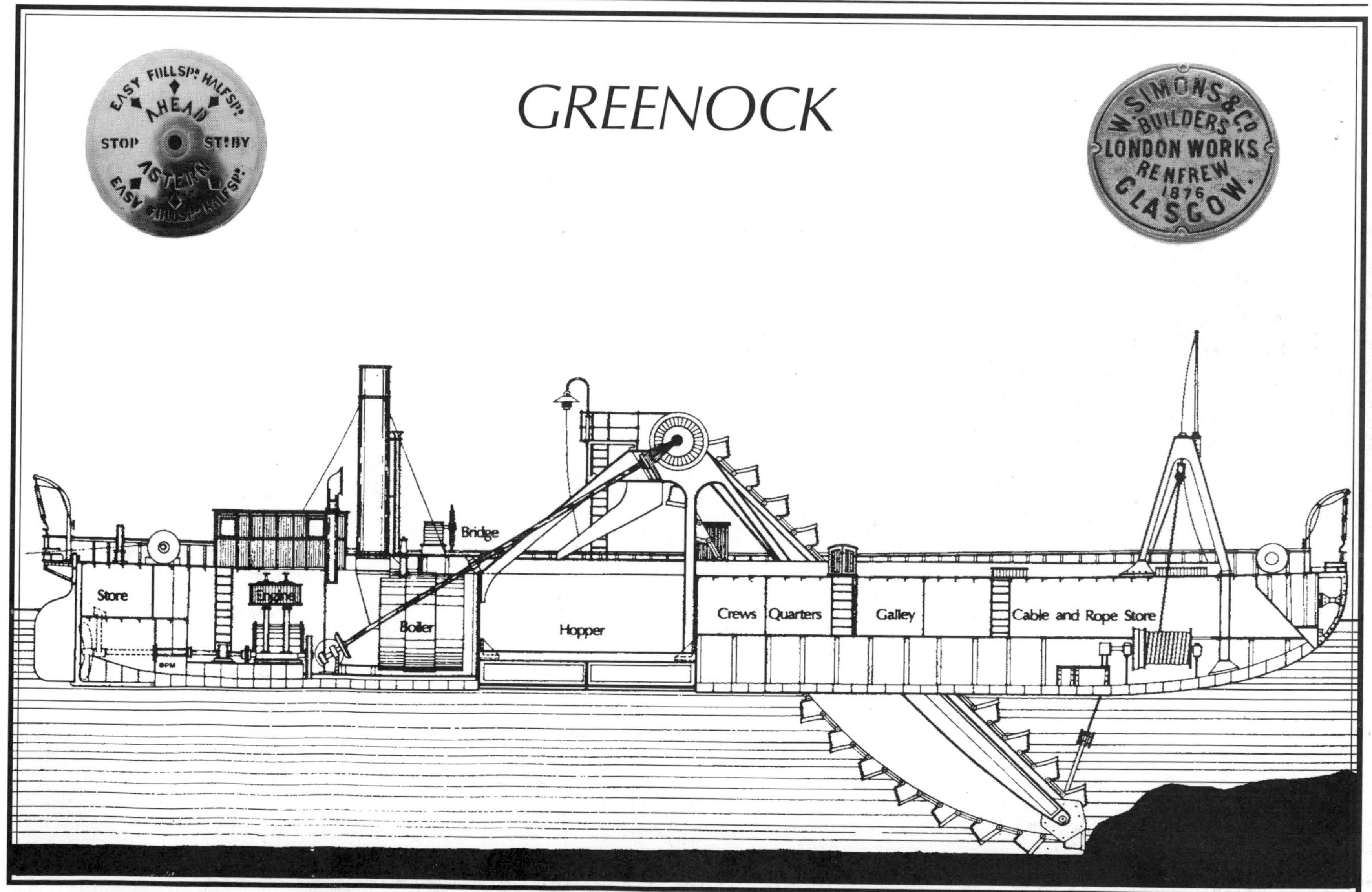
GREENOCK
EASY FULLSP! HALFSP!
AHEAD
STOP
ST!BY
ASTERN
EASY FULLSP! HALFSP!
W. SIMONS & CO.
BUILDERS
LONDON WORKS
RENFREW
1876
GLASGOW.
Store
Engine
Bridge
Boiler
Hopper
Crews Quarters
Galley
Cable and Rope Store

HERMIA

1000nt. Iron steamship.
Built by T Royden & Son, Liverpool.
Launched 1880.
(ex FROGMORE)

Dimensions 259.5' x 33.9' x 17.9'

Thursday 21st December, 1901 was not a good day for Captain Gunson of the Allan Line steamer *Carthiginian*. In the early hours of the morning, en route to Philadelphia via Liverpool, his vessel was in collision with the *SS Glenmore* off the Mull of Galloway. The *Carthiginian* had sustained extensive damage to her stem and bow plating and, as a result, Captain Gunson decided to head for Glasgow for repairs.

Twelve hours later, with tugs in attendance, the *Carthiginian* passed Port Glasgow heading up river in the failing light. On approaching the Garmoyle Lightship, the lights of an outgoing steamer were suddenly sighted a short way off. Captain Gunson immediately ordered 'engines full astern' but could not stop his vessel colliding with the oncoming steamer, the *Hermia*.

The forecastle of the *Hermia* folded like a concertina killing two Spanish crewmen asleep below. Elias Ybarra, a fireman, was also in his bunk and was unceremoniously awoken by the buckling hull plating hitting him on the head. He eventually escaped and was rescued by one of the tugs. The rest of the crew were saved and taken to the Mariner's Home in Greenock.

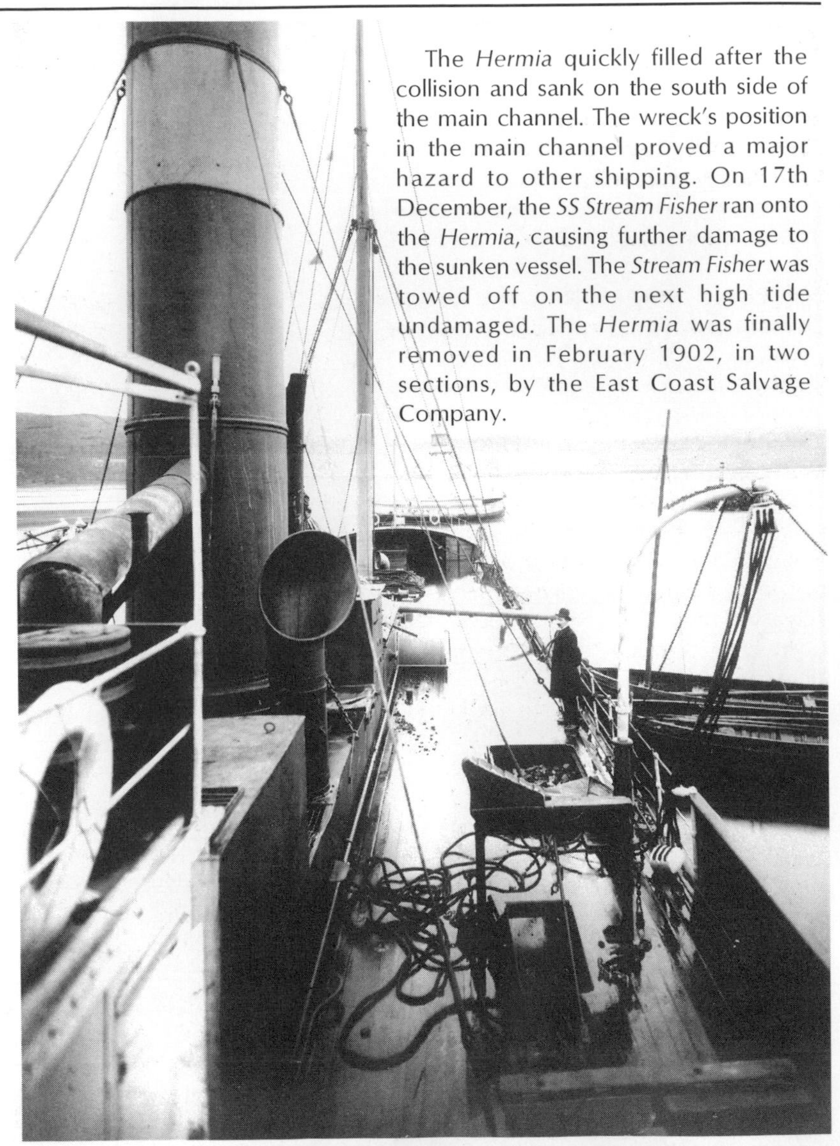

The *Hermia* quickly filled after the collision and sank on the south side of the main channel. The wreck's position in the main channel proved a major hazard to other shipping. On 17th December, the *SS Stream Fisher* ran onto the *Hermia*, causing further damage to the sunken vessel. The *Stream Fisher* was towed off on the next high tide undamaged. The *Hermia* was finally removed in February 1902, in two sections, by the East Coast Salvage Company.

IONA I

24nt. Iron paddlesteamer.
Built by J & G Thomson, Glasgow.
Launched March 1855.

Dimensions 225.2' x 20.4' x 9.0'

The fine appearance of this sleek, twin funnelled steamer and the exceptional speed provided by her oscillating engines made her very popular with the public as she sailed for her owners, William Hutchison & Company, on her regular route from Glasgow to Ardrishaig.

The history of the *Iona*, and many of her contemporary Clyde steamers, was to be dramatically changed by the events in far off America where, in the early 1860s, the Civil War raged between the Confederate southern states and the Unionist states of the north. In April 1861 President Abraham Lincoln declared a blockade on all southern ports immediately stimulating the lucrative, if risky, business of blockade running to bring essential supplies to the beleaguered citizens of these Confederate cities and towns. The fast, shallow draft steamers of the Clyde were ideal for this business and over the next few years many Clyde steamers were sold at excessive prices to Confederate agents thinly disguised as a 'Spanish firm' or the 'Emperor of China.'

The *Iona* made her last passenger sailing on the Clyde in September 1862 and then she too was sold to one of those mysterious buyers. She was stripped of all her fittings, painted grey, loaded with coal and general stores and set off from Glasgow on the morning of 2nd October, 1862. Her destination was Nassau in New Providence, the Bahamas. She spent a number of hours off Gourock plying back and forth, setting and adjusting her compasses before finally weighing anchor in Gourock Bay that evening. She steamed into the dark, clear night at a steady three or four knots.

For most of the same day the newly launched steamer *Chanticleer* had been undergoing speed trials between the Cloch Lighthouse and the island of Cumbrae and on the measured mile off Skelmorlie. She was returning to port and passed the Cloch at 6:50pm, travelling at around eight knots.

PS ***Iona I*** with Toward Point behind.

As in most of these type of incidents, the testimonies of the crew of the two vessels relate differing versions of the events which followed. The crew of the *Iona* later told how the *Chanticleer*, without lights showing, suddenly appeared out of the night bearing down on them and that, despite cries from them to alter course, she tore into the *Iona's* starboard side some twelve feet aft of the paddle box. The *Chanticleer's* bow cut through the *Iona* to within two feet of the port side so there is no doubt that the *Chanticleer* was travelling fast when the collision occurred.

The crew of the *Chanticleer*, on the other hand, said that they had put up their lights on passing the Cloch Lighthouse and, in fact, the *Iona* cut across the path of their vessel causing the subsequent collision. The pilot on board the *Chanticleer* told reporters that he had sighted the *Iona's* lights some two or three miles ahead and had turned to starboard to leave passage for the *Iona* on his port side. The two vessels continued on this course until, within a few lengths of each other, the *Iona* suddenly veered across the *Chanticleer's* bow.

The only certain fact is that the *Iona* was fatally damaged in the collision and that, after her crew and some of their possessions, plus a very shaken young stowaway, were taken off by the boats of the *Chanticleer*, her bows rose dramatically into the air and she sank, stern first, in deep water. The master of the *Chanticleer* made an attempt to push the *Iona* towards the shore but to no avail. Curiously an offer of assistance from a passing tug appears to have been declined by the captain of the *Iona* who had insisted that the master of the *Chanticleer* accept liability for payment before he would allow his stricken vessel to be taken in tow. It would also appear that many of the crew, none of whom were local, were drunk when picked up by the *Chanticleer*.

The Wreck Today

The wreck lies in approximate position 55°57.912'N, 004°47.212'W (GPS), one hundred metres south east of Whiteforeland Buoy. She lies upright in 28 metres with stern pointing in the general direction of Helensburgh. The mid section of the vessel, with paddles still clearly visible, is all that remains.

The stern and bow sections have almost disappeared into the muddy seabed. The remaining centre section is approximately 25 metres long. The engines, with their large brass counterweights, and the boilers are the most obvious visible features. The superstructure and the funnels are long since gone although the bases of the twin stacks can still be seen. The sides of the ship above deck have fallen onto the seabed, as have many other items from on board.

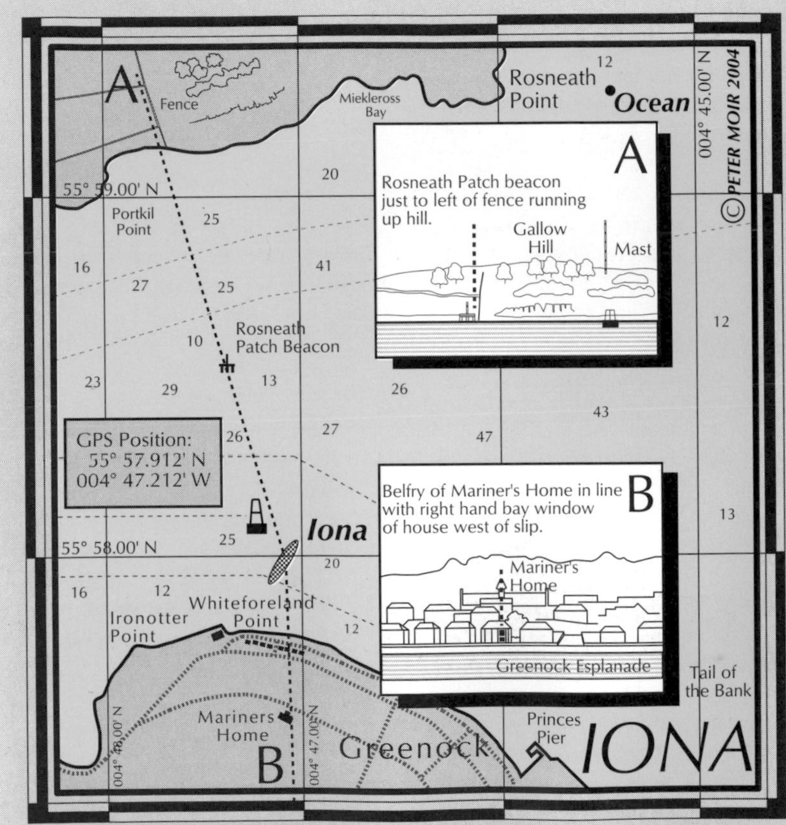

The huge store of coal for her long Atlantic voyage lies in mounds at both ends of the wreck. There are no major problems diving the wreck, however, it does lie in the shipping channel and therefore good boat cover and a sharp lookout are essential. The wreck itself is entangled with fishing line which can be a hazard in the darkness. The visibility, although always dark, is generally two or three metres. The current in this narrow part of the river can also be a problem at certain states of the tide. A dive around high water slack should give best conditions of current and visibility.

KATHLEEN and STROMBOLI

Kathleen. 1033nt. Iron steamship.
Built by R Irvine & Co, West Hartlepool.
Launched 1880.

Stromboli. 720nt. Iron steamship.
Built by Laird Bros, Birkenhead.
Launched 1870.

The narrow section of the Clyde between the Tail of the Bank and Glasgow has seen hundreds of maritime incidents over the years. These incidents have ranged in severity from vessels straying outwith the channel and stranding, to collisions, often accompanied by serious damage or even total loss of a vessel. One of the most renowned and unfortunate was the collision between the Glasgow cargo steamers *Kathleen* and *Stromboli* on New Year's Eve, 1904.

On the day in question the *Kathleen*, recently arrived from Bilbao with a cargo of iron ore, had picked up a river pilot at Princes Pier, Greenock and proceeded on the final leg of the voyage to Glasgow around 5pm. There was great anticipation among the members of her crew as, being New Year's Eve, they hoped to reach Glasgow before midnight.

Meanwhile the *Stromboli*, having left Glasgow earlier in the day for Valencia with a general cargo, was proceeding down river at around five knots. The weather at the time was hazy with visibility around half a mile. As the two vessels approached Garvel Point, a notorious place for mishaps due to the bend in the river, they both reduced their speeds.

On starting round Garvel Point those aboard the *Kathleen*, which was close in to the south side of the channel, observed the *Stromboli* taking a line inshore of her, effectively cutting the corner. The *Stromboli* crashed into the *Kathleen* on her starboard side destroying the aft engine room bulkhead.

Water poured into the *Kathleen* and she began to sink almost immediately. Most of the crew of the *Kathleen* jumped aboard the *Stromboli*, as the two vessels were firmly locked together. However, the 1st and 3rd engineers, Andrew McIntosh and James Struthers, were lost as a result of the collision, their escape blocked by the damaged bulkhead.

The ordeal for both crews was not yet over. The *Stromboli* had also been badly damaged in the collision and, in an attempt to separate his vessel from the *Kathleen*, the master of the *Stromboli*, Captain Drummond, ordered 'engines full astern' but only succeeded in backing the *Stromboli* onto the breakwater of James Watt Dock. This was the final blow as the *Stromboli* too began to fill and settle to the bottom still close by the sunken *Kathleen* on the south side of the channel. The crews of both vessels then abandoned the *Stromboli*, their escape aided by the pilot cutter *Nathaniel Dunlop* and the steamer *Cavalier*.

Daylight broke on New Year's Day to reveal both vessels lying half submerged across the channel with most of their superstructures, masts and rigging above water. The Clyde Lighthouse Trust placed a navigation light to the north of the wrecks. However, this did not prevent three vessels colliding with the stern of the *Kathleen* which protruded furthest into the channel. The most serious of these secondary collisions was that of the SS *Ardbeg* which stranded and sank on the stern of the *Kathleen* on 5th January, 1905.

Salvage work began almost immediately, with the removal of the more valuable items of the *Stromboli's* cargo which included whisky and sewing machines. After an initial delay caused by a succession of gales, which further damaged both vessels, the first priority of the East Coast Salvage Company was to 'untoggle' or separate the wrecks. This task was completed on 18th January and five days later the *Stromboli* was successfully raised. The work involved in raising the *Kathleen* was more complex due to the more extensive damage in the collision. However, on 25th February, she too was eventually raised and docked and at last the two bodies of her unfortunate engineers were recovered.

MAILLE BREZE

2441dt. Steel destroyer.
Built by Penhoet, St Nazaire.
Launched 1931.

Dimensions 424' x 39' x 16'

On the afternoon of 30th April, 1940 the French destroyer *Maille Breze* was lying in the crowded anchorage at the Tail of the Bank, Greenock. Her full crew were aboard busily making preparations for her next sortie.

Just before 3pm the quiet of the anchorage and the surrounding towns was shattered by a huge explosion. A live torpedo contained in the starboard torpedo tube which had been raised for routine maintenance had slipped from the tube and exploding as it hit the deck. It instantly killed the unfortunate crewman working on the tube and a number of others below deck. The explosion ripped a gaping hole in the deck and starboard side of the *Maille Breze* and started a fire which began to sweep through the destroyer fanned by a strong south west wind.

The anchorage immediately burst into life with vessels of all shapes and sizes rushing to the assistance of the stricken destroyer. As the *Maille Breze* began settling by the stern, the rescue ships picked up a number of survivors from the water and from the hot decks of the burning ship. The skippers of these vessels exposed themselves and their crews to considerable danger from the continuously exploding shells and ammunition on board the destroyer. Horrifically, the rescuers could hear the screams of French sailors trapped inside their burning, sinking ship, some of them even visible through the portholes and scuppers of the forward mess deck. However, despite strenuous and heroic efforts by the rescuers to save those unfortunate men trapped behind a buckled deck hatch, the screams soon died as the crewmen succumbed to the smoke and the flames.

The crews of the various ships in attendance fought for the rest of the afternoon to save the hulk of the *Maille Breze*. The tug *Marauder* even attempted to tow the wreck to the Clyde Repair slipways but eventually they surrendered the doomed vessel to the waters of the Clyde. Finally, in the early evening, five and three quarter hours after the initial explosion, she slipped beneath the waves, red hot decks hissing, sending up billowing clouds of steam as she disappeared, taking with her twenty eight of the crew.

The mast of the *Maille Breze*, protruding from the surface of the river, provided a constant reminder of the horror of that April afternoon in 1940 until the wreck was finally removed in 1954.

Frantic activity by rescue services to save those trapped below deck on the ***Maille Breze***.

MARY ANNING

797nt. Iron steamship.
Built by Palmers S B & Iron Co, Jarrow.
Launched January 1880.

Dimensions 240.5' x 30.7' x 20'

The *Mary Anning* left Glasgow on the afternoon of Friday 23rd January, 1885 under the command of Captain T Venables with a cargo of 1700 tons of coal for Odessa. She arrived at the Tail of the Bank, off Princes Pier, around 6pm and dropped anchor, intending to resume her voyage to the Black Sea the following morning.

In the early hours of the morning the coasting steamship *Argus* of Glasgow, under the charge of Captain Reid, passed Greenock on her regular run from Glasgow to Ayr. On clearing Princes Pier Captain Reid's attention was attracted by two vessels inward bound from the west and it would appear that he did not see the anchor lights of the *Mary Anning* until it was too late. The *Argus* crashed into the anchored steamer, stem on, striking her on the port side just aft of the bridge, cutting her down to the water's edge. With the exception of those on anchor watch, the crew of the *Mary Annning* were asleep. The violent collision instantly awoke them and as the realisation spread that their ship was sinking, panic ensued. Men in all states of dress spilled out onto the deck to escape from the sinking vessel. Fortunately, the two steamers remained locked together for some time and all twenty one crew members of the *Mary Anning* managed to scramble aboard the *Argus*. The *Argus* then backed away and the crews of both vessels watched as the *Mary Anning* slowly settled and disappeared from sight. The *Argus* then headed for Greenock where the survivors were landed and cared for at the Mariner's Home.

The *Mary Anning*, insured with her cargo for £23,000, was written off as a total loss. However, in March 1885, a salvage contract was let to Mr George Gush of Greenock for the removal of the wreck, as it was considered a hazard to navigation despite the fact that it lay in thirteen fathoms of water. The writers have been unable to establish the extent or success of this exercise, but it is believed that parts of the wreck still remain where she sank.

NUGGET

37nt. Wooden schooner.

Inward bound from Larne to Glasgow with a cargo of lime, the Belfast owned schooner *Nugget* was lost in a double collision on 12th November, 1910. She was approximately two and a half miles south west of the Cloch Lighthouse when the bows of a large steamship reared out of the foggy darkness and literally ran her down. Although swamped, the *Nugget* remained afloat and passed astern of the vessel, later identified as the 5400 ton Allan Line steamer *Hungarian*. Her ordeal was not yet over as, almost immediately, out of the mist loomed another steamer, this time it was the *Clan Alpine*, which, in taking avoiding action, sucked the *Nugget* under her stern, sending the schooner and her three crew to the bottom. After an unsuccessful search, the *Hungarian* returned to Greenock to report the incident. On arriving off the Esplanade at Greenock she stranded on a sandbank. The *Hungarian* was refloated two days later.

At a subsequent enquiry the masters of the *Hungarian* and the *Clan Alpine* were criticised for travelling too fast for the prevailing weather conditions. The master of the *Hungarian* had his certificate suspended for three months.

OCEAN

Motor vessel.

The *Ocean*, an ex Royal Navy aircraft carrier tender which had been converted to a pleasure cruiser by her owner Mr John Travis of Port Glasgow, left Inchgreen at 10.30am on 14th September, 1947 with twenty five people aboard for a day's outing to Ardentinny, Loch Long. As they motored downriver past Princes Pier the wind was rising causing Mrs Travis to ask her husband to stop and leave her and their daughter behind. This almost certainly was to save their lives. The rest of the party remained aboard and her husband set off towards Loch Long. He quickly saw that the weather was continuing to deteriorate and changed his plan to motor to the less exposed waters of Gareloch.

Their day went well but ominously the weather continued to worsen and, by the time they set off for the return trip, strong winds and heavy seas were sweeping across the river. For a short period Mr Travis tied up to an Admiralty buoy to see if the conditions would moderate but quickly decided to head back towards Greenock.

As the small craft ploughed into the waves, water quickly began to accumulate on deck until it was nearly a foot deep at the bow. The passengers, huddled beneath the canopy for shelter, became more and more agitated but the skipper motored on expecting to reach calmer waters on the south side of the river which would allow his friends to relax. Suddenly, when about half a mile south of Roseneath Point, the bow plunged deep into a large wave and the vessel sank within seconds. Only three people survived making this one of the worst pleasure craft disasters in the river's history.

The remains of the *Ocean* lie in position 55°59.267'N, 004°45.469'W (GPS) in 23 metres of water. The wreck has been dispersed by explosives as it lies at the edge of the channel leading into the Gareloch. The area, which is heavily patrolled by police and naval personnel due to the nuclear submarine base at Faslane, is marked as restricted on the charts making anchoring or diving off limits.

OSPREY

22nt. Iron steam yacht.
Built by Inglis & Co, Glasgow.
Launched 1877.

Dimensions 56.0' x 9.5' x 5.5'

On the morning of 28th September, 1889 the *Osprey* left her berth at the house of her owner, Mr R Brooman White, on Loch Long, to take a guest and the house gardener to Greenock to catch the train to Glasgow. She was under the command of Captain William Rogerson who had worked for Mr Brooman White for five years as the captain of the *Osprey*. He also had on board an engineer.

The *Osprey* berthed at Greenock and spent the day there waiting for the two men to return from their business in Glasgow. At 7pm that evening, with her two day trippers aboard, the *Osprey* set off into the clear dark night for the return journey to Ardarroch House. Captain Rogerson did not ignite his masthead light as he believed that all of the steamers would be finished for the day and, in any case, the night was clear and visibility good.

Meanwhile, the Caledonian Steamship Company's steamer *Madge Wildfire* was on her final run of the day from Kilmun to Gourock. She left Kilcreggan Pier at 7:37pm for the final leg of her voyage to Gourock.

Captain Rogerson was at the wheel of the *Osprey* with his two passengers on deck taking the night air when suddenly, out of the darkness, the bow of the *Madge Wildfire* loomed over them. Captain Campbell on board the *Madge Wildfire* reversed engines but it was too late. He crashed into the *Osprey* throwing the three men on deck into the water. Only Captain Rogerson survived and was recovered, unconscious, from the surface of the dark water.

The *Madge Wildfire* had sliced through the small craft, cutting it clean in two, while sustaining only minor damage to her bow. Indeed, many of the passengers on board were completely unaware of the tragedy until she came to a halt so that a boat could be lowered to pick up Captain Rogerson and search for the other men. After some time the *Madge Wildfire* set off for Gourock, leaving a boat to continue the fruitless search. Around midnight, Captain Rogerson was taken to Gourock and from there to Greenock where he regained consciousness and eventually recovered fully from his ordeal. Captain Campbell of the *Madge Wildfire* was cleared of any blame for the incident which was attributed to the lack of any light showing on the *Osprey*.

As far as we are aware, the wreck of the *Osprey* was never located nor salvaged. The authors have found the remains of a small steel wreck in position 55°58.409'N, 004°48.263'W (GPS). The wreckage consists of the bow section of a small steel vessel, lying upright in 28 metres and pointing towards Dunoon. The wreckage is badly distorted in places, as if it has almost been physically squashed. The wreckage is extremely small 10-12 metres long, and lies along the west side of a small bank.

PIONEER

30nt. Iron steamlighter.
Built by J & R Swan, Glasgow.
Launched 1859.

Dimensions 63.2' x 17.0' x 8.3'

Mechanical breakdowns and other misadventures were not uncommon in the early days of steam. The newspapers of the mid 19th century are full of stories of steam vessels having to rig sails after loosing power, or paddlesteamers machinery getting jammed in either forward or reverse. It was such a mishap that caused the loss of the Glasgow steamlighter *Pioneer* on Wednesday 1st November, 1869 while en route from Bowling to Brodick Castle.

The *Pioneer* had left Bowling the previous day and anchored overnight in the Holy Loch. She resumed her journey early the next day and steamed south passed Dunoon along the Cowal shore towards Arran.

Her passage was noted by a fishing smack off Bullwood, mainly because one of the lighter's crew was shooting seabirds with a rifle. The crew of the fishing boat returned to their work but were soon startled by a tremendous explosion and turned to see the *Pioneer* enveloped in a cloud of smoke and steam with debris hurtling through the air thirty feet above the water. As parts of the lighter landed in the sea, the bow was seen to rise up and the *Pioneer* sank by the stern, taking with her, her master Hugh Travers, and crew of two.

Boats in the vicinity raced to the scene, but little remained afloat except some hatch boards, timber debris and two cloth caps. The cause of the loss was thought to be a boiler explosion, most likely resulting from cold water entering an almost empty and overheating boiler.

The *Pioneer* was owned by a Mr James Jeffrey of Glasgow and was valued at £450, but not insured. To add to his woes, the cargo of coal had as yet not been paid for and was in his charge. The wreck of the *Pioneer* lies approximately three-quarters of a mile off the Cowal shore, just to the south of Bullwood, it is unlikely that much will remain today.

PORTLAND

581nt. Iron steamship.
Built by W D Thompson, Dundee.
Launched 1887.

Dimensions 241.0' x 33.7' x 15.8'

The *Portland* left Glasgow on her final voyage at 6pm on 5th December, 1907 bound for Belfast and London with a general cargo. She was owned by the Clyde Shipping Company of Glasgow and had a crew of twenty five on board under the command of Captain Robert Jamieson. The heavy fog that night made her voyage down the river to Greenock very slow and, on arrival there, Captain Jamieson decided to wait for clearer weather. She finally left the West Quay at 0:45am the next day and headed down river against the flood tide with visibility improving to about one mile. She edged steadily into the hazy mist at half speed.

Captain Jamieson had one of the crew posted at the bow as lookout. As the Cloch Lighthouse appeared in the distance after passing Gourock, they heard a ship's whistle through the fog. The whistle came from the 360 ton schooner rigged steamship *Welshman*, belonging to John and David Kennedy of Glasgow, which was on a voyage from Belfast to the Clyde with a cargo of limestone. Captain Donald McPherson was in command of the *Welshman* and its crew of nine.

As they approached the Cloch Lighthouse the crew of the *Welshman* also heard a steamer on their starboard bow but, although Captain McPherson telegraphed the engine room to stand by, he did not slow from his full steaming speed of eight knots. A few minutes later, as he passed the Cloch, the *Portland's* white masthead and green starboard lights were sighted ahead. The appearance of the green light placed the *Portland* to the starboard side of the *Welshman* although, later, witnesses on the *Portland* were to state that the *Welshman* was off their port bow when first sighted. This observation proved vital in arriving at the reason why the subsequent collision occurred.

SS ***Portland***.

Captain McPherson turned to port and sounded his horn to let the crew of the *Portland* know he had carried out the manoeuvre. Inexplicably, at this point Captain Jamieson on board the *Portland* responded by turning to starboard, placing his craft across the bows of the *Welshman.*

By now it was too late to take any further avoiding action and the *Welshman* ran into the port side of the *Portland* just behind the bridge. The horrendous crash, loud enough to awaken people ashore, tore a huge hole in the side of the *Portland* and broke the stem of the *Welshman.* The *Portland* was sinking fast and although the *Welshman* herself was severely damaged she stood by until the crew of the *Portland* were picked up from the boats. The *Portland* sank fifteen minutes after the collision taking with her the stoker, Mobin Moonie, who probably died or was injured in the initial collision.

(No. 7053.)

"PORTLAND" (S.S.)

AND

"WELSHMAN" (S.S.).

The Merchant Shipping Act, 1894.

In the matter of a Formal Investigation held at the Ordinary Court, Glasgow, on the 18th, and at the Debts Recovery Court, Glasgow, on the 20th, both days of March, 1907, before William George Scott Moncrieff, Esquire, Advocate, Sheriff Substitute of Lanarkshire, assisted by Rear-Admiral Henry Charles Bigge, Captain Alexander Wood, and Captain David Anderson, into the circumstances attending the loss of the British s.s. "Portland," of Glasgow, through collision with the British s.s. "Welshman," of Glasgow, off the Cloch Lighthouse, Firth of Clyde, on or about 6th February, 1907, whereby loss of life ensued.

The enquiry into the sinking found that the main cause was the error by Captain Jamieson of the *Portland* when he turned to starboard, despite clear signals from the *Welshman* that she had already turned to port. It was also held that the captain of the *Welshman* contributed to the accident by not slowing or stopping when he first heard the *Portland's* whistle through the fog.

The wreck of the *Portland* remains one of the most intriguing in the upper part of the Clyde as, to date, she has not yet been found. There are numerous reports of wrecks in the area near the Europa, the other wreck sunk in a similar collision off the Cloch in 1884, but despite many attempts, it has not been located. The most likely report to date places the wreck north west of the Cloch lying on a sloping seabed at a depth of over 80 metres in position 55°57.298'N, 004°52.788'W (GPS).

HMS SEAGULL

735dt. Torpedo gun boat.
Built Chatham Dockyard.
Launched May 1889.

Dimensions 230.0' x 27.0' x 10.5'

After her launch on 31st May, 1889 the *Seagull* was finally completed in January 1891 and ready for service. She was a Sharpshooter Class gun boat and, by the time war broke out, was commanded by Lieutenant Raymond H Dunn RN. She sailed with a compliment of 90 aboard and her twin vertical triple expansion engines pushed her along at a steady nineteen knots. She had 2 - 4.7" guns, 4 - 3 pounders and a main armament of 5 - 14" torpedo tubes.

The details of her loss are vague due to wartime restrictions and incomplete records now held in Public Records Office at Kew. However it is known that she was lost in a collision with a merchant vessel, probably SS *Corrib,* on 30th September,1918. The *Seagull* was outward bound at the time and collided with the steamer which was heading up river. Fifty lives were lost in the disaster. There were twenty one survivors reported. The exact location of her loss in also unclear although two different reports indicate that the collision took place off Wemyss Bay and two miles south of the Cloch boom.

There is a large, in tact wreck lying in 90 metres in position 55°54.323'N, 004°55.263'W (GPS). The wreck lies oriented 120/300 degrees, is approximately 65 metres long and stands some 8 metres from seabed. From the position and the measurement of the wreck it seems likely that this is the wreck of the *Seagull.*

HMS **_Seagull_**.

TIGER

44gt. Steel steam tug.
Built by G Brown & Co, Greenock.
Launched November 1902.

Dimensions 61.8' x 13.5' x 7.6'

The *Tiger*, built for the Associated Portland Cement Company of London, was intended for service on the River Medway between Sheerness and Burham.

She commenced trials on 22nd December, 1902 under the supervision of Captain Scott of the builders. The trials proceeded satisfactorily over the next two days, uncovering only minor problems with the engine and the gear used for raising and lowering the funnel. The tug had been designed and built with a funnel and mast that could be lowered and raised to allow passage below the low bridges of the River Medway. The only other problem, apparently minor, was that only one scupper had been cut in the port side. Some additional counterbalance weights were added to ease the operation of the funnel and it was agreed that two additional scuppers would be cut on the port side at a later date.

The steam tug ***Lion***, sistership of the ***Tiger***.

After a holiday on Christmas Day the trials resumed on 26th December when the *Tiger* left James Watt Dock, Greenock, along with her sister ship *Lion*, at 11:50am and headed for the Gareloch to adjust her compasses. The engineer, Simmons, had to pump eight inches of water from the engine room crank pit prior to departure. As the vessel left harbour it was observed that she had a slight list of about three inches to port.

As she headed seawards, with a complement of thirteen and watched by a crowd on the dockside, she steered into a strong west north west wind. When she was about one and a half miles from James Watt Dock and a quarter of a mile west of the guardship *Benbow*, she turned to starboard and headed directly for the Gareloch. The wind was now on the port bow and the choppy seas began shipping over the port gunwhale which had only a freeboard of eleven inches. The water immediately began to accumulate on the port side and in a very short time the list had increased so dramatically that it was obvious that she was about to sink. The pilot, Mr Gordon, left his position at the wheel and shouted to those below to come on deck. The bow swung to port and, as the sea hit the starboard side, she heeled over and foundered in one or two minutes, to the horror of those watching from the shore. All of her crew were thrown into the water as they had no time to get out the ship's lifeboat. Immediately a number of small boats rushed to the scene and succeeded in picking up nine of the crew of thirteen although unfortunately three of them died soon after on the *Benbow*.

The Board of Trade enquiry into the sinking could not establish the exact cause of the accident although, from the story related, it would appear that the vessel, which by design had a very low freeboard, was not on an even keel when she left the dock, possibly due to the counter weights added to the funnel mechanism a few days earlier. This, combined with the lack of scuppers on the port side, would appear to have been the cause of the loss in the rough seas off Greenock that December day in 1902.

The wreck was located and buoyed a few days later in approximately nineteen metres but, despite reports that attempts were made to lift her, no actual evidence can be found that this took place successfully.

Steamlighter Z

33nt. Iron steamlighter.
Approximately 60' long.

The steamlighter *Z* sank off Princes Pier, Greenock on 22nd February, 1937 after a collision with the Dutch coaster *Eland*.

At the time of the collision both vessels were passing West Quay, Greenock heading up river. The *Z* was making little headway against the strong ebb tide, so her crew decided to return to Gourock Bay. As the lighter turned she was struck by the *Eland* and badly holed on her port side. The crew immediately jumped aboard the *Eland* and were safely landed at Customhouse Quay.

In their haste to escape the crew had not stopped the lighter's engines. Still under power and afloat the *Z* steamed off down river towards the Tail of the Bank. Realising that their vessel was remaining afloat the lighter's crew, Duncan Given and John Donnelly, rushed to Princes Pier where they boarded a launch and took off in pursuit.

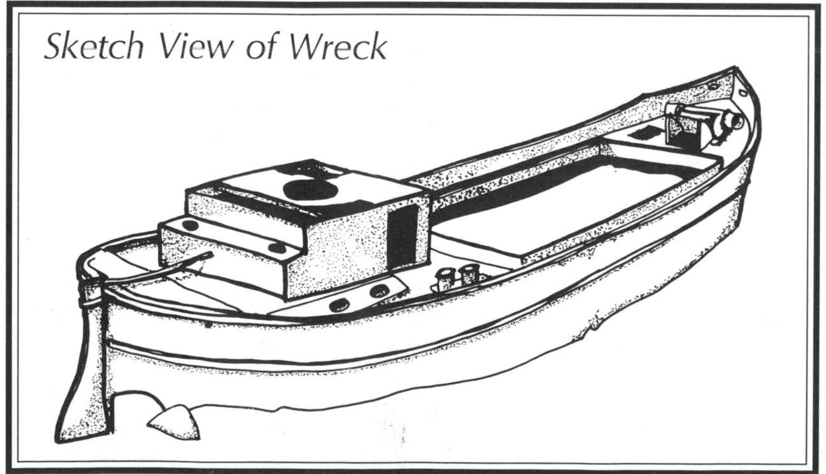

Sketch View of Wreck

Two launches eventually took the *Z* in tow, assisted by the tug *Flying Buzzard*. However, she finally sank about 800 yards north of Princes Pier, in fourteen fathoms.

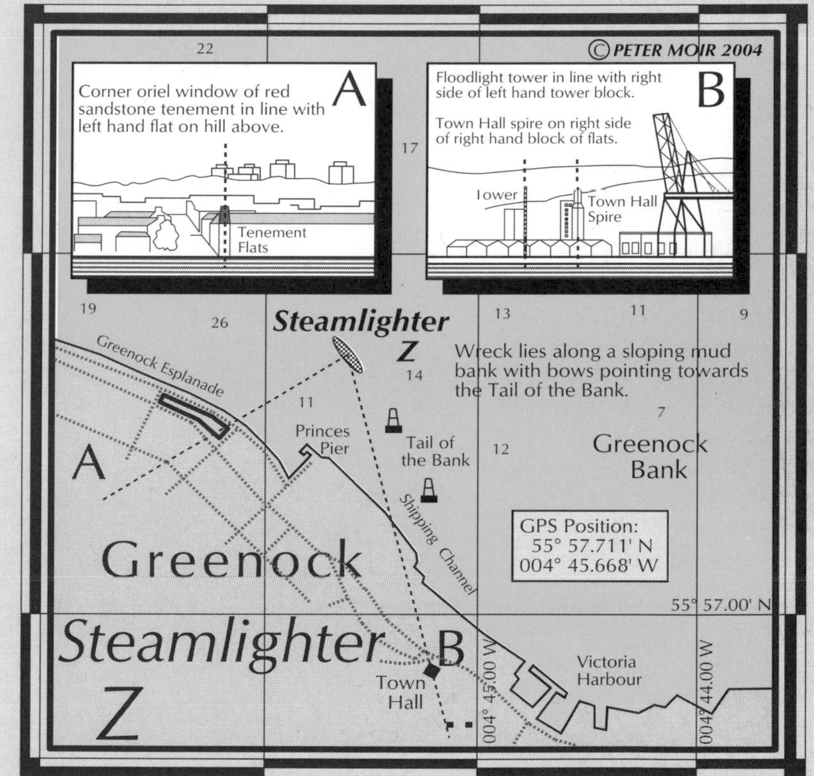

Although the wreck, lying in approximate position 55°57.711'N, 004°45.668'W (GPS) has not been positively identified as the *Z*, it is indeed the wreck of a steamlighter, lying in approximately the correct position and depth. The wreck lies along a gently sloping mud seabed between 24 and 26 metres and is oriented 140/320 degrees with bow pointing south east. The hull is virtually intact and would appear to be approximately 60' long.

UPPER FIRTH

Listed below are a selection of 65 smaller vessels wrecked within this area. This list is included as a basis for further research. Names suffixed by (S) denote extensive salvage work or total removal subsequent to date of loss.

NAME	BUILT	TONNAGE	HULL	TYPE	LOST	CAUSE	LOCATION
Active	1859	12nt	W	Sl	10.09.1867	C	Off Garvel Point
Admiral	1886	11nt	I	S.tug	25.12.1909	C	Off Greenock
Agnes	1846	31nt	I	SS	13.10.1891	S	Cove
Amelia	1856	44nt	W	Sr	28.01.1884	S	Holy Loch
Argyle		24nt	W	Sk	20.10.1873	F	Off Dunoon
Arthur	1877	30nt	I	SS	13.05.1903	F	Off Cove
Aurora	1876	31nt	I	Sr	22.12.1894	S	Gourock Bay
Betty Clark	1917	32nt	W	Sl	25.01.1822	F	Off Inverkip
Blair	1868	26nt	I	SS	15.09.1878	S	Cove, Loch Long
Brigit Smith	-	32gt	W	Sr	21.10.1874	C	Off Greenock
Castle Hill	1841	24nt	W	Sr	09.03.1851	C	Off Cloch Point
Celano(S)	-	1148gt	S	SS	10.07.1941	S	Tail of the Bank
Centenary	1839	63nt	W	Sr	17.01.1884	S	Holy Loch
Cessnock(S)			S	Drg	00.01.1968	F	Off Princes Pier
Cumberland(HMS)	1842	2214bn	W	HMS	17.02.1889	S/Fr	Roseneath Bay
Daisy	1902	50gt	W	A.Dr	25.04.1942	F	Off Greenock
Degaussing barge			I			F	Loch Goil
Dolphin	1869	37nt	W	Sk	20.08.1905	S	Strone Point
Dredger No.6	1854	400gt	I	Drg	27.08.1889	C	Off Dumbarton
Eclipse	1849	200gt	I	PS	02.09.1854	S	Gantock Rock
Effort	1845	40nt	W	Sk	16.12.1853	C	Tail of the Bank
Eliza	1846	29nt	W	SS	20.03.1884	S	Kilcreggan
Elizabeth		135nt	W	Bg	10.12.1898	C	Off Greenock
Flying Scud	1861	172nt	W	Bn	12.12.1883	S	Gourock Bay
Foison	1867	14nt	W	Sk	25.02.1910	C	Off Gourock
Forecast(S)	1925	96gt	W	A.Dr	10.04.1944	F	Off Greenock
Fredheim(S)	1898	1144nt	I	SS	24.01.1928	C	Off Dumbarton
Go Ahead	1869	16gt	W	Sk	16.03.1891	S	Holy Loch
Golden Effort	1914	86gt	W	Dr	23.09.1943	A/C	Off Greenock

NAME	BUILT	TONNAGE	HULL	TYPE	LOST	CAUSE	LOCATION
Governor Picton	1800	204bn	W	S	25.02.1803	S	Inverkip
Gowanhill	1920	96gt	S	Dr	07.05.1941	A/C	Off Greenock
Guy Fawkes	1849	34nt	I	SS	29.12.1864	C	Off Kempock Point
Harriet	1854	36nt	W	Sr	21.10.1874	S/f	Helensburgh
Hart		138bn	W	Bgn	16.02.1811	F	Off Greenock
Hibernia			W	S	03.08.1816	S	Strone, Holy Loch
Hopper No.2(S)	1862	236gt	I	Barge	13.02.1900	C	Near Erskine
Hopper No.13(S)	1871	311gt	I	Barge	14.08.1926	C	Bowling
Invergowrie(S)	1883	72nt	I	SS	23.10.1939	Exp	Off Greenock
Isabella	1844	32nt	W	Sr	01.11.1864	C	Off Greenock
James			W	SS	08.12.1851	F	Off Greenock
Kelpie		35nt	I	SS	21.02.1885	C	Off Greenock
Leading Star(S)		33nt	I	SS	03.11.1897	C	Off Greenock
Linnet	1866	33gt	I	SS	15.01.1932	C	Shandon, Gareloch
Mamo	1865	22nt	W	Sk	29.12.1899	S	Gourock Bay
Margaret	1861	26gt	W	Sk	01.03.1864	S/f	Cove, Loch Long
Marksman	1866	25nt	I	SS	14.09.1878	F	Off Cove
Maureen	1936	36gt	W	Myt	06.07.1937	S/f	Gareloch
Norma(S)		11nt	I	SS	16.03.1897	F	Gourock Bay
Olivette	1892	5nt	W	Syt	12.11.1901	F	Gourock Bay
Peep O'Day		32nt	I	SS	12.03.1867	S	Off Greenock
Provanhall		23nt	I	SS	13.03.1871	F	Off Greenock
Rebecca	1862	78nt	W	Sr	21.02.1903	S	Roseneath Point
Rhoda	1863	31nt	I	SS	20.06.1879	F	Off Lunderston Bay
Roebuck	1775	47bn	W	Sl	15.12.1803	S	Holy Loch
Royal Arch	1855	48nt	W	Sk	27.01.1884	C	Holy Loch
St Bees(S)	1883	1755gt	I	SS	15.09.1912	C	Garvel Point
Satellite(S)	1877	25nt	I	STug	05.04.1918	C	Albert Harbour, Greenock
Seagull	1906	6gt	W	Myt	27.07.1909	Ex	2m NW Gourock Pier
Sisters	1829	42nt	W	Sk	10.11.1892	C	Off Cloch Point
Sunbeam	1872	24nt	I	Sr	06.11.1882	F	Off Dunoon
Sunderland				A/c	WW II	F	Gourock Bay
Telegraph	1840	36gt	W	SS	21.03.1842	Ex	Helensburgh Pier
Valkyrie II(S)	1893	155gt	W	Yt	05.07.1894	C	Holy Loch
Vesta	1863	28nt	W	SS	02.03.1886	S	Sandbank Pier
Wild Duck	1866	25nt	W	Sr	04.08.1884	S	Near Dunoon Pier

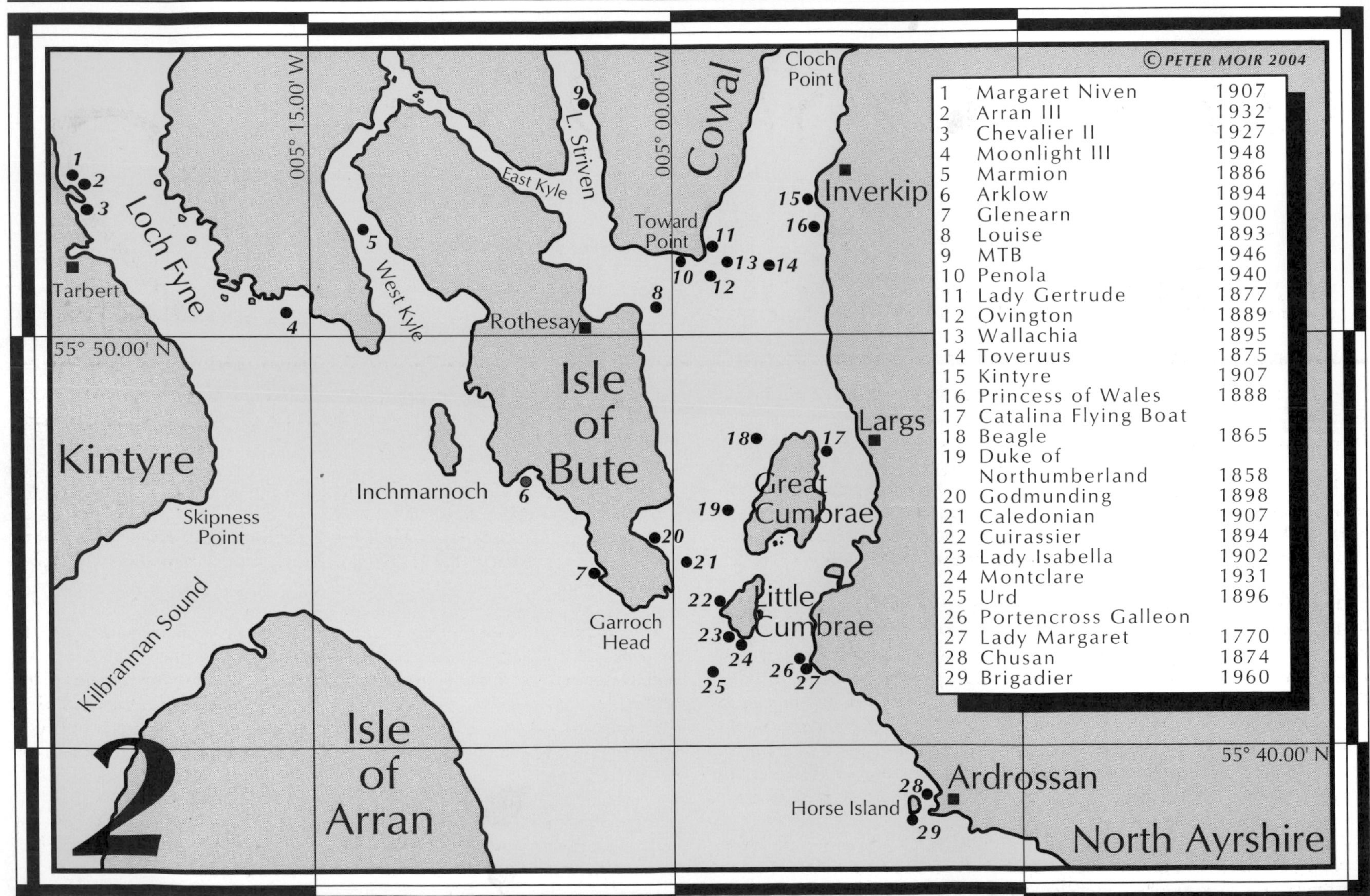

© PETER MOIR 2004
1 Margaret Niven 1907
2 Arran III 1932
3 Chevalier II 1927
4 Moonlight III 1948
5 Marmion 1886
6 Arklow 1894
7 Glenearn 1900
8 Louise 1893
9 MTB 1946
10 Penola 1940
11 Lady Gertrude 1877
12 Ovington 1889
13 Wallachia 1895
14 Toveruus 1875
15 Kintyre 1907
16 Princess of Wales 1888
17 Catalina Flying Boat
18 Beagle 1865
19 Duke of Northumberland 1858
20 Godmunding 1898
21 Caledonian 1907
22 Cuirassier 1894
23 Lady Isabella 1902
24 Montclare 1931
25 Urd 1896
26 Portencross Galleon
27 Lady Margaret 1770
28 Chusan 1874
29 Brigadier 1960
005° 15.00' W
005° 00.00' W
55° 50.00' N
55° 40.00' N
Tarbert
Loch Fyne
West Kyle
East Kyle
L. Striven
Cowal
Cloch Point
Inverkip
Toward Point
Rothesay
Isle of Bute
Inchmarnoch
Kintyre
Skipness Point
Kilbrannan Sound
Garroch Head
Great Cumbrae
Little Cumbrae
Largs
Isle of Arran
Horse Island
Ardrossan
North Ayrshire
2

CLYDE COAST NORTH

Chapter 2

INVERKIP TO ARDROSSAN

The Firth continues south from Inverkip to reach the south tip of the Cowal peninsula where Toward Lighthouse, built in 1811, sweeps out its protective beam to approaching shipping. Here the last semblance of a river is lost and the Clyde opens into a wide sea estuary with many islands and narrow channels to endanger passing ships. To the west of Toward lie the picturesque and treacherous Kyles of Bute which swing north west then south east round the northern tip of the island of Bute. Further to the west lies the long and deep expanse of Loch Fyne, which provides spectacular diving but few shipwrecks.

The major area described in this chapter centres around the islands of Great and Little Cumbrae and the south tip of Bute. Here the wide expanse of the Firth becomes two narrow channels, each just over a mile wide, one to the east and one to the west of the barren rocky island of Little Cumbrae. In 1757 the first lighthouse to be built on the river was constructed on top of Little Cumbrae to guide ships safely through these hazardous waters. With the coming of steam the dangers were further reduced as vessels no longer had to rely on the vagaries of the wind and it became usual practice to engage the services of one of the river's fleet of steam tugs to ensure safe navigation of these narrow channels.

South of Little Cumbrae the Firth widens out to over 15 miles and becomes considerably deeper, especially off the east coast of Arran, here the nature of the shipwrecks change. The open expanse of the Firth provides little or no shelter from the prevailing southerly winds and many of the vessels lost within this part of the Clyde are due to stranding or foundering in stormy weather conditions.

Diving in the area covered in this chapter is similar to that described in the previous chapter especially in the northern section. A number of fairly intact wrecks can be found north of the Little Cumbrae, again often the result of collision, sitting upright on the muddy seabed at between thirty and forty metres seabed depth.

The number of collisions significantly reduces the further south one moves, the predominant cause of loss becomes stranding in storms or fog. For the underwater explorer this also brings a change in the nature of the remains of the wrecks. As a general view, southwards from the Little Cumbrae, the accessible wrecks are in shallower water and substantially broken up, first by the activities of the many salvage firms operating on the river and second, by the action of the sea itself.

There are a number of deep water wrecks south of Little Cumbrae such as the SS *Urd*, HMS *Topaze* and HMS *Dasher*, these wrecks are now being visited and explored by teams of experienced technical divers.

ARKLOW

1474nt. Wooden sailing ship.
Built by N Moscher, Newport, Nova Scotia.
Launched 1879.

Dimensions 214.0' x' 40.0' x 13.6'

The *Arklow* ran ashore on Ardnahoe Point near Scalpsie Bay, Bute around 11pm on Thursday 20th December, 1894. She had left Greenock, in ballast, for her home port of Windsor, Nova Scotia some four days earlier, under the command of Captain T D Moscher.

A changeable weather system was prevailing over Scotland which had, in the intervening period, already forced her to return to Rothesay on two occasions. It was in fact when returning to Rothesay for a third time that the stranding occurred.

An attempt was made to "sail the vessel off" on the next high tide, but the wind strength proved insufficient. An offer of a tow from the tug *Champion* was refused as Captain Moscher considered the tug to be underpowered and was confident that other assistance would soon be offered. Unfortunately no further assistance was offered or secured and the fate of the *Arklow* was finally sealed on the night of Friday 22nd December when a hurricane swept across Scotland wreaking havoc on land and sea.

The *Arklow* was severely damaged and although a further attempt was made to tow her off on Christmas Eve she was eventually left to rot where she lay, after most of her fittings had been removed.

ARRAN III

49nt. Steel steamship.
Built by Ayrshire Dockyard Co Ltd, Irvine.
Launched March 1926.

Dimensions 99.7' x 21.1' x 9.2'

The *Arran* was owned by Clyde Cargo Steamers Ltd and employed carrying cargo between the ports of the Clyde estuary.

Early in the morning of 31st December, 1932 she left Ardrishaig on Loch Fyne with a cargo of empty beer bottles. As she headed south towards Tarbert she fought her way into a south easterly gale. Around 6:30am she ran aground on the rocky outcrop of Sgeir Leathann off Barmore Island, which lies about one and a half miles north east of East Loch Tarbert.

As dawn broke, the *Arran* could be seen high and dry on the rocks only a short distance from the shore. The company's representative in Tarbet arrived on the scene and a tug was sent for, but the *Arran* had been badly holed. As the incoming tide began to further flood the grounded vessel the crew abandoned ship and shortly afterwards the Arran slipped off the rocks into deeper water.

The Wreck Today

The wreck of the *Arran*, although substantially salvaged after her loss, lies as she sank in position 55°53.517'N, 005°24.233'W (GPS) which is on the north west corner of Sgeir Leathann. She lies on a sloping rocky seabed with her stern at 12 metres and her bow in 5 metres. The best way to locate the wreck is to enter the water towards the east end of the north side of the rock and swim west at ten metres until you reach the wreck.

SS *Arran III.*

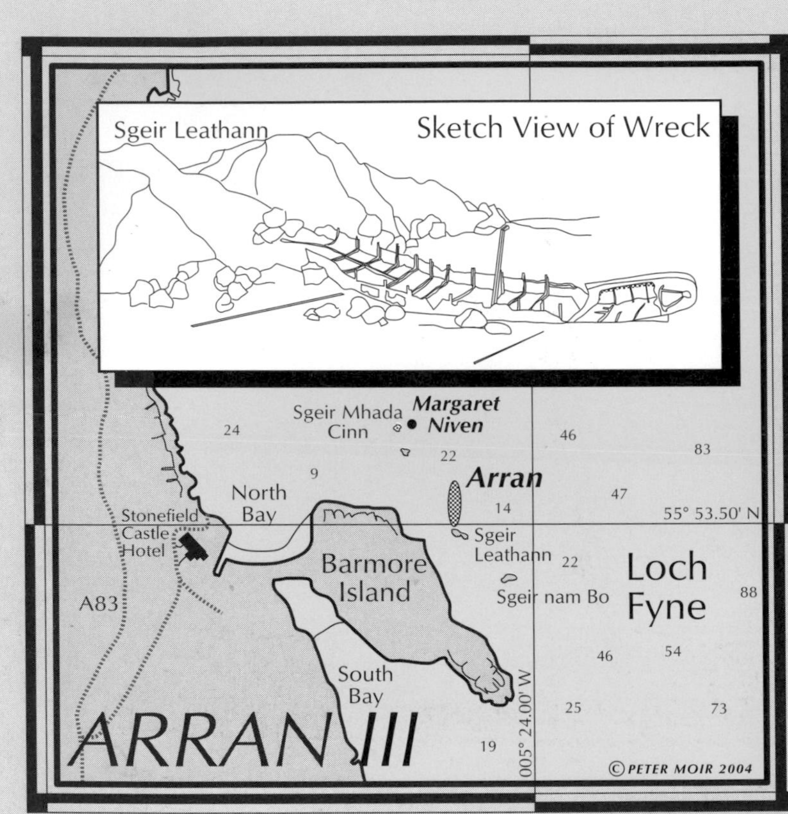

The wreck itself lies on its port side and is well broken although the stern, keel and main ribs are still fairly intact. Access to the site is only really practical by boat which can be launched at Tarbert although we believe some extremely fit divers have been known to reach the shore of Barmore Island overland through the grounds of Stonefield Castle Hotel and snorkel out to the island. Please ask for permission from the hotel owners if you choose this approach.

BEAGLE

454gt. Iron steamship.
Built by Tod & McGregor, Partick.
Launched 1864.

Dimensions 185.9' x 26.3' x 13.6'

Launched on the 21st July, 1864 to the order of Messrs G & J Burns of Glasgow, the *Beagle*, a small cargo passenger steamer, worked mainly between the ports of Belfast and Glasgow. Advertised to sail from Glasgow on Tuesdays and Fridays and from Belfast on Mondays and Thursdays, she could offer a return trip with first class cabin for 30 shillings.

It was on this service that, on 8th November, 1865 inward bound, she collided with Messrs Handyside & Henderson's steamer *Napoli* off Skate Point, Great Cumbrae and sank shortly afterwards. The *Napoli* struck the *Beagle* on her port side, twelve feet aft of her forecastle, slicing through her hull and decking to the foredeck hatch. The large open forehold of the *Beagle* quickly filled with water as the vessels separated. The crew of the *Beagle*, in all states of dress as some had been asleep, were rescued by a passing tug, the *Pearl*, which had been inshore of the *Beagle* when the collision occurred. Everyone aboard was saved but the *Beagle* quickly sank, some nine minutes later. The *Napoli* sustained damage to her stem and bow plating and returned to Greenock under her own steam. She was towed to Glasgow the following day for repairs.

The Wreck Today

The *Beagle* lies in a general depth of 34 - 38 metres, on an even keel, oriented 170/350 degrees, with stern pointing north west. The open hull has a shallowest depth of 30 - 32 metres, dependent on the state of the tide. She is marked on Admiralty charts in position 55°47.314'N, 004°56.639'W (GPS). The straight stem rises 4.5 metres out of the sand, silt seabed covered with orange and white plumose anemonae. On top of the forecastle the main anchor can be seen along with the bow steam winch. Heading aft you can descend into the forehold area, which is a profusion of silt covered debris. On the port side the huge tear of the collision damage is clearly visible.

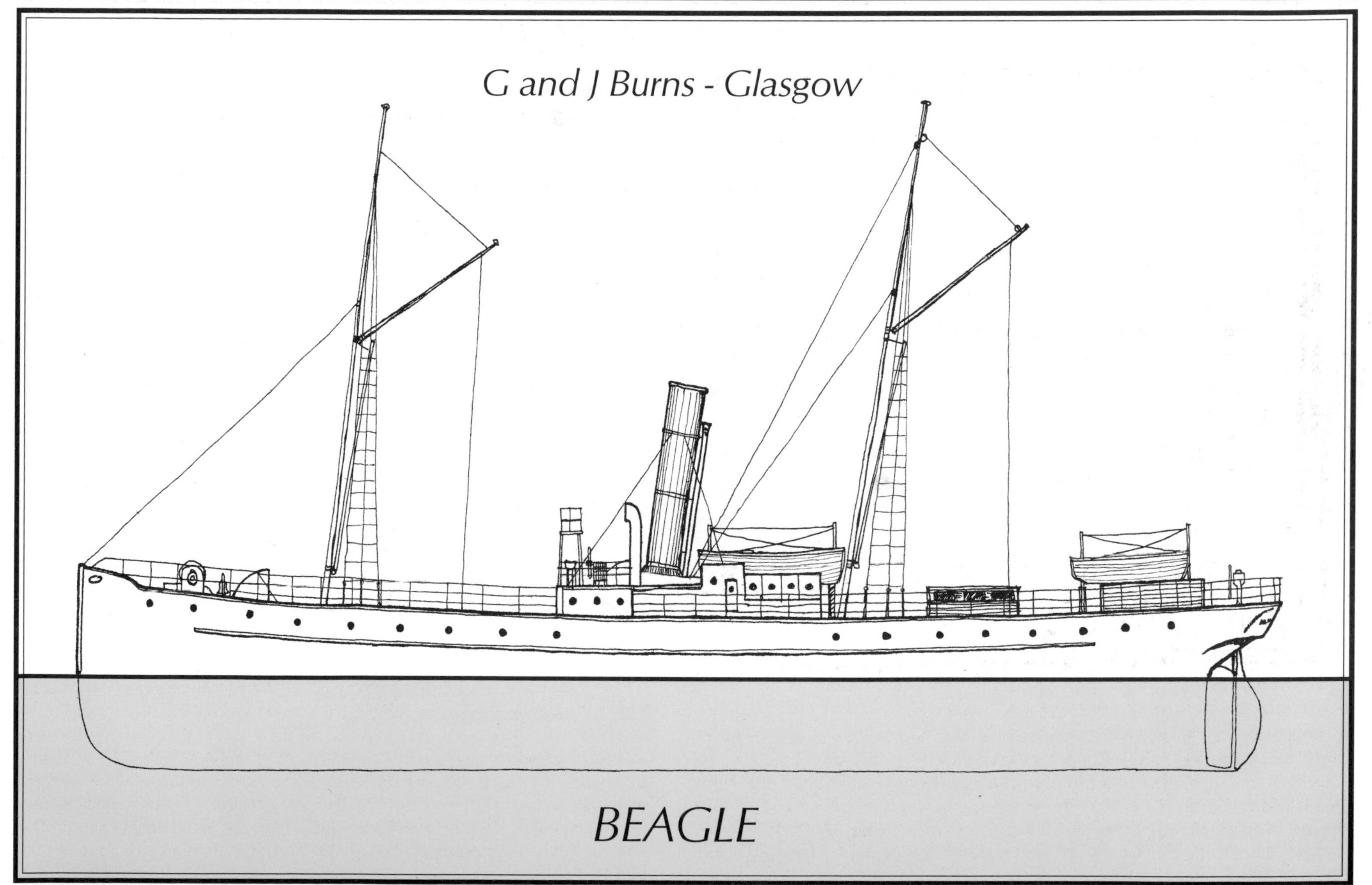
G and J Burns - Glasgow
BEAGLE

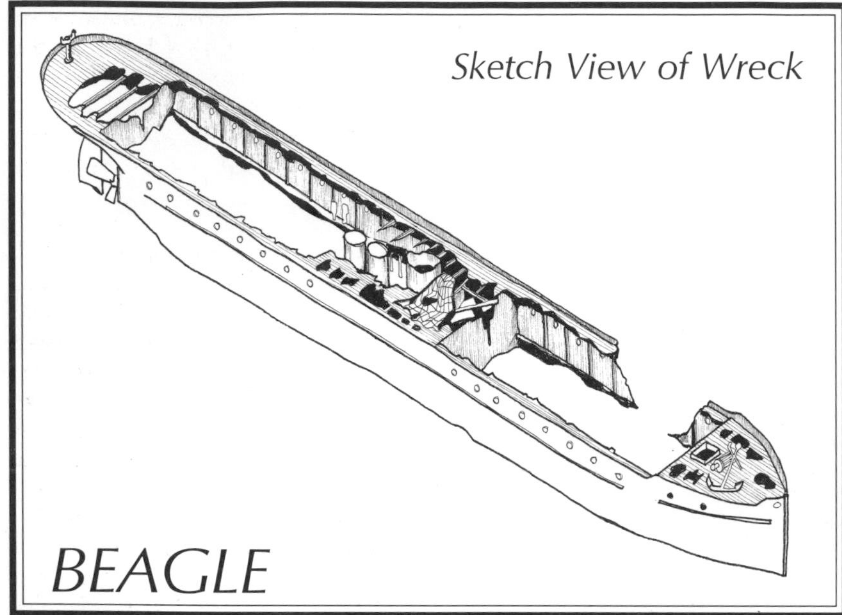

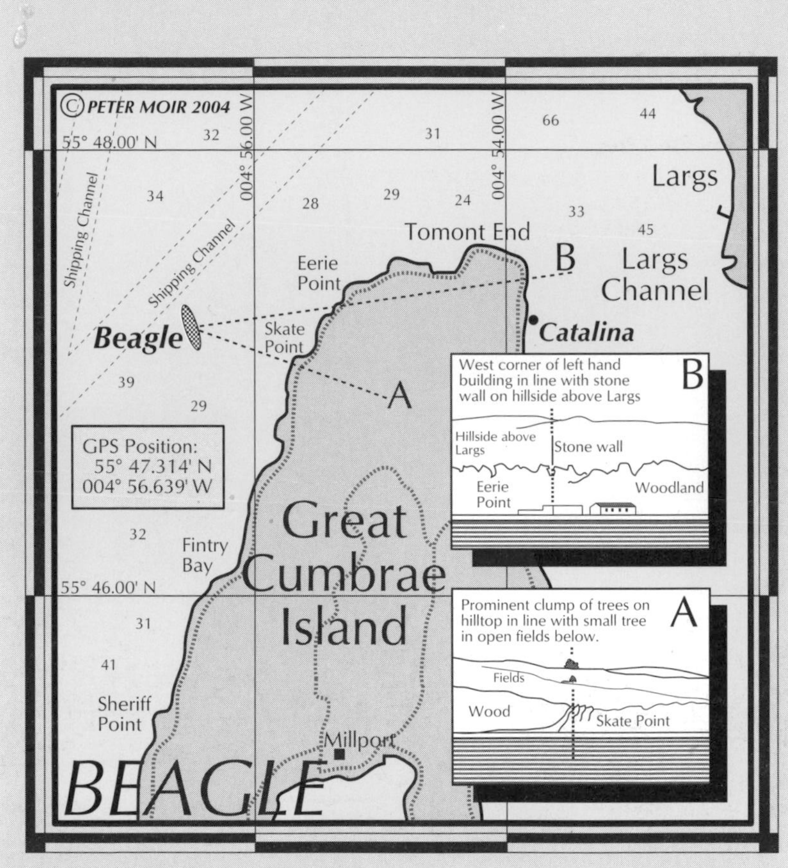

All decking and support beams have collapsed into the bow hold from above. At the rear of the forehold is the engine room forward bulkhead and the diver has to ascend to the main deck level to continue aft.

Just forward of the net shrouded boiler stack would have been the wheelhouse area, although this too has collapsed into the forehold. Astern of the boiler stack lies the engine room area and, as the aft bulkhead has crumbled, it is possible to pass into the stern section unhindered. The stern accommodation area resembles the forehold, with piles of debris and lurking conger eels. At the stern itself all that remains in board is the emergency steering post and some tangled metal debris - the remains of the stern decking. In good visibility, dropping onto the seabed can provide interesting views of the wreck. Best suited for this are the bow and particularly the stern with rudder, propeller and overhanging stern covered in soft coral and anemonae.

Visibility on the wreck averages 4-5 metres although, as with all the wrecks in this area, this will vary with the state of the tide and prevailing weather conditions. Tidal movement over the wreck is generally weak and rarely exceeds 1 knot, although surface currents running slightly harder have been experienced down to 6 or 7 metres at spring tides.

BRIGADIER

268gt. Steel tug.
Built by J Crown & Sons Ltd, Sunderland.
Launched 1942.
(Ex EMPIRE FRANK)

Dimensions 114.0' x 26.2' x 12.9'

The ***Brigadier*** ashore on Horse Island.

The Steel and Bennie tug *Brigadier* left Greenock in the early hours of the morning on Sunday 19th October, 1960 to assist two Norwegian tankers, the *Mosburg* and the *Norsefoss*, into the Shell Refinery terminal at Ardrossan.

As she approached the entrance to Ardrossan Harbour she was engulfed in a sudden snow squall and ran aground on the south tip of Horse Island, tearing her hull on a shallow reef. She immediately began to settle as water rushed in through the gash in her hull. The vessel's approach had been observed by the Harbour Pilot, Mr Neil McDonald, who guessed she had gone aground before the distress flares confirmed the *Brigadier's* predicament. He quickly set off in the pilot boat and picked up the shaken crew, some of whom had to wade through deep water in the engine room to make their escape. He later returned for Captain McKeague who had remained on board to inspect the condition of his vessel.

Salvage was carried out by Metal Industries who broke her up where she lay as removal was considered impossible. The scattered remains of the salvage operation lie in position 55°38.521'N, 004°50.567'W. It should be noted that it is not permitted to land on Horse Island as it is a bird sanctuary.

CALEDONIAN

122nt. Iron hopper dredger.
Built by Wm Simons & Co, Renfrew.
Launched 1874.

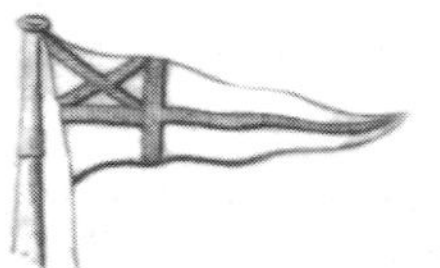

Dimensions 133.6' x 24.6' x 12.2'

The first indication of the loss of the Caledonian Railway Company dredger *Caledonian* on 4th September, 1907 was the arrival at Greenock of the steam trawler *Nettle* with severe damage to her bow plating and stem post.

Her master, Captain Jackson, reported that around 5pm the *Nettle* had been in collision with the dredger half a mile east of Kilchatten Bay, Bute. The *Caledonian* had cut across the bows of the *Nettle* while discharging her dredgings from Bowling harbour and was badly holed on her starboard side. Soon after the collision the *Caledonian* began to sink and the dredger's crew immediately launched and boarded their lifeboat. The survivors were picked up by a passing coastal steamer, the *Nightingale*, and taken to Greenock.

SS ***Caledonian***.

The engines of the *Caledonian* had not been stopped and she remained under power for nearly half an hour after being abandoned. The water level below decks eventually reached her boilers which exploded with such force that her small engine room deckhouse completely disintegrated, after which the *Caledonian* slowly sank beneath the surface in a cloud of steam. No attempt was made to locate the *Caledonian* as it was reported that she had sunk in very deep water.

CATALINA PBY - 5A

Catalina wing section - 2003.

Twin engined flying boat.
Built by Consolidated Vultee Corporation, Buffalo.
Launched circa 1941.

Wingspan 104' Length 63.9' Height 18.8'

The Catalina flying boat that lies off the ferry slip on Great Cumbrae is probably one of the most well known wrecks in the Clyde. The site has been regularly visited by divers for more than 35 years, due to its sheltered location, ease of access from the shore and suitability for diver training. The story behind the loss of the Catalina or 'Cat', as it is often referred to, is vague with various stories of accident and mishap resulting in the vessel sinking while at her mooring.

The Catalina was first developed in the early 1930's by the Consolidated Vultee Corporation of Buffalo, who won a tender to design and construct a cantilevered monoplane flying boat for the American services. The role of the aircraft would be extended patrol and bomber with a range of approximately 2,350 miles fully loaded. Production commenced in 1935 and the first variant entered service in 1936.

With the outbreak of war in 1939, the RAF soon found a need for an aircraft to undertake maritime patrol and anti submarine duties. The British Air Ministry bought a Catalina for evaluation later that year and an initial order for 50 was placed soon after, although these craft would be armed with British weapons. The initial deliveries in 1941 were the PBY-5 variant these were non amphibious, and as far as we can determine only 11 PBY-5A's, the fully amphibious versions with retractable landing gear were bought by the RAF. The Cumbrae Catalina is thought to be one of the latter amphibious variants although no remains of her under carriage remain today.

A ***Catalina*** in Oban Bay during WWII.

During WWII, Catalina's were the back bone of RAF coastal reconnaisance, working from bases at Oban, Sullom Voe and isolated outposts around the Western Isles. Catalina's became famous for their solid role, with many notable actions including the sinking of a number of U-Boats, the discovery and shadowing of the *Bismark* prior to her final battle and the rescue of many downed aviator's.

The Wreck Today

The authors first dived this wreck in 1975, when the aircraft was virtually intact, bar one of her Pratt and Whitney Wasp engines which lay directly inshore on the beach. At this stage the wreck sat parallel to the shore, facing north, with starboard wing down. In good visibility it was possible to swim around and through what was a substantial and very scenic wreck, that was carpeted in colourful marine growth and inhabited by the near mythical conger eels.

The mixture of saltwater and aluminium have taken their toll over the years and the remains can now only be compared to wreckage. Most recently, in 2003 a scallop trawler towed through the wreck and broke up most of what remained of the hull, sections of the wing remain intact but are badly damaged, and are now at seabed level.

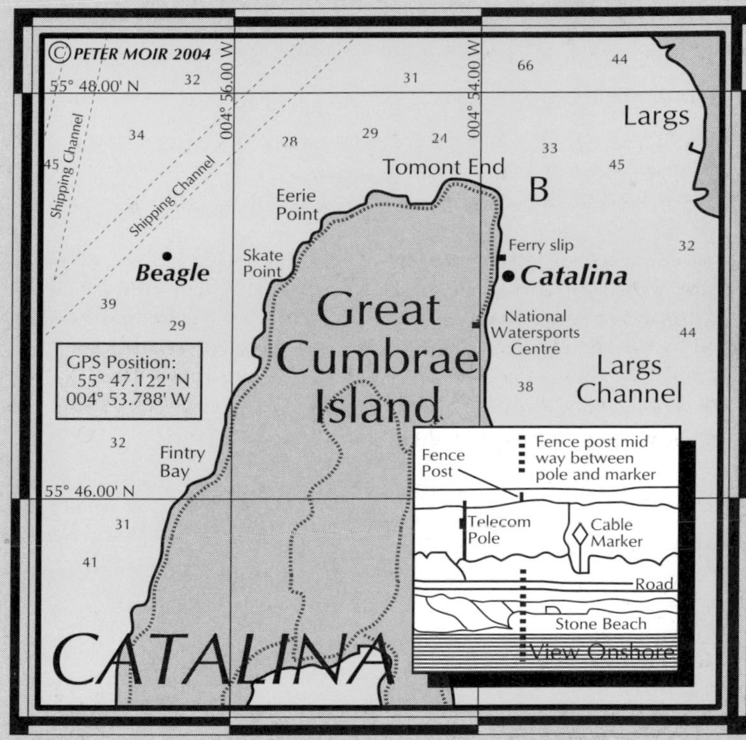

The wreck lies approximately 100 metres south of the concrete RoRo ferry slip on Great Cumbrae in position 55°47.122'N, 004°53.788'W (GPS), and can be dived from the shore or by boat. The wreckage lies in approximately 19-21 metres, although some parts can be found slightly deeper.

CHEVALIER

121nt. Iron paddlesteamer.
Built by J & G Thomson, Glasgow.
Launched 1866.

Dimensions 211.0' x 22.2' x 9.3'

PS ***Chevalier*** ashore south end of Barmore Island.

Although various minor incidents and strandings of paddlesteamers have occurred since, the last vessel of this type to become a loss in the Clyde area was the *Chevalier* on Friday 25th March, 1927.

The *Chevalier* was owned by David MacBrayne and was on her usual route from Glasgow to Ardrishaig when she was disabled two miles north of Tarbert, Loch Fyne when her starboard paddlewheel gave way. Drifting helpless and broadside to a southerly gale, her anchors were cast but did not hold and she was driven onto the rocks at the south east end of Barmore Island. The ship's boats were immediately launched and the twenty passengers, their luggage and the crew were safely landed ashore near Stonefield Castle.

The *Chevalier* was subsequently refloated but, after detailed inspection, the extensive repairs required were deemed to be uneconomical and the *Chevalier* was scrapped.

CHUSAN

1381gt. Iron paddlesteamer.
Built by J Elder & Co, Govan.
Launched September 1874.

Dimensions 300.0' x 50.2' 10.0'

The *Chusan* was owned by the China Steam Navigation Company. She was an unusual craft, more reminiscent of a Mississippi steamboat than a Clyde steamer. Power was provided by three hundred horse power beam engines driving two huge paddlewheels which extended fifteen feet from the side of the ship.

She left Glasgow on 8th October, 1874 for the long voyage to Shanghai via Suez and Singapore, under the command of Captain Johnson with a crew of forty two. She reached Waterford in Ireland but had to return to the Clyde due to a fault in her engines. She left Waterford for the Clyde on 21st October and reached Arran by 3am the next morning before encountering a violent storm which forced her to run for shelter in Ardrossan Harbour. The *Chusan* was within two hundred yards of the safety of the breakwater but was swept, out of control, onto Crinan Rocks and immediately began to break up in the huge seas.

The frantic efforts of those ashore to save the stranded crew were hampered by the absence of the Coastguards, who were away on exercises. The sea quickly broke the *Chusan* in two as the crew of a small tug bravely tried to get a rope to the stricken vessel. The smaller forepart of the wreck was washed into the harbour and those on board this section were saved. The remainder of the ship was stuck fast on the rocks and was soon smashed to pieces as the horrified crowd looked on helplessly. Fifteen of the crew, including Captain Johnson, were drowned. The remains of the wreck were salvaged at a later date but a dive round Crinan Rocks could still prove rewarding.

CUIRASSIER

54nt. Steel steamship.
Built by Richardson Duck & Co Ltd, Cleveland.
Launched 1860.

Dimensions 95.4' x 19.6' x 7.8'

The *Cuirassier*, a small rear engined coastal steamer, was owned and managed in Glasgow by Duncan Gardner. Purchased a few years previously from an English owner she worked the west coast routes carrying mainly small general cargoes. On Sunday 15th July, 1894 while outward bound from Glasgow to Bonawe with machinery and horse bedding, the *Cuirassier* ran ashore near Little Cumbrae Lighthouse. The seabed around this part of the island drops steeply and, as the tide rose, she slipped from her precarious position and sank. Contemporary reports indicated that she had gone down in twelve fathoms.

The Wreck Today

The remains of the *Cuirassier* lie approximately 250 metres north of the lighthouse in position 55°43.066'N, 004°57.766'W (GPS). Lying up and down a steep shingle and rock slope, she lies in depths much deeper than reported at the time of her loss.

The wreck lies in 30 - 36 metres from bow to stern. The wreck is well broken with the only recognisable part being aft from boiler to stern. The wreck is best located by following an underwater cable which is just visible among the rocks above the high water mark. This cable, which twists and turns as it descends the steep slope, eventually runs right through the bow section of the wreckage.

Visibility on this wreck can at times be very good, and the wreck provides a good site for trainee divers on their first deep dive while providing the safety of the seabed for reference.

Tides along this section are noticeable at spring tides but do not run much more than 1 knot.

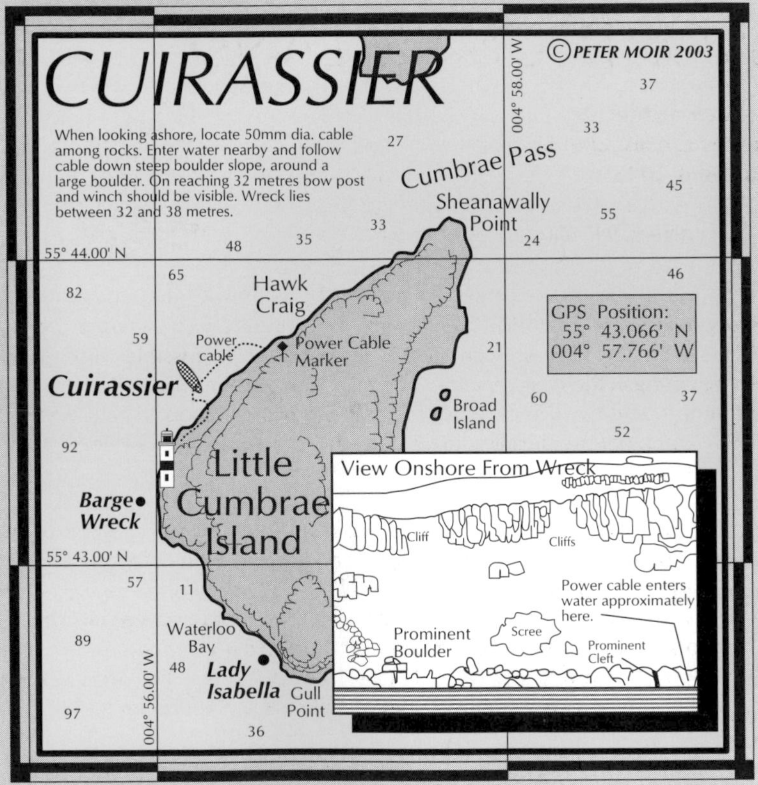

CUIRASSIER

©PETER MOIR 2003

When looking ashore, locate 50mm dia. cable among rocks. Enter water nearby and follow cable down steep boulder slope, around a large boulder. On reaching 32 metres bow post and winch should be visible. Wreck lies between 32 and 38 metres.

GPS Position:
55° 43.066' N
004° 57.766' W

Cumbrae Pass
Sheanawally Point
Hawk Craig
Power cable
Power Cable Marker
Cuirassier
Broad Island
Little Cumbrae Island
Barge Wreck
Waterloo Bay
Lady Isabella
Gull Point
55° 44.00' N
55° 43.00' N
004° 58.00' W
004° 56.00' W

View Onshore From Wreck
Cliff
Cliffs
Power cable enters water approximately here.
Prominent Boulder
Scree
Prominent Cleft

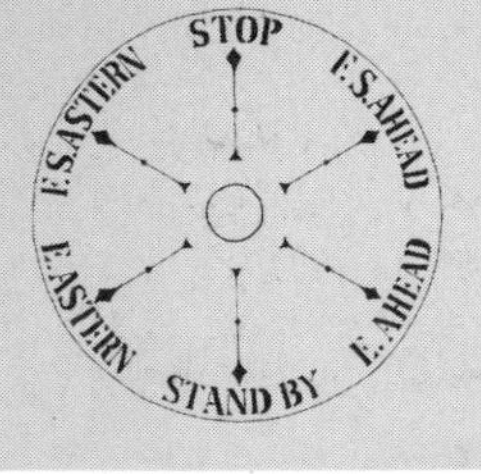

STOP
F.S.AHEAD
E.AHEAD
STAND BY
E.ASTERN
F.S.ASTERN

DUKE OF NORTHUMBERLAND

Wooden paddle tug.
Built by C Chisholm, Shields.
Launched 1856.

Dimensions 94' long

Large sailing vessels entering and leaving the Firth of Clyde invariably used the services of a tug. This service saved time and even possible mishap while manoeuvering in the busy restricted shipping lanes of the Upper Firth. It was not uncommon on days of little or no wind for departing vessels to be towed as far as Ailsa Craig, before unfurling their sails and setting off alone on their voyages round the world.

It was en route to find such work, south of the Cumbraes, that the Clyde Shipping Company tug *Duke of Northumberland* was lost in collision with the SS *Thistle* on Tuesday 18th May, 1858. The collision occurred in the early hours of the morning off the west coast of Great Cumbrae, the tug eventually sinking in 25 fathoms. The *Thistle* circled the scene of the accident for more than an hour, but could not find any survivors. Luckily the tug's crew had made a quick escape in their boat and finally landed at Millport some one and a half hours later.

The Wreck Today

The wreck of the *Duke of Northumberland* can be found in position 55°46.419'N, 004°57.582'W (GPS). She lies on a muddy seabed oriented approximately 130/210. The remains generally consist of the machinery and vertical boiler, although we suspect much of the keel and lower hull lies within the deep mud seabed. This wreck is only for the experienced and suitably trained diver.

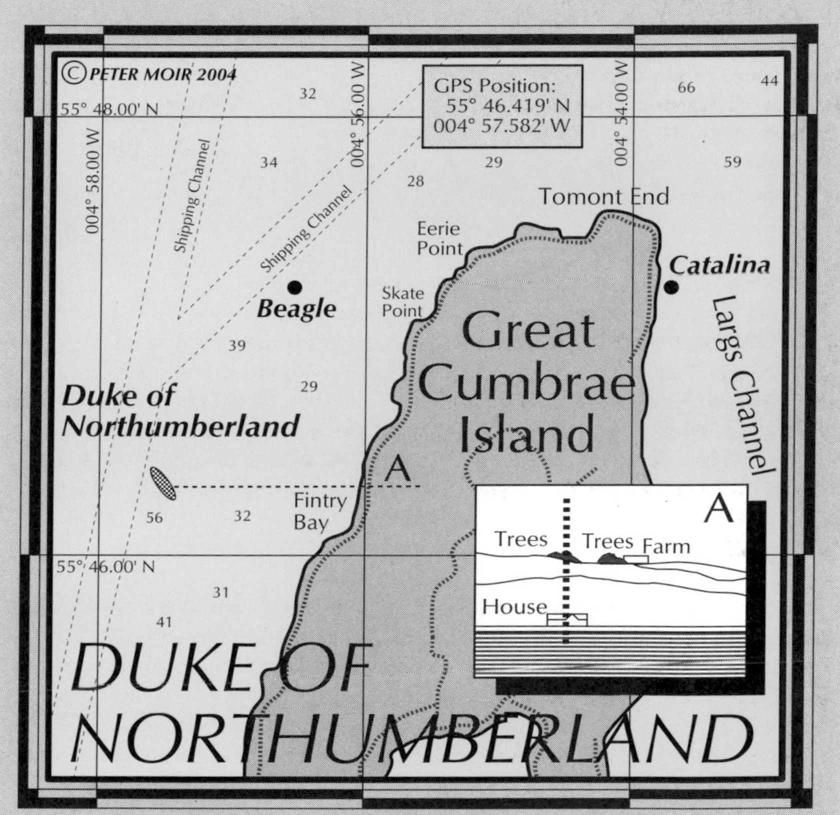

General seabed depths around the wreck are 54 metres, the wreck rises a maximum of 1-2 metres, the seabed also rises by around 1 metre in the general vacinity of the debris. The remains are certainly of an old wooden hulled paddle ship, and although we have not as yet found any conclusive proof of the wrecks identity, we believe taking the underwater evidence and the position of loss that this is indeed the *Duke of Northumberland.*

GLENEARN

1624nt. Iron steamship.
Built by London & Glasgow Engineering & Iron S B Co Ltd, Glasgow.
Launched 1873.

Dimensions 330.1' x 35.3' x 24.8'

The loss of the Glasgow steamship *Glenearn* by stranding on 10th February, 1900 was primarily due to a breakdown of official communications.

The *Glenearn* left Glasgow for Alexandria on 13th December, 1899 and commenced her return voyage via various Mediteranean ports on 11th January, 1900. Meanwhile, on 18th December, 1899 the Clyde Lighthouse Trustees issued a notice to the effect that the character of the leading light on the Little Cumbrae was to be altered. This alteration took effect on 6th February, the lights changing from a fixed light to a grouped flashing light.

Around 4:30am on 10th February the *Glenearn* was off Whiting Bay, Arran, with the captain and crew completely unaware of the recent changes made to the light of the Little Cumbrae. About this time the bow lookouts reported a flashing light off the starboard bow to the north. After consulting the most recent Notices to Mariners on board, Captain Laurence identified this light as Ardrossan Harbour. The confusion was compounded by the fact that Ardrossan Light had also recently been amended from a fixed to a group flashing light. Captain Laurence ordered a change of course to port to take the *Glenearn* up by Cumbrae Heads. He then went below leaving instructions with the mate to report to him when the fixed light of Little Cumbrae was sighted.

Around 5:30am Captain Laurence, uneasy with the situation, returned to the bridge. The mate reported that the fixed light of Little Cumbrae had not yet been sighted, but a flashing light was clearly visible, close on the starboard quarter. Almost immediately the dark form of land was sighted dead ahead and the *Glenearn* drove ashore in Dunagoil Bay, Bute. Fortunately no one on board was injured and the crew got safely ashore.

Salvage operations were started almost immediately to try and recover not only the vessel, but her valuable cargo of wine and fruit. However, much of the cargo in her bow holds washed out, leaving surrounding beaches strewn with citrus fruits. This resulted in the wreck locally being referred to as the "Orange Boat."

THE DUNAGOIL WRECK.

GODMUNDING

779nt. Iron steamship.
Built by Blyth Shipbuilding Co.
Launched February 1888.

Dimensions 242.0' x 33.0' x 16.5'

Around 10:30am on Saturday 14th May, 1898 the Glasgow and South Western Railway Company steamer *Viceroy* collided with the *Godmunding* about two miles north of Little Cumbrae Lighthouse. The *Godmunding* was inward bound from Cadiz with a cargo of iron ore and empty wine casks. Though severely damaged on her starboard quarter she was successfully beached four hundred yards east of Kilchatten Pier. No one was injured and the eighteen crew landed safely at Kilchatten.

Recovery operations by the Glasgow Salvage Company commenced almost immediately resulting in the vessel being substantially salved in situ. Her hull was finally refloated later that year.

Salvage work underway on the SS ***Godmunding*** with Great Cumbrae beyond.

KINTYRE

94nt. Iron steamship.
Built by Robertson & Co, Greenock.
Launched 1868.

Dimensions 184.7' x 22.9' x 11.5'

The small cargo passenger steamship *Kintyre* is generally acknowledged to have been one of the most graceful steamers of her type to sail on the Clyde. Owned by Campbeltown & Glasgow Steam Packet Joint Stock Company, she was familiarly referred to as the Campbeltown Yacht, because of her raked lines and clipper bow.

On Wednesday 18th September, 1907 the *Kintyre* was lost in collision with the 3500gt steamer *Maori* about four hundred yards south west of Wemyss Point. The *Maori,* only recently completed by her builders Denny of Dumbarton, was undergoing speed trials on the measured mile at Skelmorlie. On completing a run northwards, she passed Wemyss Bay Pier and altered course to port before swinging in a wide arc back into Wemyss Bay for her next run south. Meanwhile the *Kintyre,* en route to Tarbert via Campbeltown, was steering a course close to the Renfrewshire coast. When the vessels were about half a mile apart signals were exchanged, the *Maori* making it clear she was continuing her long turn to starboard. At this point the *Kintyre* should have slowed to let the larger vessel pass in front but, either due to some misunderstanding or more likely a desire not to waste time by slowing, no order to that effect was given by her master, Captain MacKechnie. Steaming at full speed the *Kintyre* cut across the path of the *Maori* which, by now, was very close. The engines of the *Maori* were put full astern but her momentum could not be checked before she crashed into the starboard side of the *Kintyre* near the aft hatch. The two vessels remained locked together long enough for most of the crew of the *Kintyre* to clamber aboard the *Maori.* Meanwhile the *Kintyre* was beginning to sink and, with water quickly filling the engine room and aft cabin, her stern soon became submerged.

SS ***Kintyre***.

Captain MacKechnie and William Lennox, her engineer, remained on the bridge of the *Kintyre* and made a brave attempt to beach her. However, four minutes after the collision, a hissing sound came from the engine room, followed by a muffled explosion and then, in twenty seconds, the *Kintyre* slipped beneath the surface. As the *Kintyre* sank the two men still aboard were thrown into the sea. Captain MacKechnie had a miraculous escape. Dragged down by a piece of wreckage tangled around his legs, he managed to free himself and floated to the surface, where he was picked up by a small boat. Suffering from exhaustion, he was taken to the Wemyss Bay Hotel where he was treated by a doctor. William Lennox was less fortunate and could not be found after an extensive search. In December 1907 the owners of the *Kintyre* took William Denny & Bros to court, trying to recover £10,000 damages for the loss of their vessel. Lord Salvesen presiding held that the collision was caused solely by the actions of those aboard the *Kintyre* and her owners had to shoulder the burden of an uninsured loss.

The *Kintyre* can be located approximately 400 metres south south west of Wemyss Point and some 200 metres off shore in position 55°53.178'N, 004°53.974'W (GPS). Lying on an even keel on a steeply sloping seabed, she is oriented 90/270 degrees with her bow pointing towards the shore. The *Kintyre* is somewhat deeper than most of the diveable wrecks in the area, the depths around the wreck ranging from 38 to 49 metres bow to stern. Rising on average 3 metres from the seabed, the hull is substantially intact except for an area on her starboard side aft of the engine room.

SS ***Kintyre*** at Lochranza, Isle of Arran.

Apart from the depth, the wreck itself provides few problems for the diver. Hold and accommodation areas either side of the engine room centre section are open and easily accessible. The remains of deck beams, winches and alike can be found protruding from the deep silt. The clipper bow, the most visually dramatic part of the wreck, rears some 4 metres out of the seabed. The plating around this area has fallen away to expose the cage like structural members of her hull which are now covered in orange and white plumose anemonae.

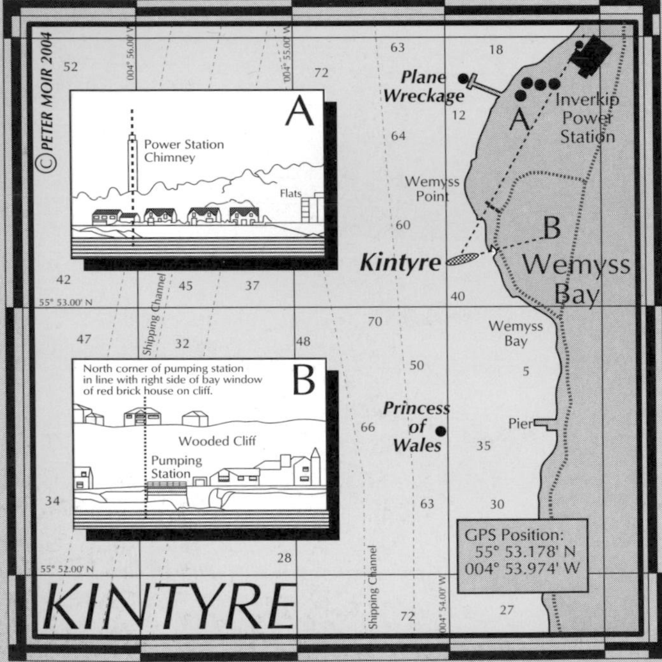

It is possible to dive this wreck from the beach by following the sewer outfall pipe from the concrete structure inshore of the wreck. On reaching 42 metres head north along the slope, the wreck lies some 10 - 15 metres north of the pipe. However, due to the depth of the wreck and the distance from the shore the authors would strongly advise against this method of diving the wreck.

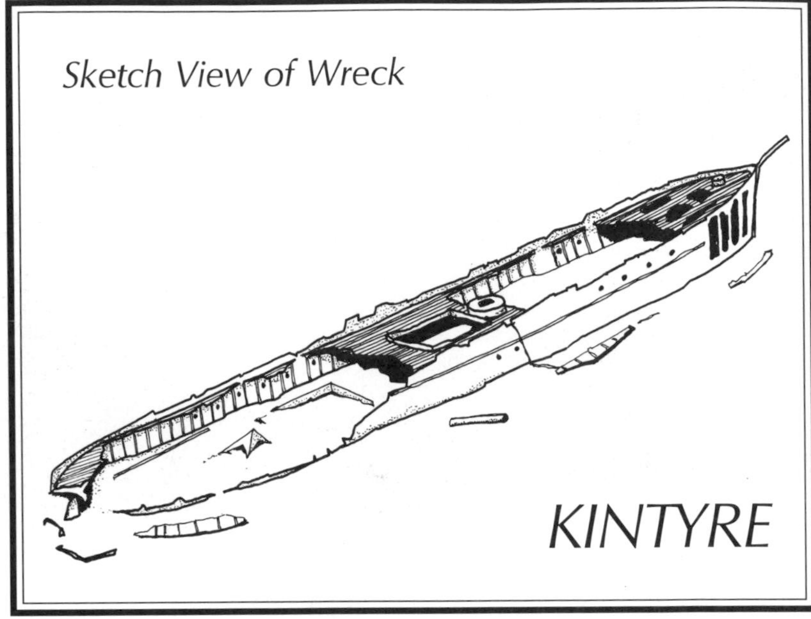

LADY GERTRUDE

167gt. Iron paddlesteamer.
Built by Blackwood & Gordon.
Launched 1872.

Dimensions 190.0' x 18.0' x 7.6'

The *Lady Gertrude* was powered by a diagonal engine and, typical of steamer design of the period, was flush decked with a single funnel. She was owned by Gillies & Campbell and employed as their fleet flagship on the Wemyss Bay to Rothesay run.

PS *Lady Gertrude*.

It was on this usual run that she approached Toward Pier on 16th January, 1877. As she drew alongside the pier, the captain attempted to reverse engines to bring her to a halt. However, due to an unknown mechanical problem, this proved to be impossible and the *Lady Gertrude* ran aground.

The passengers, although somewhat shaken by the incident, were safely disembarked from the stern onto the pier. It was confidently expected that the *Lady Gertrude* would be refloated without serious damage. First the steamer *Inveraray Castle*, then two tugs, attempted to pull her off but without success. Shortly afterwards she broke her back and became a total wreck. Salvage of the wreck was carried out, including the removal of her engine which was reused later that year in the steamer *Adela*. To this day the remains of her hull can sometimes be seen protruding from the sand.

LADY ISABELLA

1396nt. Iron barque.
Built by A McMillan & Son, Dumbarton.
Launched August 1882.

Dimensions 255.7' x 38.3' x 20.6'

On 27th August, 1902 the *Lady Isabella* left the French settlement of Tehio, New Caledonia, with a cargo of nickel ore, for her first visit to her native river since her maiden voyage in 1882. She was under the command of Captain McKinlay and carried a crew of twenty three. Her voyage was to be an eventful one and was to end in tragedy only a few miles from her destination. She struggled against a succession of violent storms and, by the time she finally reached the Clyde some four months later, she had jettisoned one hundred tons of her cargo, which had shifted in one storm, and lost a member of her crew overboard off the west coast of Scotland in another.

During the night of 17/18th December, she passed Arran under a favourable, but increasing, breeze closely attended by the tug *Flying Phantom*. Just after 3am Captain McKinlay spotted the beckoning flicker of Little Cumbrae Lighthouse through the darkness and set a course towards it but, as he approached the island, the steady south west wind suddenly increased to a violent squall and veered to the north west. As the sails of the ship flapped useless in the wind, the crew struggled to regain control and steerage. The *Lady Isabella* was driven relentlessly towards the rocky south west coast of the barren island. The captain ordered anchors away in an attempt to save his vessel from the impending disaster, but to no avail. The *Lady Isabella* struck the seabed fifty yards from the shore and immediately began to fill with water.

Wreck of the ***Lady Isabella***.

The ***Lady Isabella*** ashore.

The distress rockets were fired but, as it appeared that they were in no immediate danger, they decided to remain aboard till morning when they could, more safely, make their way ashore in the ship's lifeboat. Captain McKinlay was on the poop deck examining the position of his ship when, suddenly, she lurched by the stern as a wave swept over her. He was washed overboard and would certainly have drowned had the next wave not miraculously swept him back onto the *Lady Isabella* where he managed to grab hold of the mizzen mast rigging. The same wave smashed the ship's lifeboat, leaving the crew marooned on the wreck. The courageous sailmaker, Anderson, seeing the plight of the ship and his comrades, volunteered to swim the cold fifty yards to the shore with a rope. He succeeded in securing the line to the shore and, one by one, the crew pulled themselves ashore, with Captain McKinlay being the last to land.

The ship's carpenter examined the *Lady Isabella* shortly before coming ashore and reported that there was water in every hold. She was now completely submerged at the stern making successful salvage very unlikely. Divers surveyed the hull later in the month and reported severe damage to the keel and hull plates, plus four holes in the starboard side. She was abandoned to the sea, which quickly broke her to pieces, although she was extensively salvaged by James Gush of Greenock over the next few years.

The remains of the *Lady Isabella* lie 200 metres north west of Gull Point, Little Cumbrae in approximate position 55°42.716'N, 004°57.500'W (GPS). She lies where she struck approximately 50 metres from the shore, on a sloping sand and rock seabed, with depths ranging from 5 - 15 metres. The wreck lies more or less at right angles to the shore with only a few hull plates and part of the keel remaining.

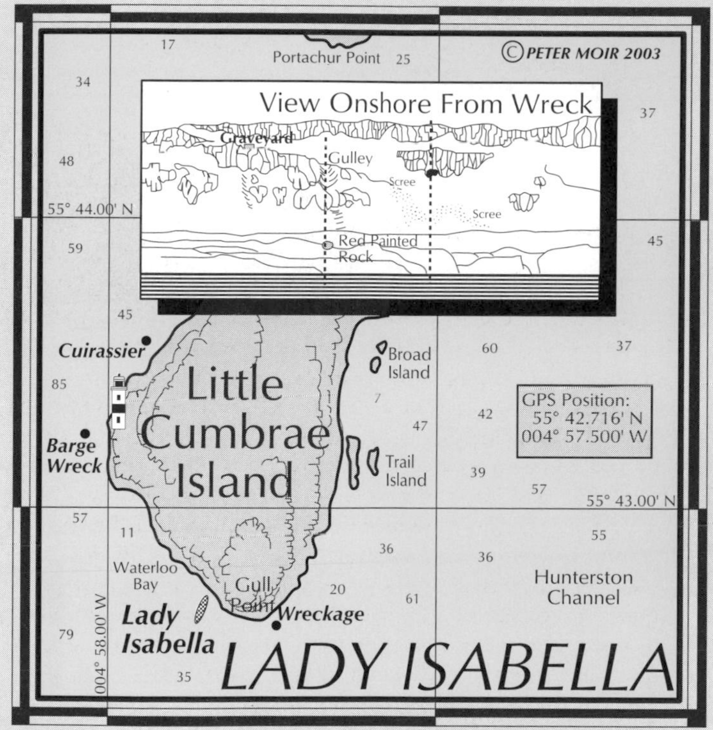

The highest part of the wreck stands 2 metres from the seabed and some machinery, wood and ropes are also clearly visible. Some interesting pieces of non ferrous metal have been found over the years but little remains now. There are no problems diving the wreck, once located, although the site is exposed to the prevailing south west winds and as such is often subject to substantial swell.

LADY MARGARET

Three masted wooden sailing ship.
Launched 1769.

The *Lady Margaret* had lain in Greenock for some weeks taking on a valuable general cargo for her destination of James River, Virginia. This cargo included substantial amounts of haberdashery, wrought iron, crockery, saddles, bridles, stirrups and many other miscellaneous items. She left Greenock on 17th January, 1770 under the command of Captain James Kippen, probably the brother of the owner, Mr George Kippen of Glasgow.

As she turned west into the North Channel and passed Tory Island off the Irish coast, she was hit by a violent storm. Captain Kippen decided to return to a safe port to ride it out and finally chose to return all the way to Greenock. By 23rd January the *Lady Margaret* was off Arran and steering northwards using the islands on the Clyde as shelter from the strong south west winds. Just after 10pm, as she passed close to Little Cumbrae, the wind suddenly shifted to the north west, leaving the *Lady Margaret* helpless as her sails flapped out of control in the now violent gale. The wind and the seas swept her eastwards and onto the rocks south of Portencross Castle, despite desperate efforts by the crew to avert disaster by cutting away the fore and main masts.

The next day dawned with the *Lady Margaret* high on the exposed rocks with her holds already awash. A hastily set up committee of the merchants owning the cargo despatched one of their number, Mr Alex Fisher, to the scene to make every effort to salvage as much of the cargo as possible. He immediately suggested that the ship, which was worth £2,600, should be scuttled to ease the removal of the cargo, valued at some £14,000. The owners reluctantly agreed and a large hole was cut in her side, followed by the removal of much of her lower decking, allowing for a substantial part of her cargo to be successfully removed. On Sunday 11th February, 1770 the *Lady Margaret* finally broke up and succumbed to the waves which had pounded her stranded hull almost continually since she went ashore.

LOUISE

43gt. Iron steamlighter.
Built by Swan & Co, Maryhill, Glasgow.
Launched 1870.

Dimensions 65.2' x 14.3' x 5.5′

The *Louise* was powered by a fifteen horsepower direct acting engine and carried cargo between the ports of the Upper Clyde for her owner, Mr Hay of Renfield Street, Glasgow.

On the morning of 3rd February, 1893 she left Rothesay for Falkirk under the command of her master, John Steel, with two crew. Her cargo consisted of sixty three tons of tar and ammoniacal liquor in casks. The loading of the casks left the top row protruding from the hold making it impossible to secure the hatches that would normally cover the hold. This was to be a fatal mistake.

As the *Louise* left Rothesay Bay the sea was calm but, as she reached Bogany Point at the south end of the bay, she left the shelter of the land and the sea immediately became rough. Mr Steel decided to return to Rothesay and await calmer weather. As he turned to port his little vessel was hit, side on, by a series of heavy seas and, as a large wave pushed his port gunwhale beneath the surface, the water rushed into the open hold. The master and his two crewmen leapt into the *Louise's* lifeboat which was being towed astern but, before they could untie the painter, another large wave struck the *Louise* and she sank by the stern taking the lifeboat and the two crew with her. Mr Steel survived by clinging to a floating hatch cover.

The wreck of the *Louise* lies on a sloping sandy seabed off Bogany Point in a general depth of 43 metres in position 55°50.674'N, 005°00.946'W (GPS). The wreck has eluded the attentions of divers for years as it is fairly difficult to locate and rises only two metres from the seabed. There are many mounds in the seabed close by making location by echo sounder difficult. The wreck lies more or less parallel to the shore with the bow facing in the general direction of Rothesay.

The boiler stands as the wreck's highest point with the remaining hull wreckage heavily silted and breaking up. The visibility is usually poor as the silt is easily disturbed quickly leaving the diver disoriented or even off the wreck onto the muddy seabed. Although off the main shipping channel the wreck lies in an area which is busy with pleasure craft making good boat cover essential.

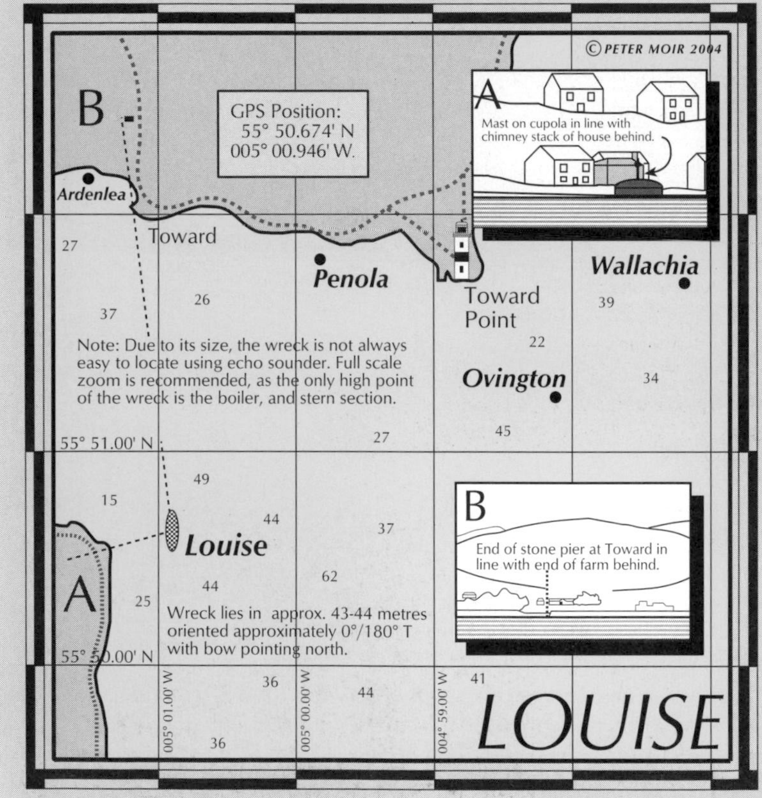

MARGARET NIVEN

24nt. Iron steamlighter.
Built at Port Glasgow.
Launched 1866.

Dimensions 63.2' x 16.5' x 5.0'

There are very few details available of the loss of this small steamship. She ran aground on a rock known locally as the 'Bald Heid' north east of Barmore Island, Loch Fyne on 21st August, 1908. She was carrying a cargo of stone chips from nearby Crarae and was en route to Glasgow in poor visibility when the accident occurred. The ship must have sunk very quickly as the rock is small and the heavy cargo would have pulled her down as she filled. Thankfully the crew made it the short distance to shore safely.

The Wreck Today

The wreck lies on a shingle seabed 50 metres north east of the rock in position 55°53.693'N, 005°24.396'W (GPS). The rock itself is marked by a rather fragile looking metal pole. It is a small wreck lying on a sloping seabed in depths of 28 to 32 metres.

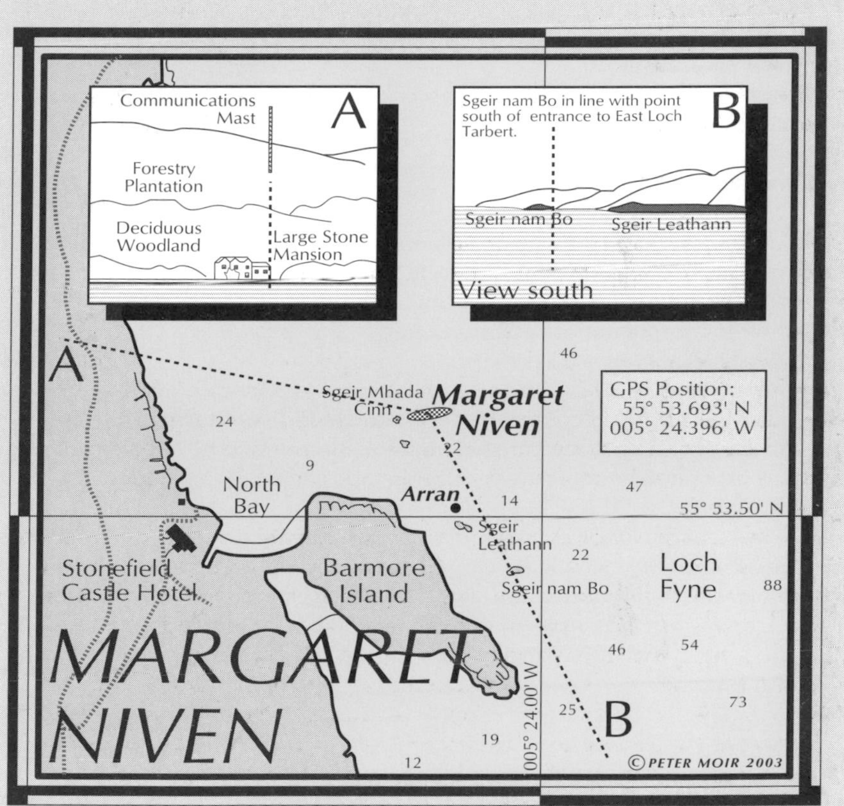

The hull, with the stern and its cast propeller facing east north east, is still basically intact and the single boiler stands proud of the deck level making it the most obvious item aboard. Otherwise, the cargo of road chips fills the rest of the hull. There is some additional scattered wreckage on the seabed. The wreck should be located using an echo sounder but, if this is not available, could probably be fairly easily found by descending the steep face of the rock itself and swimming along the 30 metre contour. The site is fairly sheltered except from the north and the east and is not subject to tidal flows.

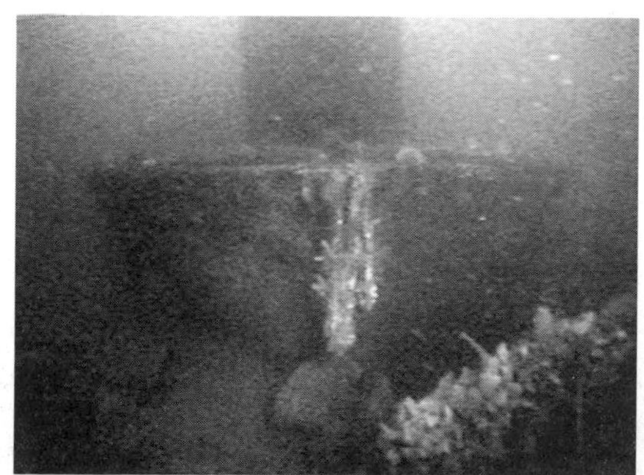

Stern shot of the ***Margaret Niven*** with rudder lying to starboard.

MARMION

32nt. Iron steamship.
Built at Maryhill, Glasgow.
Launched 1864.

Dimensions 65.7' x 16.2' x 5.9'

The details surrounding the loss of the small steamlighter *Marmion* are somewhat sketchy, to the extent that her loss was not recorded in newspapers at the time. Indeed, it was not until the outcome of the Board of Trade inquiry in December 1887 that any formal report was published in the local press.

The *Marmion* was owned by a Mr. J Campbell of Greenock and was lost on 12th October 1886 while en route from Maryhill to Arran with a cargo of gas lime. At the time, the *Marmion* was under the command of Alistair McKinnon who was assisted by another two crew members.

The cause of the loss was never fully proven, nor was any conclusion made at the inquiry other than a fault developing below water level giving rise to a rapid ingress of water. The master and crew stated that the build up of water below deck level was not fully realised until it was too late, and that they abandoned ship when the waves from a strong northerly wind began to break over the stern of the *Marmion*.

The crew abandoned ship in their small boat and landed safely ashore on Bute. The drama had developed while they were proceeding south down the West Kyle and they eventually abandoned ship off Kilmichael Farm on the north west coast of Bute, opposite Kames. The *Marmion* remained afloat for at least 30 minutes after she was abandoned, eventually sinking in deep water at the lower end of the West Kyle. The Sheriff in summing up at the Board of Trade inquiry remarked that the crew could have stayed aboard and attempted to beach the vessel, as they were only a stones throw from the shore when they rowed away.

The authors have been unable to find any reference to her salvage , it is likely she remains in deep water somewhere near Carry Point.

MOONLIGHT II

41nt. Steel steamship.
Built by Larne Shipbuilding Co, Larne.
Launched 1913.
(ex ORMSA)

Dimensions 66.7' x 18.4' x 8.5'

The Light Shipping Company's *Moonlight* left Furnace for Ormidale, Kyles of Bute under the command of relief skipper Stewart Ross with a cargo of granite chips on 25th August, 1948. On board the four crewmen and their one passenger, the engineer Alexander Mair's wife Jean, expected an uneventful voyage but, as they steamed south towards Ardlamont Point, the wind steadily building towards gale force. Eventually, as they were hit by a fierce squall and took two or three heavy seas over the bow, Captain Ross decided to turn back and sit it out in the shelter of Skate Island. They turned round and ran with the wind back towards the island which lies just north of Ardlamont Point.

SS ***Moonlight II*** as ***Ormsa***.

Huge waves continued to buffet the ship but the crew were beginning to relax when suddenly the pressure of water on deck burst into the forecastle and the ship began to fill. She quickly took on a heavy list and began to founder. The people on board had very little time to prepare before the ship sank beneath the surface throwing them into the open water. James Cooper, the deckhand, was the only lucky survivor. He struggled in the stormy seas to reach and grab hold of the upturned lifeboat and held on grimly as the wind and waves pushed him the mile or so to the shore.

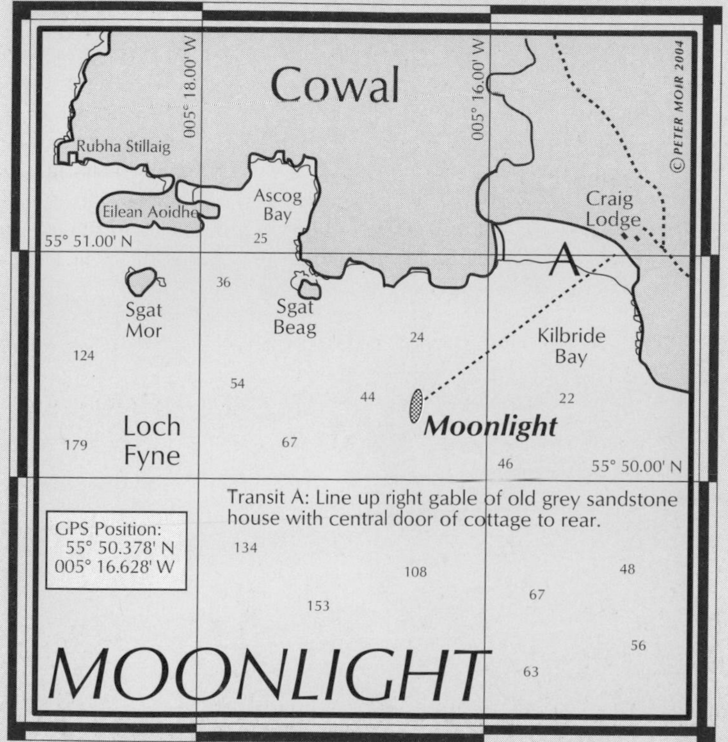

Ashore, a woman guest at J W Turnbull's estate had witnessed the sinking and James Beveridge, the gamekeeper, rushed to the shooting lodge's motor boat with a guest to attempt a rescue.

However they too were soon in difficulties as the boat's engine was flooded in the heavy seas. Luckily they drifted ashore and escaped safely. Meanwhile, Turnbull himself organised a shore search party who found Captain Ross' body.

Before another rescue attempt could be launched the exhausted deckhand staggered to the lodge and after knocking at the door collapsed on the step. Mrs Beveridge helped him indoors and quickly revived him with a hot meal and a change of clothing. The bodies of the three other people aboard the *Moonlight* were never found. A single lifebelt with the name *Moonlight* was the only trace of the ship washed ashore.

The wreck of the *Moonlight* can be found in position 55°50.378'N, 005°16.628'W (GPS). Lying on an even keel on a gently sloping seabed, she is oriented 010/190 degrees with her bow pointing south south west. Depths around the wreck range from 38m at the bow to 36m at the stern. The wreck rises on average 3-4 metres above seabed level. The wreck is substantially intact although her engine casing appears to have been damaged on the starboard side, perhaps by a fishermans trawl. There are no hazards to diving this wreck which often provides an excellent dive with shoals of fish and good visibility.

MONTCLARE

9,724nt. Steel steamship.
Built by John Brown & Co, Ltd.
Launched 1922.

Dimensions 549.5' x 70.2' x 40.2'

The Canadian Pacific liner *Montclare* was inward bound to Glasgow from St.John's, New Brunswick when she stranded just north of Gull Point, Little Cumbrae. She had arrived in the Clyde in the early morning of Saturday 21st March, 1931 and encountered thick fog around Pladda, and her speed was reduced to dead slow.

The impact was felt throughout the ship, and remarked upon by one passenger as 'three bumps and all stop'. Her master immediately checked for damage but none was visible above waterline, so an attempt to reverse off was made, but she held fast and as the tide was falling no further attempts were made. Tugs were immediately called to assist and those aboard waited for help to arrive.

As the tide receded the *Montclare* began to list badly and her master decided to abandon ship, much to the consternation of the passengers aboard who thought they were safe and the vessel would be refloated on the next high tide. All the passengers were ferried to Largs by the tugs *Flying Eagle* and *Wrestler* and a large crowd turned out to greet the cold and somewhat bewildered survivors arriving in a small west coast town after dark. A local restaurant was opened up and meals prepared and hastily eaten before they boarded a train for Glasgow.

As for the *Montclare*, she was refloated the following day and docked at Greenock, leaving soon after under her own steam for Liverpool.

MTB's - Loch Striven

The wrecks located around Brackley Point in Loch Striven are very popular with local divers as they provide a range of dives for various levels of experience, in a sheltered location with shore access. Deep water is also close by for more advanced training and the wreck of a motor gunboat or torpedo boat lies offshore but requires boat access.

A key feature of the site is the location of a number of small wrecks and wreckage around Brackley Point, all within a 200 metre radius. Three of the wrecks would appear to originate from WWII, and be the remains of wooden motor torpedo or gunboats, the fourth is a small steel barge. The Loch was used for classified experimental work during both World Wars, it is understood that the wrecks were either a result of this work or scuttled at the end of hostilities.

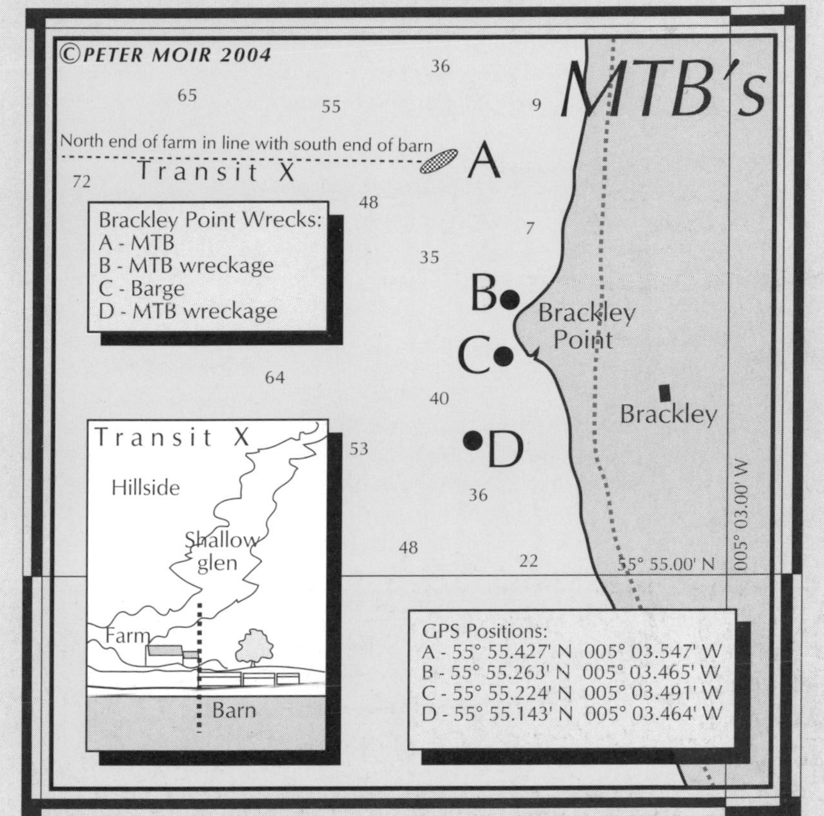

The three gunboat wrecks are of classic timber construction and would have been built with diagonal mahogany planked hulls with plywood or solid framing, with timber housing to engine space and deck house. This type of vessel was developed at the start of WWII to meet the needs of the Royal Navy for a fast seagoing patrol boat, and a hard chine fast planning hull was developed as the basic shape. Built primar*ily* as a MTB (motor torpedo boat), a number were built with machine guns fore and aft and designated MGB (motor gunboats) others were developed for specific purposes, with customised armament on the basic hull.

The most interesting of these wrecks, due to its state of preservation, is the wreck of a wooden MGB lying some 250 metres north of the point in position 55°55.143'N, 005°03.538W (GPS). The wreck is oriented approximately 030/210 and lies between 36 and 42m with bows pointing south west. This should be considered a boat dive due to depth and the slight flow across the wreck on spring tides.

Two wrecks are located at Brackley Point and are easily accessible from the shore. Wreckage from an MGB or MTB lies in the shallows north of the point in position 55°55.263'N 005°03.465'W. Lying on a steep sand slope the wreckage extends from 5 to 14 metres diagonally across the down slope. On the west side of the point lie the remains of a small steel dumb barge in 12 metres of water. The wreck, which at time of writing is still intact, lies in position 55°55.224'N, 005°03.491'W on a more gentle sand slope.

Lying approximately 200 metres to the south of the point and directly offshore from a small cottage (Brackley) on the hillside lies the wreckage of yet another MGB/MTB. This vessel would appear to have been extensively salvaged although parts of hull, engine and tanks remain in position 55°55.143'N, 005°03.464'W. The wreckage lies on a sand and mud slope between 11 and 21 metres.

OVINGTON

444nt. Iron steamship.
Built by Osbourne & Graham, Sunderland.
Launched 1873.

Dimensions 187.0' x 28.3' x 14.3'

The *Ovington* left Glasgow around 9pm on 28th December, 1889 bound for Hamburg with a general cargo, mainly of charcoal and ammonia. Her captain was William Gorley and she had a crew of twelve. At 11:15pm they landed the river pilot at Greenock and continued down river. As the *Ovington* reached Toward Point a couple of hours later the weather, which had been poor up to that point, suddenly deteriorated with further fog and snow squalls. Captain Gorley decided to drop anchor and await clearer weather before proceeding. It is curious that Captain Peter McEwan of the other steamer involved in this tragic incident, the 1500 tons SS *Queen Victoria*, reported the weather dark but clear prior to the collision.

What is certain is that, as the *Ovington* slowed to a halt and prepared to drop anchor with all lights burning, the *Queen Victoria* appeared out of the night on her port bow and collided with her, tearing a huge hole between the bridge and the forecastle.

The actual cause of the collision was later revealed as an error made by Captain McEwan and his crew on board the *Queen Victoria*. They were returning from a voyage to Antwerp and had reached the Clyde the previous evening. On reaching Cumbrae, they took a bearing for Toward Lighthouse. It seems likely from the weather report of Captain Gorley of the *Ovington* that the lighthouse itself was shrouded in fog and snow, despite the clear weather further south. At around 2am the lookout on the *Queen Victoria* spotted a light ahead and Captain McEwan, thinking the light to be the Skelmorlie Buoy, turned slightly to port to pass the light to the west. By the time they realised that the light was in fact the stern light of another steamer it was too late and, despite desperate efforts to avoid the collision by reversing engines, they ploughed into the side of the vessel lying across their path.

The two ships held together for a few minutes allowing a number of the crew of the *Ovington* to scramble onto the bow of the *Queen Victoria* but, within five minutes of the original impact, the *Ovington* sank by the bow taking with her five of her crew. As she sank she was ripped apart by a huge explosion, leaving the surface littered with debris and wreckage. Indeed a large part of the bridge, including the compass binnacle and bell, was washed ashore on Bute the following day.

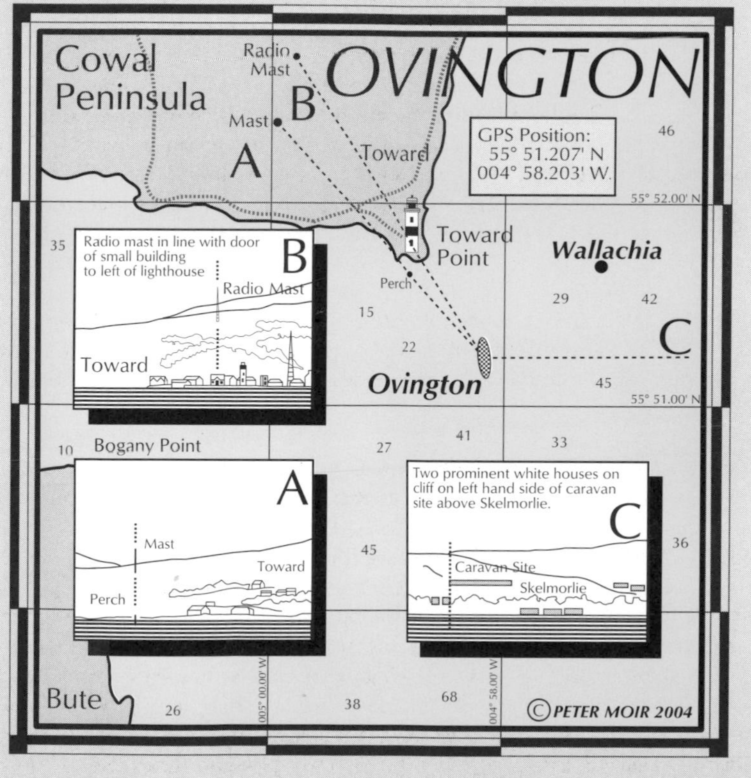

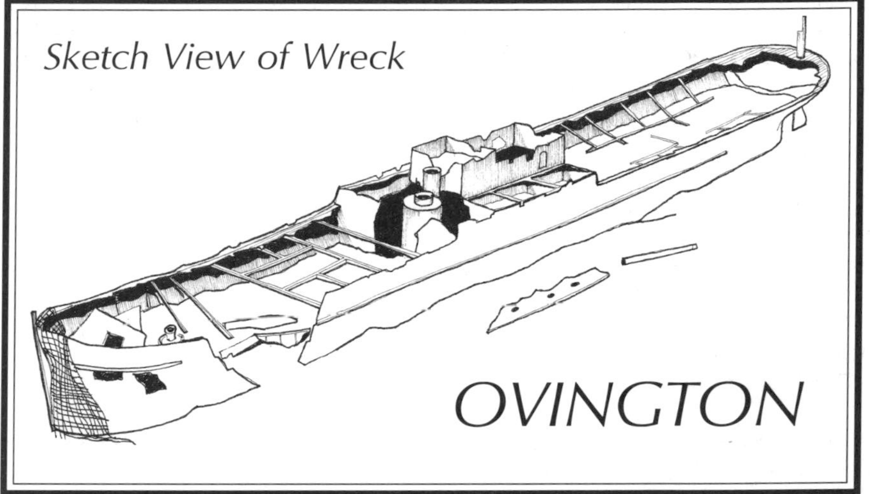

The Wreck Today

The *Ovington* lies in position 55°51.207'N, 004°58.203'W (GPS) approximately one mile south of Toward Lighthouse. She lies upright in a general depth of 35 metres with deck level at around 32 metres.

The hull is still substantially intact, although the port side, where the collision occurred is gradually breaking apart and falling onto the seabed. The hardwood decking has rotted away, leaving the main supporting deck beams exposed. However, since the wreck was first discovered in March 1984, all the deck beams in the stern section have collapsed. This fact should be considered when descending below deck level in the bow section.

The most interesting area of the wreck is the midship section where the bridge area, engine room, galley and stores can be found. The only hazards associated with diving the wreck are the usual darkness, depth and its generally poor structural condition. At certain states of the tide the site can be subject to currents and it is also quite exposed to swell. The site also lies close to the Wemyss Bay to Rothesay ferry route so good boat cover and a prominently displayed 'A' flag are essential.

PENOLA

138nt. Wooden auxiliary schooner.
Built by E Bonne, Kerity, France.
Launched 1908.

Dimensions 106.0' x 24.1' x 11.6'

On the morning of 9th November, 1940 as the grain schooner *Penola* sailed up the Clyde, she was in collision with another vessel near Toward Point and later sank. The crew took to the lifeboats and made their way to the shore. The *Penola,* which settled upright with masts and part of her deck above water at high tide, later broke up and became a total wreck. Her remains are charted and lie in shallow water in approximate position 55°51.717'N, 004°59.667'W, just west of Toward Lighthouse.

The ***Penola*** under tow.

PRINCESS OF WALES

111.7nt. Steel paddlesteamer.
Built by Barclay Curle & Co Ltd, Glasgow.
Launched 1888.

Dimensions 216.0' x 21.15' x 8.2'

Recently launched to the order of the Southampton and Isle of Wight Royal Mail Steam Packet Co, the *Princess of Wales* left Glasgow on the morning of Saturday 16th June, 1888 to run speed trials along the measured mile at Skelmorlie. Aboard were between fifty and sixty people consisting of guests, workmen and crew.

PS ***Solent Queen,*** sistership of the ***Princess of Wales.***

Arriving off Wemyss Bay shortly after midday, she completed her first run down the measured mile about 1pm. She immediately commenced her return run at dead slow speed. Around this time, the steamer *Balmoral Castle* entered Wemyss Bay to the north to run down the measured mile at full speed. The two vessels closed on their respective courses for a few minutes, with the *Balmoral Castle* initially taking a line slightly inshore of the *Princess of Wales*. As the *Balmoral Castle* entered the northern end of the mile it would appear that her pilot, James Parker, considered his course too close inshore and headed his vessel to starboard, further off shore. On seeing this manoeuvre, pilot James Barrie aboard the *Princess of Wales* immediately altered his course to suit, although both vessels were still at this stage passing starboard to starboard.

The distance between the two vessels closed rapidly. When a further change of course to starboard was made by the *Balmoral Castle* she was within two hundred yards of the other steamer and a collision was unavoidable. The engines of the *Princess of Wales* were put full ahead but she was unable to clear the path of the oncoming steamer. The *Balmoral Castle* cut through the paddle steamer, aft of the engine room, sending the people aboard sprawling across her decks. Amidst the confusion the one remaining undamaged lifeboat on the *Princess of Wales* was quickly launched and the ladies were safely landed at Skelmorlie. Most of those remaining aboard were rescued by other small boats sent from the shore, yachts nearby and boats from the *Balmoral Castle*. Around fifteen of the survivors sustained serious injuries and, once landed, were cared for by a local doctor.

The stern section quickly sank after the collision taking with it three workmen who had been putting finishing touches to the aft saloon. Meanwhile the forepart of the wreck remained afloat, saved by the engine room bulkhead. A passing steamer, the *Adela,* on her usual run from Rothesay to Wemyss Bay took the forepart in tow in an attempt to beach her at Wemyss Bay. However, before they could do so, the forepart heeled over and sank off Wemyss Bay Pier.

There are conflicting reports among contemporary sources as to exactly where the forepart sank, with depths of five, ten and twenty five fathoms being mentioned. Five days after the collision Captain Burns of the Glasgow Salvage Association, established her position from oil seeping to the surface off Wemyss Bay Pier, in approximately thirty fathoms. Due to the depth of the water salvage was considered impractical, being too deep for divers to work safely. The *Princess of Wales*, still under the ownership of the builders, was written off as a total loss thus ending one of the shortest careers of any vessel built on the Clyde.

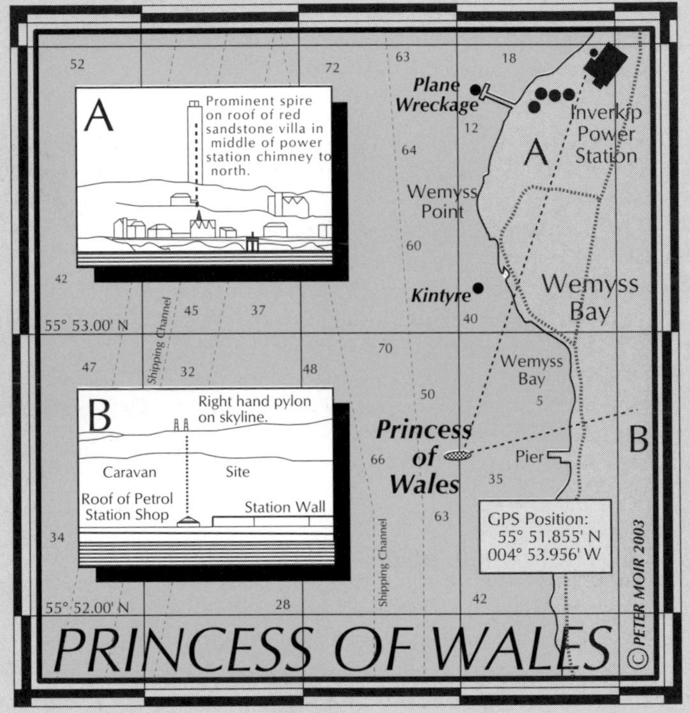

The wreckage of the fore section of the *Princess of Wales* was located in 1992 lying in 62 metres in position 55°52.525'N, 004°54.084'W (GPS). The wreckage is reported to be lying upside down on a muddy seabed. Clearly this wreck is beyond the safe limits of normal sports diving and, as such, diving her is not recommended. There are no confirmed reports of the location of the stern section although there are many rumours of a wreck off the Sklemorlie shore line. Most of these reports place the wreck in deep water. The seabed in this area shelves very steeply, even close to the shore, to depths of 60 metres or more.

TOVERUUS

476t. Wooden barque.
Built in Russia.
Launched 1874.

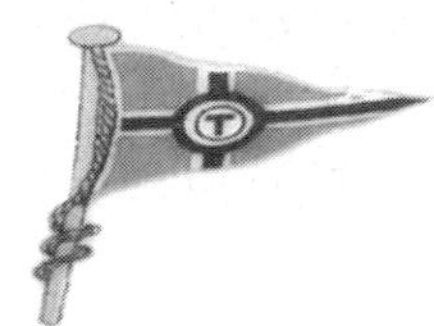

Bad weather, poor visibility and the lack of a proper lookout all contributed to the loss of the Russian barque *Toveruus* on Thursday 23rd December, 1875.

Her master, Captain Malmquist had overseen the loading of 500 tons of coal and 200 tons of pig iron bound for Genoa, the previous week. As they slipped anchor from the Tail of the Bank on 19th December gusts of wind filled her sails, and an ominous grey sky signalled unsettled weather ahead. The *Toveruus* sailed south until reaching Toward Point, by which time a full gale had arisen. Captain Malmquist decided to anchor up and ride out the southerly winds and heavy seas. Two anchors were set on the south side of the Skelmorlie Bank; lights were set to mark her position, and the crew settled down to wait for a lull in the weather. They remained at anchor for a number of days with no sign of any improvement in the weather.

In the early hours of 23rd December, Gustave Greenberg and a seaman called Hendricksen were on anchor watch, the weather was thick with frequent rain showers. Shivering from the cold they patrolled the deck of the barque occasionally glimpsing breaking wave tops illuminated by the anchor lights. Suddenly, Greenberg saw the lights of an incoming steamer dead ahead, unable to take any action to move his vessel, he quickly roused the crew by ringing the ship's bell and fortunately most were on deck when the inevitable collision occurred. The incoming vessel proved to be the Bristol steamer *Clutha*, and she crashed into the *Toveruus* on her port side sending most aboard sprawling across the decks. The collision caused extensive damage to the wooden hull of the barque and she immediately began to sink. Most of the crew were able to get aboard the *Clutha* while they were locked together, but the heavy seas eventually separated the two vessels and the *Toveruus* sank some eight minutes after the collision, three person were missing.

The following morning, the Millport to Wemyss Bay steamer *Largs* passed the site of the wreck, as her three masts were visible from some distance. To their amazement, they saw a man clinging to one of the masts, but were unable to get alongside due to the weather conditions. They immediately made for Gourock for help and succeeded in rescuing the man after towing the lifeboat south to the wreck site. The final loss of life stood at two, being the ship's cook and carpenter.

The wreck lay for some weeks on the south side of the bank in seventy feet of water. A salvage contract was let to Charles Gush of Greenock who succeeded in removing all the mast, rigging and deck structures, the hull was reported as being left as it was in deep water out with the main shipping channel. The authors have looked for the remains of the hull but to date have not been able to find any trace, it is possible it could have been recovered or may have rotted away over time with assistance from the voracious teredo worms.

URD

1108nt. Iron steamship.
Built by Raylton Dixon & Co, Middlesborough.
Launched 1877 (ex MARLBOROUGH).

Dimensions 264.5' x 33.4' x 18.8'

The Norwegian steamship *Urd*, inward bound from Oran to Glasgow with a cargo of iron ore and esparto grass, was lost in collision with the steamship *Elk* on Thursday 26th March, 1896. The collision occurred approximately one and a half miles south of Little Cumbrae Lighthouse around 5am. The *Elk* hit the *Urd* on her port side midships which resulted in the sinking of the *Urd* some five minutes later with the loss of two of her crew.

Two months later a formal investigation was held in Glasgow during which it was established that the cause of the collision was careless and improper navigation of the *Elk*. Although not positively identified as such, due to the general seabed depths of 90 metres or more, the authors are of the opinion that the wreck charted by the Admiralty at 55°41.951'N, 004°58.251'W (GPS) is in fact the *Urd*.

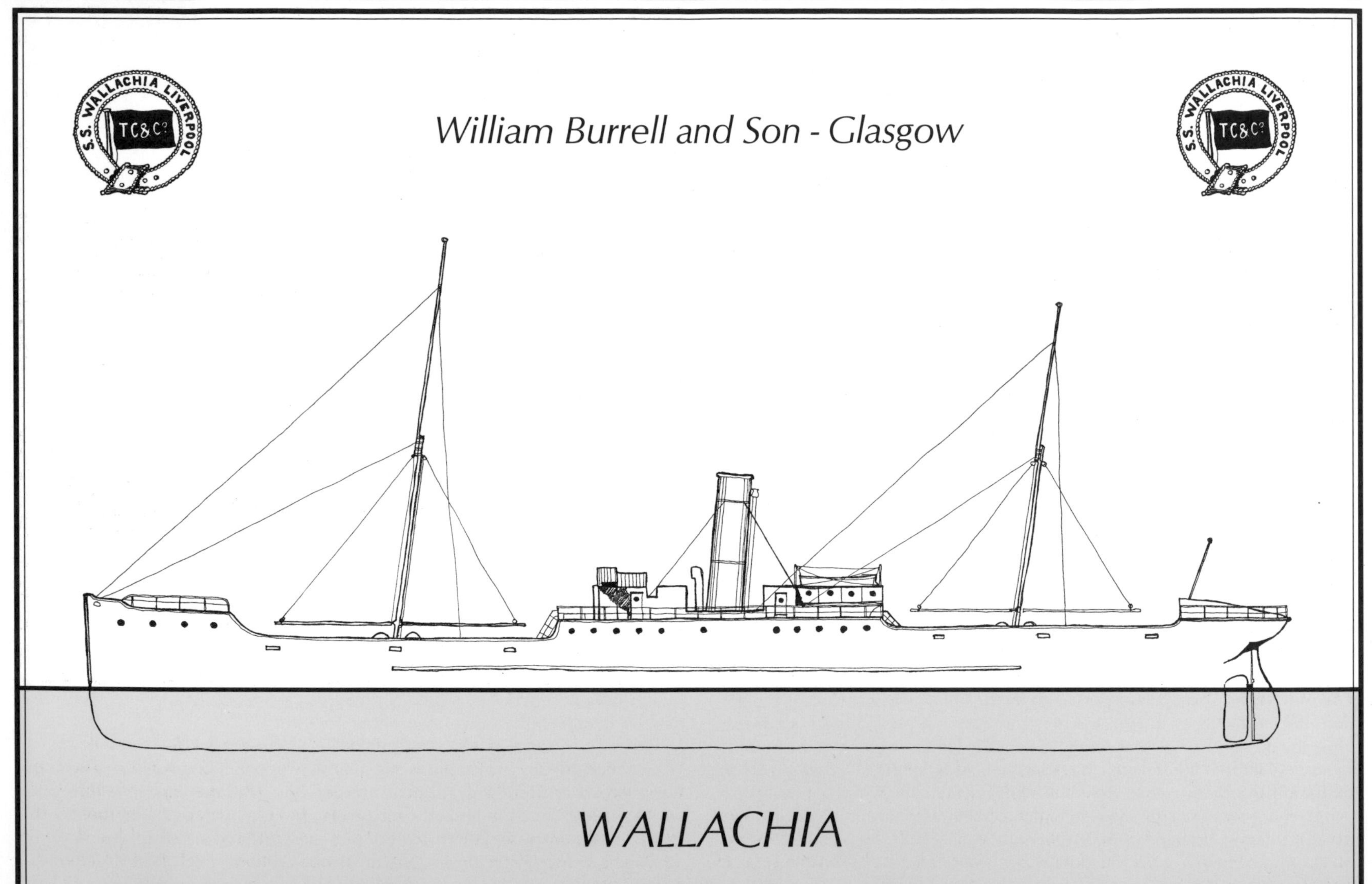
S.S. WALLACHIA LIVERPOOL
TC&Co
William Burrell and Son - Glasgow
S.S. WALLACHIA LIVERPOOL
TC&Co
WALLACHIA

WALLACHIA

1077nt. Iron steamship.
Built by Oswald Mordaunt & Co, Southampton.
Launched March 1883.

Dimensions 259.2' x 36.1' x 18.0'

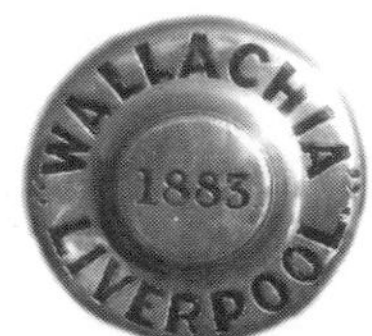

The *Wallachia*, a single screw steamer, was originally owned by Taylor & Cameron of Liverpool and used on the Black Sea run. She was bought by William Burrell & Son of Glasgow in 1893 and employed on regular trips between Glasgow and the West Indies.

On 29th September, 1895 she left Queen's Dock, Glasgow at 10am bound for Trinidad and Demerara. Captain Walton and his crew of twenty one had on board a valuable general cargo including whisky, gin, beer, acids, glassware, and earthenware plus building materials and footwear. They also had one passenger aboard.

The weather was foggy and she was held up, around noon, off the Tail of the Bank. As the fog lifted slightly in the early afternoon Captain Walton set off, keeping to the channel on the Cowal side of the river. Just before 4pm, as the fog thickened once more, the *Wallachia* grounded off Innellan Pier but quickly refloated on the rising tide. Shortly afterwards, as they felt their way gingerly down river, Captain Walton was startled by the appearance of a large steamer off his starboard bow. It was the 1406 ton Norwegian steamer *Flos*. It was obvious that they would collide and he only had time to order everybody clear of the forecastle before the bow of the *Flos* crashed into the starboard side of the *Wallachia* ten feet from the stem.

The captain of the *Flos* kept his engines ahead to keep the vessels together while the *Wallachia's* lifeboats were launched. The first capsized as it was lowered into the water but the crew and the single passenger were soon safely aboard two of the remaining three boats. A plan to tow the *Wallachia* to shallow water was quickly abandoned when the *Flos* backed away, as the *Wallachia* immediately began to settle at the bow.

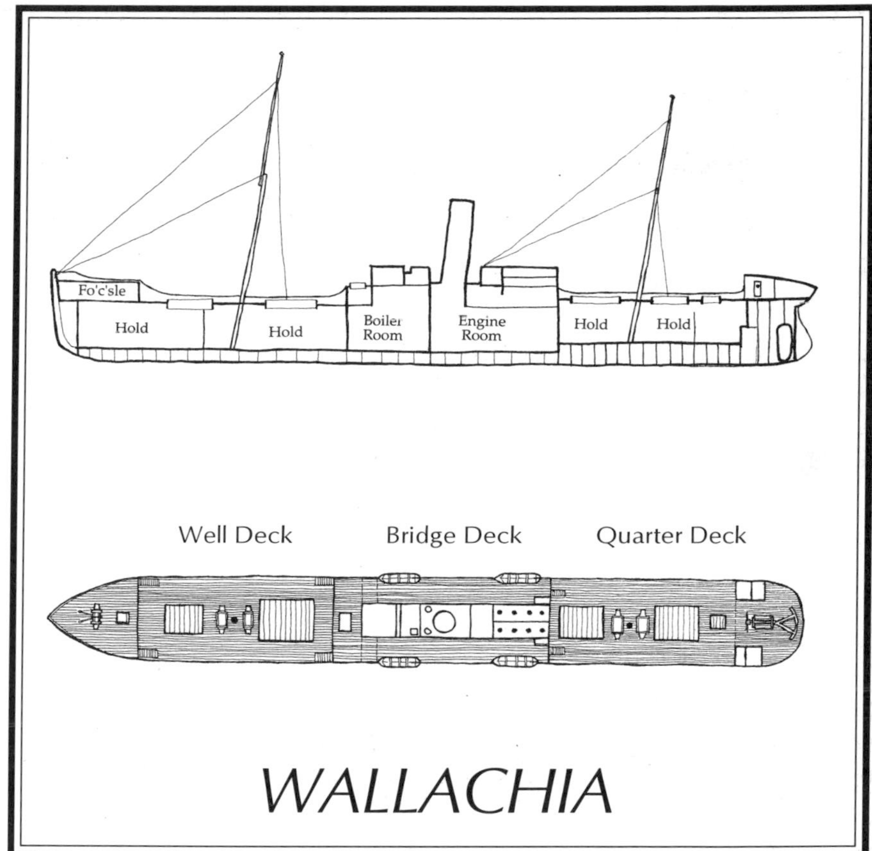

Twenty five minutes after the original collision the *Wallachia* sank by the bow, with a terrific explosion as she plunged beneath the surface. The crew rowed safely to Toward Lighthouse. In October, 1895 the salvage ship *Torch* was reported over the wreck with divers down to remove her masts. The *Wallachia* was then forgotten for eighty years until rediscovered by divers in 1977 who were diving on an unknown obstruction which had entangled a fisherman's nets.

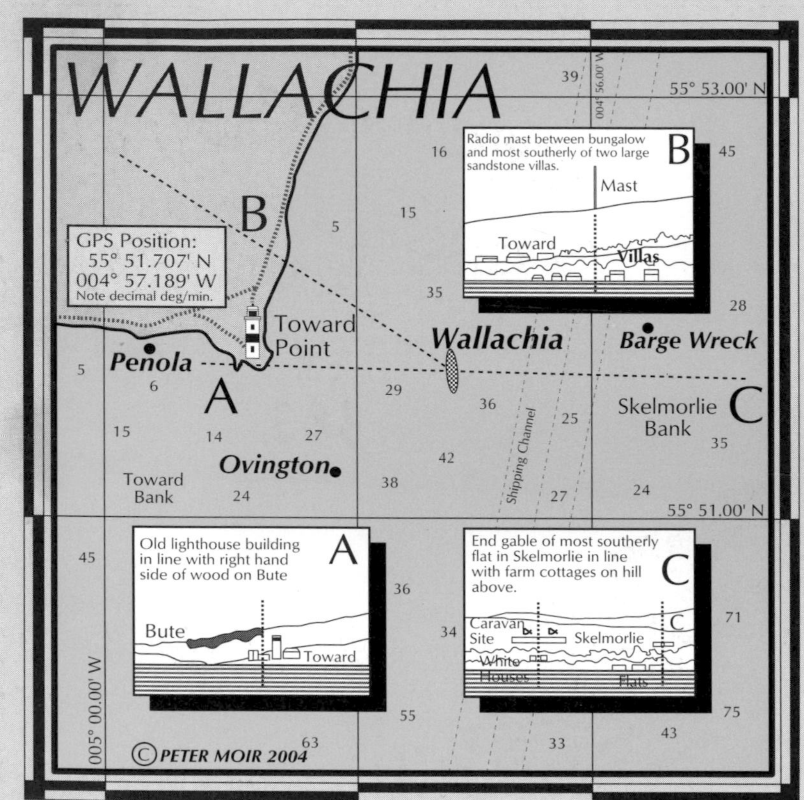

The wreck of the *Wallachia* lies upright on a muddy seabed at 34 metres in position 55°51.669'N, 004°57.189'W (GPS). Her bow points approximately north and the average depth over the wreck is 30 metres.

The raised forecastle has a large winch on top and can be safely entered and exited by the two rear facing bulkhead doors. As with many of the wrecks, care should be taken as the visibility will quickly reduce to nil as finning disturbs the deep silt. The gash of the collision on the starboard bow is clearly visible. There is a large heavy fishing net entangled on this part of the wreck, therefore care is essential.

The foredeck has three holds, each of which is deep with silt, although some interesting items of cargo have been recovered from these holds. The remains of the foremast lie across the middle hold. The raised bridge deck housed the captain's quarters and provided access to the engine and boiler rooms. The funnel has disappeared but provides an interesting entry to the engine room as it is possible to swim down the remains of the funnel and aft, below deck level, into the engine room and out through the roof. The wooden decks on each side of the superstructure have rotted giving access to cabins, galley, bathroom and coal bunkers below. The rear deck has three more holds and, just aft of the engine room, lie the remains of the deck cargo of stannous chloride in earthenware jars. Each jar carries the inscription 'Richard Smith, Acid Maker, Glasgow,' a company still in existence today.

The rear deck holds contain thousands of bottles of beer. The corks are inscribed with the name of the maker - McEwans. The covered stern houses the emergency steering gear, toilet and store. The depth and probable darkness of the *Wallachia* provide the major hazards for the diver, plus the relatively unpredictable currents that can be experienced at the site.

The wreck is beginning to show further signs of deterioration with large cracks appearing in the stern deck around the middle hold, and the front of the bridge has fallen away, brought down by the collapse of steam steering gear in bridge. Extreme care should therefore be taken when entering any overhead environment on this wreck. The wreck lies close to the Wemyss Bay to Rothesay ferry route and the shipping channel, so good boat cover, with clearly visible 'A' flag, is essential.

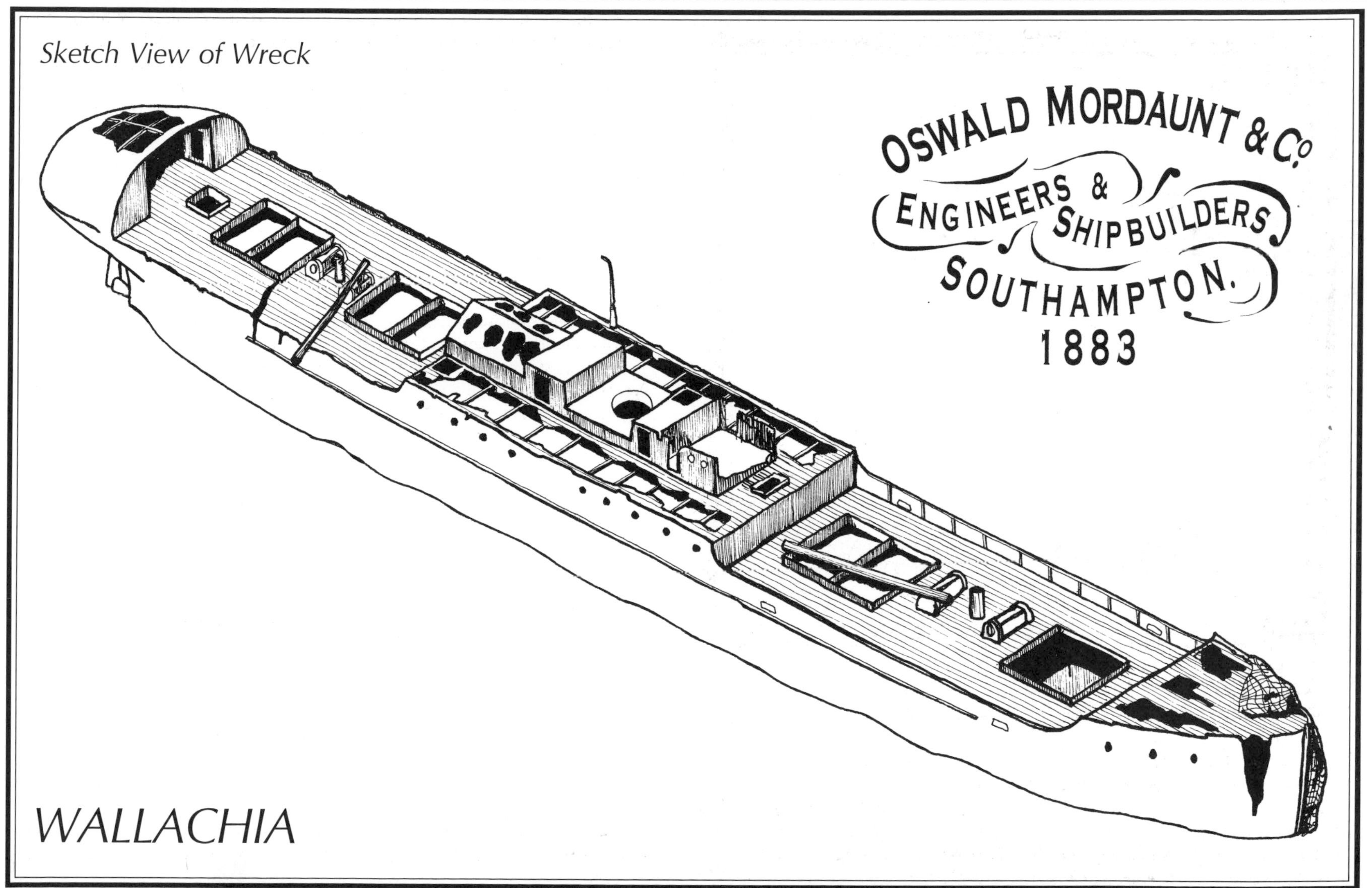
Sketch View of Wreck
OSWALD MORDAUNT & Co
ENGINEERS & SHIPBUILDERS
SOUTHAMPTON.
1883
WALLACHIA

CLYDE COAST NORTH

Listed below are a selection of 65 smaller vessels wrecked within this area. This list is included as a basis for further research. Names suffixed by (S) denote extensive salvage work or total removal subsequent to date of loss.

NAME	BUILT	TONNAGE	HULL	TYPE	LOST	CAUSE	LOCATION
Abigail	1833	138nt	W	Bg	24.01.1883	S	Arranman's Barrel
Amy	1886	35nt	I	SS	08.02.1899	F	Off Innellan
Annetta	1865	376nt	W	Bk	22.11.1881	S	Horse Island
Ardenlea	1859	1217nt	W	Bk	22.11.1881	S	Kirkfindlay Bay
Arsenal	1933	150nt	S	S.Tr	16.11.1940	C	Off Kilchatten Bay
Beryl	1895	15nt	W	Syt	20.06.1902	S	Craigmore, Bute
Champion	1857	18nt	W	P.Tug	15.12.1858	C	Off Small Cumbrae
Clio		143nt	W	Bg	19.12.1880	S	Ardrossan
Countess of Eglington		68nt	I	PS	27.03.1845	S	Millport Bay
Dolphin	1869	37nt	W	Sk	07.01.1898	S	Wemyss Bay
Dumb Barge			S	Barge	11.07.1928	F	N end Skelmorlie Bank
Eagle	1861	171nt	W	Bn	01.03.1882	S	Loch Fyne
Ellen	1900	4nt	W	Syt	27.06.1927	Fr	Off Skelmorlie
Flying Childers			I	PS	31.03.1862	C	Off Wemyss Point
Follow Me			W	Dr	24.01.1928	C	Loch Striven
Forth	1863	25nt	I	SS	04.08.1903	S	3m N of Largs
H	1850	33nt	I	SS	13.03.1885	F	Loch Fyne
Halcyon	1885	2nt	W	Syt	04.06.1891	S	Rothesay Bay
Helios	1867	430bn	W	Bk	02.12.1891	C	2m S of Toward Point
Hugh Crawford	1810	374bn	W	S	22.01.1820	S	The Bridges, Innellan
Hunter	1852	32nt	I	SS	18.02.1858	S	Ardscalpsie Point, Bute
I	1874	33nt	I	SS	18.12.1886	F	Off Small Cumbrae
Ianthe	1873	68nt	I	SS	25.10.1899	S	Ardscalpsie Pt, Bute
Ilma	1889	22nt	I	Syt	20.10.1896	S	Millport Bay
Isabella	1842	42nt	W	Sk	28.12.1882	S	Etterick Bay, Bute
Janet	1869	34nt	W	Sk	10.01.1879	F	Off Inchmarnock
Jenny	1803	215bn	W	Bgn	22.12.1814	S	Scalpsie Bay, Bute
John Craich	1841	58nt	W	Sr	03.10.1889	F	Off Skelmorlie Bank
LCV 584			W	LCV	15.03.1943	F	Off Innellan

NAME	BUILT	TONNAGE	HULL	TYPE	LOST	CAUSE	LOCATION
Linnet	1892	9nt	W	SS	31.05.1907	F	Rothesay Bay
Loch Etive	1892	58nt	I	SS	29.09.1906	F	Near Tarbert, Loch Fyne
Loven	1855	256nt	W	Bg	22.12.1894	S	Horse Island, Ardrossan
Maggie	1877	31nt	W	K	26.08.1935	S	Clonaig, Skipness
Maggie Lauder	1891	8nt	W	SS	23.09.1903	C	Tarbert, Loch Fyne
Margaret	1866	25nt	W	Sk	24.11.1885	C	Off Millport
Maritana(S)	1882	30nt	I	Syt	03.09.1902	S	Skelmorlie
Mars	1844	94nt	I	PS	10.04.1855	S	Gogo Burn, Largs
Martha	1873	20nt	W	K	25.02.1894	S	Etterick Bay, Bute
Mary	1837	33nt	W	Sr	08.04.1880	C	Loch Riddon
Mary	1889	11nt	W	Sr	23.09.1898	C	S of Skate island, Loch Fyne
Matchless	1857	45nt	W	K	03.12.1892	C	Off Wemyss Bay
Matilda Hilyard	1868	589nt	W	Bk	28.02.1880	S	Horse Island, Ardrossan
Merse	1914	296gt	S	S.Tr	22.05.1917	M	Off Garroch Head
Moonlight(S)		35nt	I	SS	29.03.1879	S	Horse Island, Ardrossan
Otter	1886	35nt	I	SS	09.09.1859	F	Off Garroch Head
Petchlee	1851	364nt	W	Bn	20.03.1884	S	Near Ardrossan
Petrel	1865	74nt	W	Sr	13.12.1890	S	Garroch Head
Phoebe	1845	65nt	W	Sr	09.09.1859	S	Kilchatten Bay
Queen of May	1888	42nt	W	Sr	14.03.1893	S	Tarbert, Loch Fyne
Reaper	1875	131gt	W	Sr	12.03.1923	S	Toward Point
Regenti	1850	278gt	W	Bq	05.11.1871	S	Ardrossan
Restless	1851	19bn	W	SS	21.02.1862	S	Horse Island
Sarah Ann	1863	102nt	W	Sr	04.02.1879	S	Near Ardrossan
Sea Bird	1870	75nt	W	Sr	13.12.1890	S	Garroch Head
Seagull	1868	12nt	W	Sk	02.01.1892	S	Loch Striven
Springbok	1862	182nt	W	Sr	24.12.1881	S	Great Cumbrae
Sutherland	1874	346nt	W	Bn	07.02.1881	S	Garroch Head
Tarbert Castle	1836	100nt	I	PS	07.01.1839	S	Ardmarnock, Loch Fyne
Valtos	1903	3nt	W	Sl	03.07.1903	F	Off Wemyss Point
Walker	1865	9nt	W	P.Tug	27.10.1887	C	Off Small Cumbrae
Wallace	1883	38nt	I	SS	12.03.1913	S	1m E of Skipness Point
Warlock	1871	23nt	I	SS	19.11.1905	F	3m S of Skate Island, Loch Fyne
Welcome	1861	32nt	W	Sk	17.12.1891	S	Horse island, Ardrossan
Winsome	1902	46gt	W	M Dr	18.11.1941	F	Off Fairlie
Witch	1872	31nt	I	SS	15.08.1890	F	Off Skipness Poimt

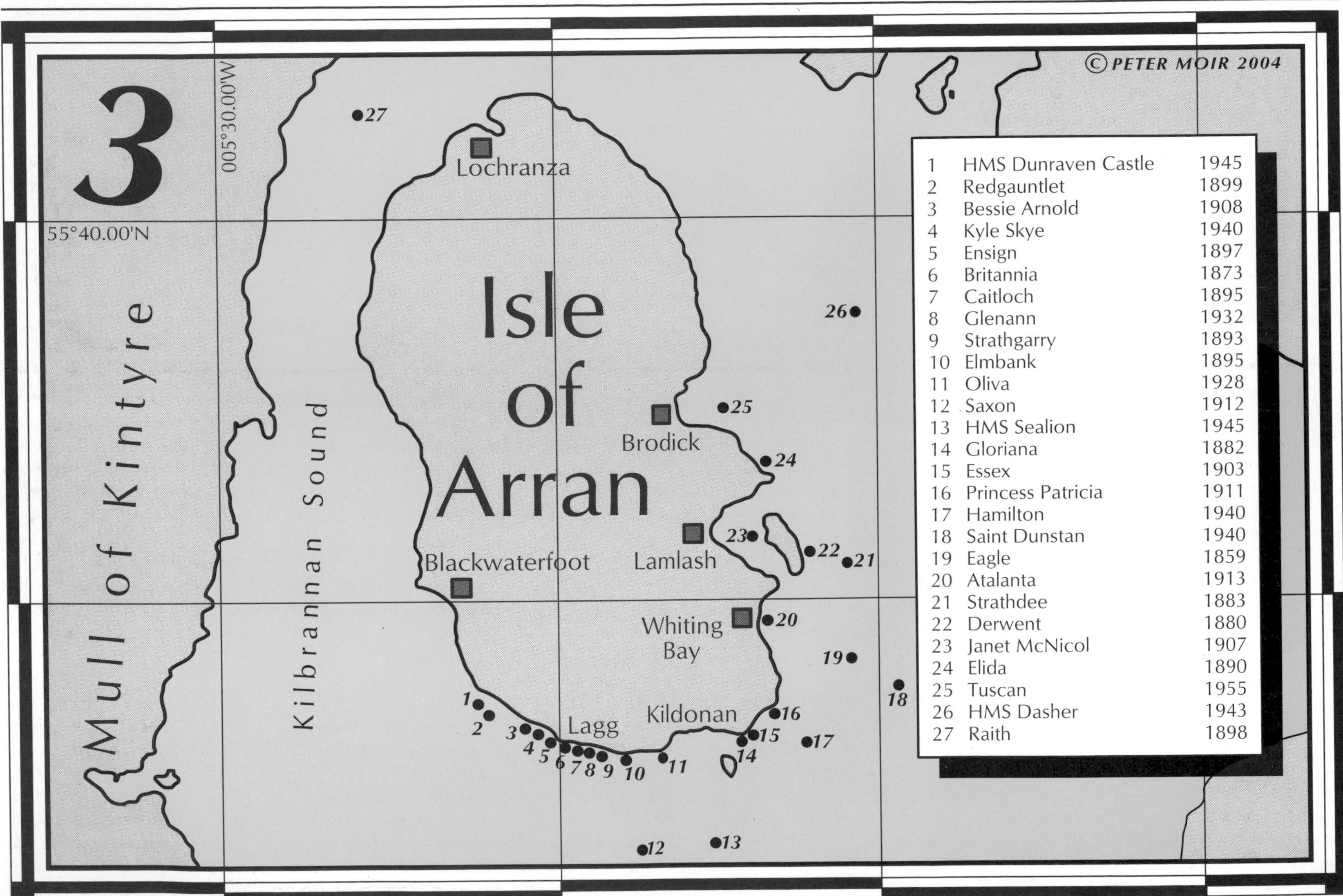
3
© PETER MOIR 2004
005°30.00'W
55°40.00'N
Mull of Kintyre
Kilbrannan Sound
Isle of Arran
Lochranza
Brodick
Lamlash
Blackwaterfoot
Whiting Bay
Lagg
Kildonan
1 HMS Dunraven Castle 1945
2 Redgauntlet 1899
3 Bessie Arnold 1908
4 Kyle Skye 1940
5 Ensign 1897
6 Britannia 1873
7 Caitloch 1895
8 Glenann 1932
9 Strathgarry 1893
10 Elmbank 1895
11 Oliva 1928
12 Saxon 1912
13 HMS Sealion 1945
14 Gloriana 1882
15 Essex 1903
16 Princess Patricia 1911
17 Hamilton 1940
18 Saint Dunstan 1940
19 Eagle 1859
20 Atalanta 1913
21 Strathdee 1883
22 Derwent 1880
23 Janet McNicol 1907
24 Elida 1890
25 Tuscan 1955
26 HMS Dasher 1943
27 Raith 1898

ARRAN

Chapter 3

The dramatic, mountainous island of Arran provides the subject matter for the third chapter. The island lies west of the main shipping flow up and down the Firth, and has seen more than its fair share of shipwrecks, as vessels attempted to hug her shoreline, using the island as shelter from the prevailing west and south west winds or as they ran for shelter provided by the bays at Lamlash and Brodick. Many more were smashed to pieces on her exposed south west shore in violent storms or ran aground there in fog or at night. The exposed nature of this coastline and its attraction for shipwrecks led to the construction of the lighthouse on Pladda, the small rocky islet on the south tip of Arran, in 1790, the second lighthouse to be built on the Clyde. Despite this precaution, the shallow waters hereabouts continued to be a graveyard for many more ships over the ensuing years.

The landlocked bay at Lamlash was a favourite haven for ships seeking shelter and it was not uncommon for more than a hundred ships to be anchored there in bad weather. The steep dark slopes of Holy Isle and the hills of the main island provide shelter to one of the best anchorages on the west coast of Scotland. The bay was also used by the Navy during the war and was guarded by anti-submarine nets at both entrances, some of these nets now lie in deep water in the middle of the bay. There are a number of wrecks close to the bay and around Holy Isle, and most of these are of small coastal sailing vessels.

The south end of Arran has the main concentration of shipwrecks, as can be seen from the map opposite. The sea here is relatively shallow and the coastline very exposed to the prevailing south westerly wind. As such, most of the wrecks are well broken and often some distance from the shore as they grounded on one of the many outlying reefs. The attentions of salvage firms have further dismantled the wrecks leaving them bare, broken and often difficult to identify.

The northern half of the island is characterised by steep sandy slopes descending into depths of 50-70 metres or deeper, and most wrecks here have been lost as a result of collision or foundering in open water. As a result there are few if any within air diving range, any that have been lost in shallow water have since completely disintgrated.

Diving around Arran is fairly straight forward with few complications and generally better visibility than other areas in the Clyde. The weather, which caused many of the shipwrecks, in turn proves to be the main hazard to the diver. On the exposed south west coast the prevailing winds and swell often making diving impossible or, at best, dangerous. However, the advantage of diving on an island is that it is always possible to dive somewhere, no matter how poor the weather or from which direction the wind is blowing. Boat launch facilities are suprisingly sparse, although the slip at Lamlash provides access to many of the better sites, compressed air should also be available on the pier.

ATALANTA

199nt. Steel steamship.
Built by John Brown & Co Ltd, Clydebank.
Launched May 1906.

Dimensions 210.4' x 30.1' x 10.5'

SS ***Atalanta*** ashore.

The *Atalanta*, owned by the Glasgow & South Western Railway Company Ltd, was among one of the first turbine steamers to work commercially on the Clyde. On Thursday 8th May, 1913 shortly after leaving Whiting Bay Pier for Ardrossan, she came to an abrupt halt due to a mechanical fault and was quickly washed ashore by heavy seas. The twelve passengers and her crew got safely ashore and later continued on their journey aboard the PS *Jupiter* which had been sent as a replacement. The *Atalanta*, although badly damaged, was successfully refloated by the Clyde Shipping Company tug *Flying Mist* later that month and taken to Glasgow for repair.

SS ***Atalanta*** ashore with ***Flying Mist*** beyond.

BESSIE ARNOLD

104nt. Wooden schooner.
Built by Ferguson of Chester.
Launched 1872.

Dimensions 86.6' x 22.2' x 11.4'

One of Arran's most dramatic wrecks and rescue attempts was the loss of the schooner *Bessie Arnold* and four of her crew on Monday 28th December, 1908. En route to Clydebank with a cargo of iron ore, she was caught in a violent storm and driven ashore near Sliddery on the south west coast.

As soon as news of the disaster reached Kildonan telegrams were dispatched to Campbeltown for the assistance of the lifeboat, which left its Kintyre base around 10am. She made her way across Kilbrannan Sound under reefed sail, arriving off Sliddery around 1pm. The lifeboat anchored up wind of the *Bessie Arnold* and kedged inshore on her anchor rope. As the lifeboat approached the schooner, three men were seen huddled together on her bow trying to shelter from the waves and the freezing spray.

Heavy seas were pitching the lifeboat around in all directions making it impossible to get alongside the wreck which was lying beam to the shore. After numerous attempts to get alongside, a large wave bodily lifted the lifeboat thirty yards and sent her crashing onto the deck of the *Bessie Arnold*, causing considerable damage to her keel and rudder. At the time the bowman, Neil MacKenzie, was swept overboard and two others, including the coxswain, were severely injured. Fortunately, the backwash of the next wave lifted the lifeboat off the wreck and she swung free again on her anchor rope. Neil MacKenzie meanwhile, had managed to hold onto the schooner's rigging and, as the lifeboat approached again, jumped into the sea and was eventually hauled aboard.

As the lifeboat had a hole in her bottom and her rudder was useless, her coxswain decided to return to Campbeltown as she could not be controlled in the prevailing weather conditions. Shortly before the lifeboat left the *Bessie Arnold*, the rocket brigade apparatus and crew arrived from Kildonan. A line was eventually secured to the wreck and the remaining crew members brought ashore. Of the three remaining aboard, two eventually died of exposure. It was discovered later that two members of her crew had been washed overboard shortly before the *Bessie Arnold* went ashore. Some of the crew were later buried in Kildonan cemetery.

BRITANNIA

1118nt. Iron steamship.
Built by Tod & McGregor, Partick, Glasgow.
Launched June 1863.

Dimensions 261.5' x 33.1' x 21.5'

One of the largest vessels to become a total wreck round the shores of Arran was the cargo passenger steamship *Britannia*. Owned by the Anchor line of Quebec and Montreal, the *Britannia* stranded off Torrylin beach in the early hours of Tuesday 28th January, 1873 on the final leg of a voyage from Alexandria to Glasgow via Malta. She had encountered strong winds accompanied by dense fog in the North Channel causing her to veer far off course.

News that a large vessel had gone ashore on the south west of Arran soon reached Glasgow. The salvage steamer *Dispatch* and the tug *Flying Squall* left Glasgow the same day with representatives of the owners and a salvage team aboard. Initial attempts to refloat the *Britannia* were hampered by continuing bad weather. However, part of her cargo of wheat, beans, cotton, and olive oil was successfully removed during the following week, along with her sails, ropes and loose fittings.

SS ***Britannia***.

Attempts to refloat the *Britannia* were finally abandoned on the 1st February as damage to her hull had become so extensive she was considered beyond economical repair. The authors have been unable to establish what eventually happened to the wreck, other than the fact that she did not appear in the Shipping Register after this date. However, it would seem reasonable to suggest that a wreck of this size would have been salvaged in some form at a later date.

CAITLOCH

1264nt. Iron barque.
Built by R Duncan & Sons, Port Glasgow.
Launched December 1874.

Dimensions 235.0' x 37.0' x 21.8'

The *Caitloch* was built by R Duncan for T O Hunter & Company of Greenock in 1874. In February 1891, while in Hamburg harbour, she capsized and sank after sitting down on the anchor of the barque *Dunnerdale*. She was successfully raised and repaired and subsequently sold to C A Banck & Company of Helsingborg, Sweden.

On 13th February, 1895 she was inward bound to the Clyde from Falmouth with a cargo of sugar valued at £25,000 for the Glebe refinery in Greenock. On reaching the approaches to the Clyde she was taken in tow by the Clyde Shipping Company tug *Flying Eagle*. This was the usual method of manoeuvering a large sailing ship in the waters around Arran, Cumbrae and Bute. Despite this precaution, at around 9:30pm that day, the *Caitloch* stranded on Torrylin beach, south Arran in a strong south westerly wind. The *Flying Eagle* struck a reef, snapping off her funnel and severely damaging her hull and was left with her stern high and dry on the rocks and clear of the water. The *Caitloch* was quickly holed as she was bumped against the rocky shore and soon filled with water, leaving her decks awash in the rough seas.

The lifeboats from both the *Flying Eagle* and the *Caitloch* herself were quickly lowered into the pounding waves in an attempt to reach safety. The crew of the *Flying Eagle* reached the shore but the crew of the *Caitloch* decided to weather the storm in the lee of their wrecked ship and land in daylight after seeing their first lifeboat washed ashore and smashed to pieces on the rocks. They spent a long, cold night continually drenched by the huge waves crashing over the *Caitloch* but landed safely in the morning. Although most were suffering from exposure as they landed, for once, no one was killed or seriously injured in the incident on either of the two vessels involved.

Salvage crews visited both wrecks over the next week and the *Flying Eagle* was successfully refloated on 20th February. There is no record of successful salvage of the *Caitloch*, although her sails and fittings were removed by the crew within a week of her wrecking. It is also certain that some salvage would have been carried out due to the shallow depths of the wreck.

HMS DASHER

13,785dt. Steel escort carrier.
Built by Sun Shipbuilding Co, Hoboken, USA.
Launched 1941.
(ex RIO DE JANEIRO)

Dimensions 492' x 66' x 23'

Work commenced on the SS *Rio de Janeiro* at the Sun Shipbuilding Company in late 1940. The diesel powered passenger/cargo ship was to have a very different future to that envisaged by her designers and builders. As the war in Europe intensified and the need to defend and supply Allied countries increased, she was sold to the Royal Navy under the lease/lend agreement set up between Britain and USA. On completion, the *Rio De Janeiro* was taken to Brooklyn Naval Yard where, by July 1942, she had been converted into the Archer Class Escort Carrier HMS *Dasher*.

These escort carriers were never popular ships as the rush to get them into service left them poorly finished and, many thought, unsafe. The cheap nature of their construction resulted in their unfortunate, if appropriate, nickname - 'Woolworth's carriers.' In one incident, during convoy duty near Iceland, the crew of the *Dasher* below decks were horrified to see a seam on the side of the ship burst open, almost to the water line, giving them a clear view of the convoy destroyers through the side of the ship. However, she made it back to Scotland

and was repaired at the Caledon yard in Dundee allowing her and her two squadrons of Hurricanes and one squadron of Swordfish to take part in the successful invasion of North Africa, codenamed Operation Torch. In an even more sinister prelude to the *Dasher's* final loss, her sister ship *Avenger* was lost after a submarine attack in the Atlantic - she was hit by a torpedo from *U-155* but was lost, with most of her crew, in the huge explosion which followed the initial hit.

In March, 1943 the *Dasher* was stationed in the Clyde and late in the month was carrying out some exercises off Arran. On the morning of the 27th she left the safety of the anchorage at Lamlash at 11am and after a day of practice flights off the east coast of the island she headed back to the protection of the Clyde anchorage off Greenock. In fact, Captain Boswell had already radioed ahead that he expected to reach the boom at the Cloch Lighthouse by 6pm that evening. Her five hundred and twenty eight officers

View from a rescue ship shortly after the ***Dasher*** sank.

and crew were already anticipating some time ashore in Greenock or maybe even a trip into Glasgow for a respite from stress of wartime convoy duty. It has never been absolutely established what happened next but at 4:42pm, as the last of the Swordfish were being refuelled, there was a rumbling explosion followed almost immediately by a second, larger explosion. These explosions completely destroyed the Fleet Air Arm deck and blew the lift between the hanger and the aircraft deck high into the sky and into the sea on the port side of the *Dasher*. The ship was plunged into darkness as the lights and machinery failed and a strange silence descended on the fatally wounded ship. Within six minutes the *Dasher* lifted her bow almost vertically to the sky and sank. Many of her crew didn't even make it to the deck before she sank and even more were lost when they jumped overboard into the sea only to be killed in a huge fire when the aviation fuel floating on the surface was ignited by the flames aboard the ship. Of the men and women aboard only one hundred and forty nine were saved by the vessels that rushed to the scene.

The subsequent official enquiry, held aboard her sister ship HMS *Archer*, could only point to possible causes of the disaster and even these were influenced by the politics of the situation and the controversy that followed between Britian and the United States. It was clearly established that a small, but potentially serious, petrol leak had been discovered two weeks before the disaster and that a hole leading from the petrol storage area into the shaft tunnel existed. It is also known that ammunition and sixty eight depth charges were stored close by. The official enquiry concluded that somehow the petrol leak had caused a build up of petrol vapour in the shaft and storage areas and that these fumes had been ignited causing the first explosion heard by the survivors. The second larger explosion, possibly ammunition or the depth charges, ruptured the ship's hull causing the rapid sinking. Due to the security surrounding the movements of shipping during the war, the relatives of the unfortunate crewmen killed in the incident only learned the true nature of the accident many months later.

The wreck of the *Dasher* lies upright in 170 metres in position 55°37.750'N, 005°00.883'W (GPS) close to the ferry route from Ardrossan to Brodick. She is lying east/west with her wooden flight deck 30 metres above the seabed.

DERWENT

232nt. Wooden brig.
Built in Workington.
Launched 1795.

The *Derwent* was employed by her owner, Mr J Little, carrying cargo between Ireland, north west England and south west Scotland.

On 19th December, 1880 she was on a voyage from Maryport to Londonderry with a cargo of coal under the command of Captain R Little, when she ran ashore in a storm close to the lighthouse on the south east end of Holy Isle. Her crew escaped safely onto the island as the wreck was very close to the shore.

The wreck of the *Derwent* lies in approximately 10 metres in position 55°31.167'N, 005°03.583'W (GPS). She is about 100 metres from the shore and a quarter of a mile north east of the lighthouse lying almost parallel to the shoreline.

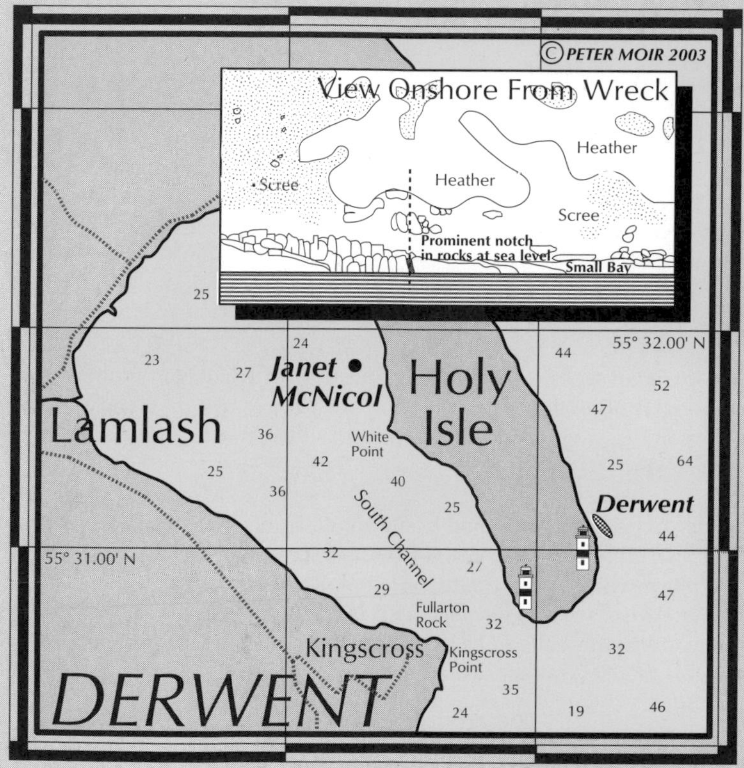

The wreck itself is very broken with only a few wooden spars and planks visible above the sandy seabed. The sternpost rises about 4 metres from the seabed and is ablaze with anemonae and dead men's fingers. At first glance the wreck appears uninteresting but some interesting artefacts, including the ship's bell, have been discovered buried in the sand around the wreckage.

HMS DUNRAVEN CASTLE

276nt. Steel trawler.
Built by Smith's Dock Co Ltd, Middlesborough.
Launched 1917.
(ex SWANSEA)

Dimensions 125.5' x 23.4' x 12.8'

Around 7pm on 29th January, 1945 the secretary of the Campbeltown lifeboat received a telephone call requesting that the lifeboat be sent to the Iron Rock Ledges on the south west coast of Arran where a Naval trawler, with twenty five people aboard, was ashore in heavy seas. Due to wartime restrictions, the customary maroons to summon the crew could not be fired so each member had to be mustered individually. The lifeboat's departure was further delayed while permission to open the boom defence nets across the mouth of Campbeltown Loch was arranged.

The lifeboat, *City of Glasgow*, left Campbeltown at around 7:50pm and arrived off 'the Irons' at 9:15pm. The weather conditions were atrocious, with sub zero temperatures, a southerly gale, mountainous seas and frequent snow showers. Coxswain Duncan Newlands initially approached the trawler from the south west, but found his route blocked by a reef. He managed to manoeuvre the lifeboat around the reef and, on the second attempt, secured a line to the trawler. The crew of the *Dunraven Castle* were safely transferred to the lifeboat which then backed out around the reef and headed for Campbeltown.

The crew of the lifeboat were highly praised for their fine service under such severe conditions and her coxswain, Duncan Newlands, later received a medal of commendation. As to the fate of the *Dunraven Castle*, it is thought that she was successfully refloated, as she appears in official records as continuing service in the Royal Navy until the end of September 1945.

EAGLE

220nt. Iron steamship.
Built by Denny Bros, Dumbarton.
Launched July 1857.

Dimensions 160.0' x 23.0' x 18.5'

For the previous few days the full rigged ship *Pladda* had limped towards the Clyde fully waterlogged, only staying afloat on her cargo of Canadian timber. Around 10pm on 28th November, 1859 she was met by the tug *Reckless* off the south coast of Arran and taken in tow for the remainder of her voyage to Glasgow.

The *Pladda* remained under tow until around 11:30pm when, with a freshening wind, her captain decided to let go the tow rope and proceed under sail. Shortly after the two vessels parted the bow lookout on the *Pladda* sighted lights of another vessel close by off the port bow. The *Pladda* had not, as yet, set her sails and was not fully under control. As the two vessels closed, Captain Ingram attempted to turn the *Pladda* to starboard, but she did not respond quickly enough and she crashed into the port side of the oncoming vessel.

The other vessel proved to be the McConnel & Laird steamer *Eagle* on her usual run to Londonderry with fifty six passengers, twenty crew and her main cargo of two hundred sheep aboard. The *Eagle* was immediately enveloped in smoke and steam causing a state of panic aboard. The two vessels remained locked together for ten minutes, allowing most of the passengers and crew to scramble aboard the *Pladda*. However, unfortunately not everyone aboard was able to escape before the vessels parted and the *Eagle* filled and sank. The initial death toll was thought to be as high as twenty but, after checking with the ticket receipts and the survivors, it was ascertained that only eleven had lost their lives. The stewardess from the *Eagle* had a lucky escape. Still aboard the *Eagle* as she sank, she was thrown into the sea and managed to stay afloat by holding onto two sheep until she was rescued. After an extensive search for survivors by the *Reckless* and the boats from the *Pladda*, the tug took the *Pladda* in tow once more and headed for Greenock.

The collision was reported to have taken place no more than a mile east of Lamlash. However the authors are of the opinion that the incident took place further south, off Whiting Bay.

ELIDA

537nt. Wooden barque.
Built in America.
Launched 1839.

Dimensions 125.6' x 29.2' x 20.6'

The Norwegian barque *Elida* stranded north of Clauchlands Point on 10th December, 1890 in thick fog. She had left Glasgow two days earlier bound for Tonsberg in Norway, under the command of her master, Mr A Bugge, with a crew of eleven.

Details of how the stranding occurred are somewhat vague. Contemporary sources give conflicting accounts of exactly where she went ashore, some noting Lamlash Bay, while others mention Hamilton Rock which lies near Clauchlands Point. Initial research was further complicated by the coincidental loss of another Norwegian barque called *Ellida* on 12th December near Port Ellen, Islay. The reports on the Islay wreck were in some cases published before those of the Arran wreck.

The Wreck Today

The wreck, which lies 250 yards north of Clauchlands Point in approximate position 55°33.417'N, 005°05.288'W (GPS), is well known as the *Elida* although, to the authors' knowledge, nothing has been recovered from the wreck that absolutely confirms its identification. The wreck lies close inshore off a narrow rocky shoreline which is backed by featureless cliffs some 50 metres high.

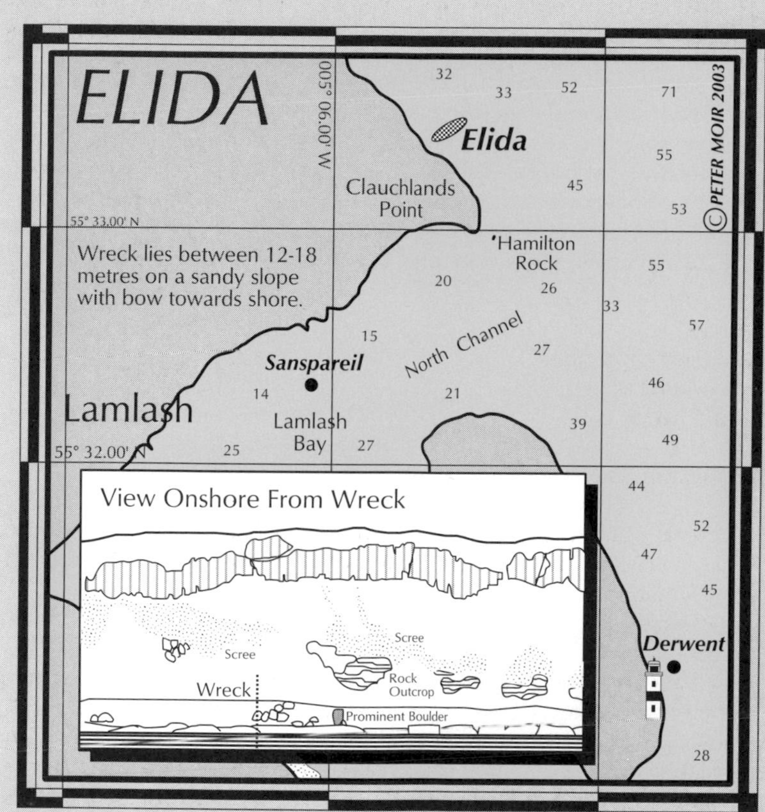

Unfortunately the nature of the shoreline gives few conspicuous marks to aid location of the wreck. The only shore level landmark nearby is a prominent square column of rock about 1.5 metres high which lies just north of the wreck. The diver should enter the water here and swim south along the base of the boulder slope in 12 metres. The wreck lies approximately 30 metres south on the sand slope between 12 and 18 metres. All that remains of the wreck above the seabed are parts of her main frames, deck beams, hull and ballast stones.

ELMBANK

2188nt. Iron barque.
Built by Russell & Co, Port Glasgow.
Launched April 1890.

Dimensions 279.0' x 41.9' x 24.2'

The *Elmbank*, owned and managed by Andrew Weir & Company of Glasgow, was one of the many large sailing vessels which formed part of the Glasgow based Bank Line.

On Saturday 6th January, 1895 she left Le Havre bound for Greenock under tow by the Clyde Shipping Company tug *Hercules*. Around 10pm on Tuesday 9th January, in poor visibility and squally conditions, she bottomed on rocks off the Mull of Galloway. The tug's crew immediately cut the tow cable thinking that they might also be dragged ashore. However, shortly afterwards, the *Elmbank*, which was under partial canvas, managed to sail off shore apparently undamaged. Due to the deteriorating weather conditions the *Elmbank* could not regain her tow so she continued on her journey closely followed by the *Hercules*.

The barque ***Elmbank***.

During the night the easterly gale had blown the *Elmbank* off course and, by 6am on 10th January, Pladda was sighted approximately seven miles to the north east. The gale force winds and heavy seas slowly pushed the *Elmbank* closer to the south coast of Arran. She tacked and headed north east but it soon became evident that she would not clear Arran and her anchors were cast in the hope of holding her off shore. The anchor cables were no match for the violent conditions and finally parted. The *Elmbank* was eventually washed ashore at Shannochie approximately two miles west of Bennan Head.

The crew were rescued by the Kildonan Lifeboat and safely landed there around midday. Fortunately Captain Greig's family, who were travelling aboard the *Elmbank*, had been transferred to the *Hercules* the previous evening. The *Elmbank*, insured and valued at £20,000, eventually became a total loss, a result of further gales and heavy seas during the following week. Some initial salvage was undertaken and the sale of the recovered items raised £18.15.4d. Towards the end of February, 1895 a salvage contract was let to the Glasgow Salvage Association on a "no cure, no pay" basis, but little more than ropes and fittings were recovered.

Wreck of the ***Elmbank***.

ENSIGN

399nt. Iron steamship.
Built at Rutherglen.
Launched 1883.

Dimensions 155.5' x 23.2' x 11.5'

The *Ensign* left Workington for Port Glasgow on the morning of 22 December, 1897 with a cargo of pig iron for her owner Mr William Robertson of Glasgow. At first the voyage was good but, as they steamed up the Galloway coast, the visibility deteriorated to the extent that, when they passed Corsewall, they could not see the light. Still, the captain and crew were not concerned and a course was set for Pladda.

Half an hour later they were aground on the rocks at Clauchog Point, Arran. The captain, seeing the heavy list of his ship, ordered the crew into the boats and they safely reached the shore. The Glasgow Salvage Association were called in to help refloat the vessel and for the next three days preparations went well and the weather remained calm and foggy.

However on Christmas Day the fog cleared, the wind got up and soon the wreck was being pounded by a southerly winter gale which continued, unabated, until 3rd January. By this time the *Ensign* was well battered but surprisingly the hull was only penetrated at one place and her keel was still intact. The respite from the weather was short as the next day another gale blew up and the salvors recommended she be sold where she lay. The auction, at Crown Halls, Glasgow took place on 19th January when she was sold to the shipbreaking company of Ross and Marshall who eventually refloated and repaired her. She sailed on for many years under the new name *Leelite*.

ESSEX

206nt. Wooden brigantine.
Built by Vaughan, Newport, Nova Scotia.
Launched 1866.

Dimensions 110.0' x 27.0' x 12.6'

The *Essex* stranded opposite Kildonan coastguard station around 10:30pm on 21st January, 1903. She had left Portrush in ballast the previous day bound for Maryport, but had been caught in a storm in the North Channel and was forced to run for shelter in Lamlash Bay. Unfortunately, in the darkness and the heavy snow showers, her master, Mr Skillen, did not see Pladda Lighthouse nor the land ahead before his vessel stranded on the reefs off Kildonan.

The Coastguards immediately attempted to rescue the six men aboard with rocket apparatus. However, the equipment broke down as the first man was on his way to the shore. Fortunately he was eventually rescued, but none of the others could be brought ashore in this manner. Telegrams were immediately dispatched to Campbeltown and, at 6:10am, the lifeboat *James Stevens II* sailed out of Campbeltown Loch into the full force of the storm.

The *James Stevens* arrived off Kildonan at 9am and her crew watched as wave after wave swept over the *Essex* and her crew who had by now climbed into the rigging. The lifeboat manoeuvred near to the *Essex* which provided a certain amount of shelter from the confused seas. The crew eventually boarded the lifeboat and were later landed at Lamlash.

The *James Stevens* and her crew of fifteen left Lamlash around midday but, due to the direction of the wind, found that they had to row from Pladda to Campbeltown. The *James Stevens* arrived home after 11:30pm having been at sea for seventeen and a half hours in extreme weather conditions. It is interesting to note that the seven members of the shore party who helped launch the lifeboat each received six shillings while each member of the crew, for all their efforts, recieved only fifteen shillings. The *Essex* eventually broke up and became a total wreck.

GLENANN

140nt. Iron steamship.
Built by McIlwaine Lewis & Co, Belfast.
Launched March 1884.
(ex THEME ex CULTRA ex VOLTANTE ex THEME)

Dimensions 159.2' x 23.0' x 11.3'

The *Glenann* was owned by the Antrim Ore Company. On Thursday 21st January, 1932 she was on a voyage from Belfast to Glasgow to pick up a cargo, when she ran aground in thick fog near Kilmory on the south coast of Arran.

The Campbeltown lifeboat was called out and quickly arrived on the scene but, as the weather was calm, the crew had been able to get ashore unaided. Initially, due to the calm seas, it was hoped that she could be quickly refloated as she was more or less undamaged, lying parallel to the shore.

SS ***Glenann***.

The Steel & Bennie tug *Strongbow* was sent for and arrived at the scene of the wreck around 11am. Unfortunately, by the time she reached Kilmory, the weather had deteriorated significantly with waves breaking over the *Glenann* filling her empty holds. The bad weather continued for the next few days and by 23rd January it was obvious that she would become a total wreck.

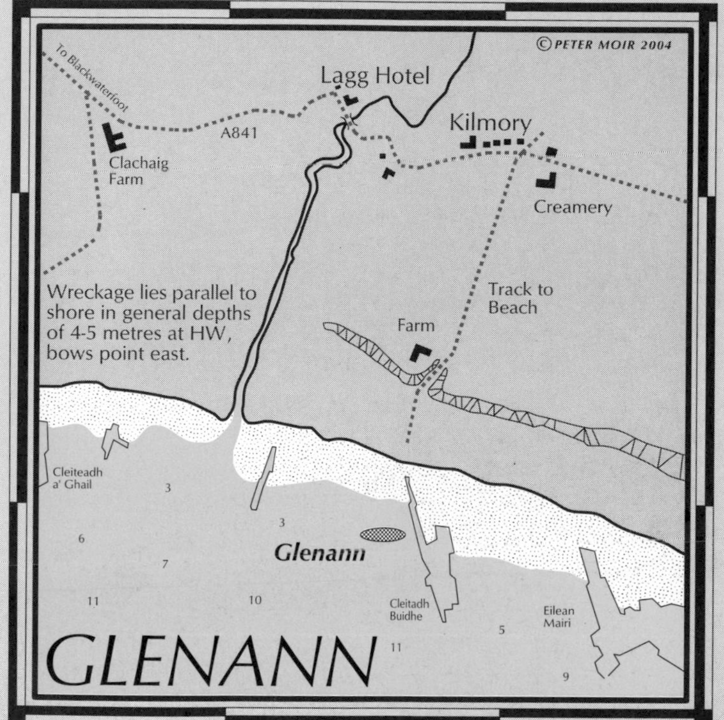

The wreck of the *Glenann* lies in approximate position 55°26.100'N, 005°13.800'W (GPS), off Torrylin beach. She can be dived from the shore which is reached by a track down the west side of Kilmory cemetery. She has been extensively salvaged over the years, although items such as her rudder, propeller and shaft, main frames and plates from her hull still litter the seabed in 4 metres of water. Part of the wreck may still show at low water.

GLORIANA

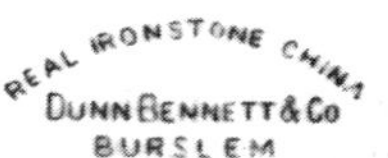

7nt. Wooden paddle tug.
Launched 1862.

Dimensions 80.0' x 16.2'

The *Gloriana* was owned by the Bowling and Greenock Towing Company. On 20th November, 1882 she ran aground on Kildonan Rock. She sustained considerable damage to her bow beneath the water line and, although a tug was dispatched from Brodick with pumps, she quickly filled with water and became a total wreck. Her crew landed safely near Kildonan Castle.

HAMILTON

68nt. Steel steamship.
Built by Scott & Son, Bowling.
Launched 1905.

Dimensions 97.5' x 20.1' x 8.2'

Four lives were lost when the small coaster *Hamilton* foundered off Pladda on 16th February 1940, fortunately a fifth member of the crew survived.

Owned by the Shira Steam Shipping Company of Glasgow, the *Hamilton* had left Ayr overnight on the 16th, bound for Campbeltown with her regular cargo of coal. Later that night, fishing boats working off the east coast of Arran were alerted by distress flares and made for the spot. Unfortunately by the time they arrived on the scene the vessel had foundered although they managed to recover three bodies.

A heavy sea was running at the time, and the boats made for shelter in Lamlash where they were able to land the only survivor, Buchan McLean who was taken to the Arran War Memorial Hospital.

SS ***Hamilton***.

The authors believe that the wreck of the *Hamilton* is one of a number of wrecks which lie in deep water within 2 miles of Dippen Head, Arran. As to the cause of the wreck, we can only assume that the coaster foundered in the bad weather conditions.

JANET McNICOL

19.4nt Wooden smack.
Built by J & H Halliday, Rothesay.
Launched 1875.

Dimensions 42.5' x 14.8' x 6.4'

The *Janet McNicol* left Irvine harbour around 10:30am on 8th October, 1907 bound for Brodick with a cargo of bricks. Aboard were John McNicol, son of her owner, Alexander McNicol of Brodick, Neil Stewart, mate, and Alexander Russell, deckhand. As a result of deteriorating weather conditions during their passage across the Firth John McNicol decided to spend the night in the shelter of Lamlash Bay and anchored the smack off the north west side of Holy Isle shortly after 4pm.

Around 2:30am the following morning the Belfast steamer *Glentow* entered Lamlash Bay from the south and made for the north west shore of Holy Isle. As the *Glentow* entered the anchorage she struck the *Janet McNicol* on her port quarter, carrying away part of her stern. The *Janet McNicol* quickly filled with water and sank taking with her the three crew members.

At a subsequent enquiry, James Kissock, who had been in command of the *Glentow*, was found solely responsible for the loss of the *Janet McNicol* and her crew. He was severely censured as he held no master's certificate, and ordered to pay £10 towards the costs of the enquiry.

The remains of the *Janet McNicol* lie approximately 200 metres west of the small jetty on Holy Isle in position 55°31.850'N, 005°05.450'W . The remains consist of a pile of bricks and wooden debris, lying in 6 metres.

The ***Janet McNicol***.

KYLE SKYE

116nt. Steel steamship.
Built by Rennie, Ritchie & Newport, Glasgow.
Launched 1922.
(ex NANCY THOMAS)

Dimensions 130.3' x 22.6' x 9.8'

The *Kyle Skye* ran aground on Cleits Beach near Kilmory on Saturday 26th October, 1940 and later became a total wreck. She now lies in position 55°26.417'N, 005°15.600'W (GPS), approximately 100 metres from the shore.

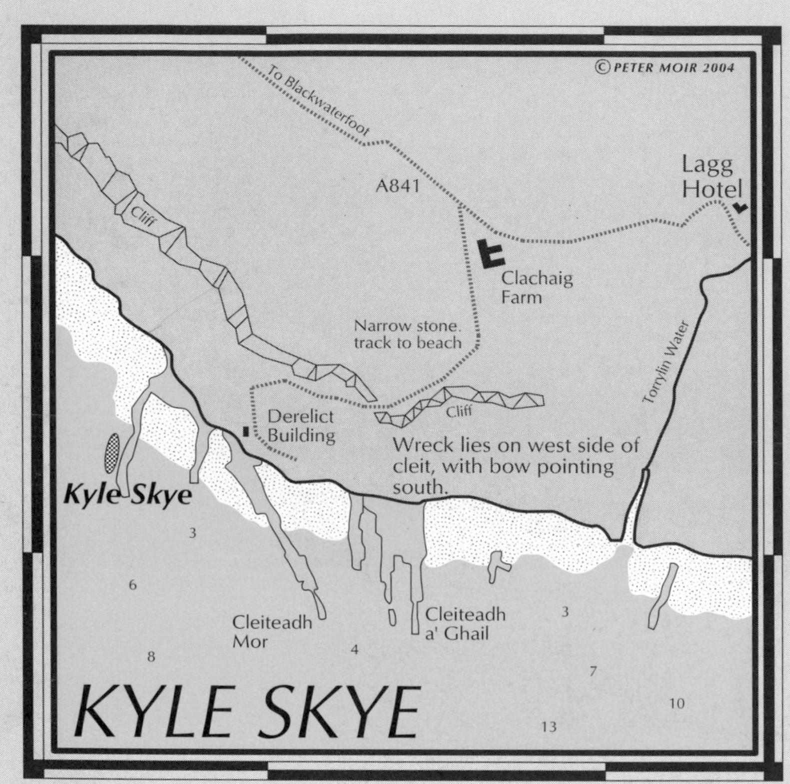

The *Kyle Skye* is well dispersed, with sections of the wreck on either side of the cleit (dyke). However the main part, the stern section, lies on the west side and appears to rest on its port side which is buried in the pebble and shingle seabed. Parts of the wreck occasionally show at very low spring tides.

Access to Cleits Beach is via a farm track half a mile west of Kilmory and is signposted on the main road between Kilmory and Blackwaterfoot.

SS ***Kyle Skye***.

OLIVA

335nt. Steel oil tanker.
Built by Swan Hunter &
Wigham Richardson Ltd, Newcastle.
Launched July 1916.

Dimensions 412.2' x 53.5' x 31.1'

The British oil tanker *Oliva*, bound for Ardrossan with a cargo of 5500 tons of benzine, went ashore near Bennan Head on Monday 17th September, 1928. As the *Oliva* scraped over the outlying reefs one of her tanks was pierced and she was soon engulfed by fumes from the escaping oil. The vessel was evacuated as quickly as possible with the aid of the Campbeltown lifeboat crew and breeches buoy. Members of her crew returned to extinguish all fires aboard to prevent further mishap from a possible explosion.

The Liverpool and Glasgow Salvage Association started work on 21st September, by which time ten of her eighteen tanks and pump room were badly holed. The damage could not be repaired from the outside and the nature of the cargo made it impossible for divers to safely work inside. In order to salve the *Oliva* 1200 gallons of benzine were jettisoned into the sea balancing her remaining cargo.The *Oliva* was finally refloated around 7am on 29th September and towed to Lamlash Bay where the remainder of her cargo was transferred to another vessel. She was later towed to Greenock for repair.

SS ***Oliva*** ashore near Bennan Head.

PRINCESS PATRICIA

275 nt. Steel steamship.
Built by Caledon S B & Eng Co Ltd, Dundee.
Launched 1903.

Dimensions 225.3' x 32.1' x 14.9'

SS *Princess Patricia*.

SS *Princess Patricia*.

The *Princess Patricia* was owned by M Langlands & Son of Glasgow. On 4th October, 1911 she ran aground near Dippen Head on the south east coast of Arran. Initially the incident, which was a fairly common occurrence on the Clyde, created little concern and plans were quickly made for refloating her. A tug from the Clyde Shipping Company soon arrived on the scene, closely followed by the Liverpool & Glasgow Salvage Association, who set about patching the hole in the vessel's hull below the water line and pumping her out.

However, as the days passed, concern increased as a number of unsuccessful attempts were made to pull her off until, on 27th October, as the weather deteriorated, salvage operations were suspended. The storms continued for over a week and when the salvage teams finally returned to the wreck they could see that their task was now hopeless. The *Princess Patricia* had been driven higher onto the rocks and had broken her back. She was abandoned as a total wreck and substantially salvaged for scrap over the subsequent months.

RAITH

23nt. Iron steamship.
Built 1856.

Dimensions 72.8′ x 15.2′ x 7.5′

The *Raith* was a small coastal steamer which was lost in the Kilbrannan Sound on 17th September, 1989. She had been recently purchased by a Belfast shipowner for £230, who had spent a further £500 overhauling the vessel.

The *Raith* left Glasgow for Belfast on 14th September but was beached at Lochranza on 15th to carry out an inspection and cleaning of her hull and rudder. Once complete she proceeded on her journey on 16th under the command of James McMaster with a crew of three.

The weather that night was very poor with strong winds and rain. All proceeded well and the *Raith* travelled south down the Sound until just after midnight when water was discovered in the engineroom. The donkey pump was immediately started but the level continued to rise until the master ordered the boiler fire to be extinguished. Captain McMaster remained aboard but ordered the remainder of the crew to abandon ship and standby in the ships boat where they remained for over an hour.

Unable to stem the flow, Captain McMaster reluctantly abandoned ship shortly before it foundered off the north west coast of Arran.

At a later Board of Trade inquiry both Captain McMaster and the mate alleged the engineer was drunk and unable to work the pumps. However the court found that the pair did not make enough effort to trace the leak and were both found at fault, with Captain McMaster being ordered to pay costs of £10. The *Raith* foundered in deep water and was never recovered, she was insured for £400.

The authors are of the view that the wreck located in position 55°43.804'N, 005°22.524'W is the *Raith*.

REDGAUNTLET

107 nt. Steel paddlesteamer.
Built by Barclay Curle & Co Ltd, Glasgow.
Launched 1895.

Dimensions 215.0' x 22.1' x 7.4'

The *Redgauntlet*, owned by the North British Railway Company ran ashore off the south west coast of Arran on Wednesday 16th August, 1899. She had been on a pleasure cruise round Arran and, as she turned east out of Kilbrannan Sound, she struck the Iron Rock Ledges at full speed.

The 290 passengers and crew managed to get safely ashore and later continued on their journey aboard the PS *Waverley* from Whiting Bay.

The *Redguantlet* remained on 'the Irons' for the next week while representatives of the Clyde Salvage Company inspected her hull. She was refloated on 25th August and taken to Glasgow for repair.

The ***Redgauntlet*** ashore.

SAINT DUNSTAN

3566nt Steel steamship.
Built by Northumberland SB Co, Newcastle.
Launched July 1919.

Dimensions 400.0' x 53.0' x 32.8'

The *Saint Dunstan* was originally ordered as part of the First World War standard ship programme, which was put in place in 1916 to keep pace with the heavy casualties from enemy action. Many of these vessels were built overseas in the United States, Canada and the Far East and as the programmes name suggests; standardisation of hull design, engines and specification was introduced. Her order name was *War Keep*, but on her completion in 1919 she was sold to the Saint Line of Liverpool as *Saint Dunstan*.

Details surrounding the loss of the *Saint Dunstan* are somewhat vague due to wartime restrictions. She was torpedoed off Northern Ireland on 25th August 1940 while on convoy from Glasgow to Baltimore in ballast, and unfortunately fourteen of her sixty-three crew were lost. The submarine assigned with her demise was the *U-57* that at the time, was under the command of the U-boat ace Erich Topp. The *Saint Dunstan* remained afloat and was taken in tow for the Clyde the following day, but later sank on the 27th August, approximately 4.75 miles north east of Pladda.

The wreck of the *Saint Dunstan* lies on a muddy seabed in position 55°27.249'N, 004°58.717'W. Survey details from the Hydrographic Department of the Royal Navy record that the wreck lies in general seabed depths of 82 metres with a least depth over the wreck of 67 metres, the wreck is oriented 030/210 degrees. The *Saint Dunstan* is a sizable wreck and would make a challenging dive to those suitable trained and equiped.

SAXON I

85gt. Iron steamship.
Built by J & J Hay, Kirkintilloch.
Launched October 1894.

Dimensions 65.8' x 18.0' x 8.4'

The *Saxon* was a typical Clyde puffer which was owned and operated by her builders for the first 6 years of her life. In 1901, she was chartered to Murison and Campbell of Montrose, who eventually purchased her the following year.

In June 1906, while inbound to the Forth with a cargo of grain and fish, she ran aground on the north end of the Isle of May and became a constructive total loss. The wreck was bought by the Hay brothers later that year and towed back to Kirkintilloch where she was repaired and returned to the coasting trade until 1912 when her fate was finally sealed.

Inward bound to the Clyde, the *Saxon* was lost in collision with the Norwegian steamship *Waterloo* around 6am on Thursday 24th October, 1912. The collision took place approximately 4 miles south west of Pladda in calm conditions and good visibility. Unfortunately two of her crew were below at the time and went down with the *Saxon*, Two further crew managed to jump overboard and were picked up by the *Waterloo*, they were later landed at Ardrossan and the *Waterloo* proceeded on her voyage to St Petersburg.

The wreck of the *Saxon* lies in position 55°20.199'N, 005°20.699'W (GPS) in general seabed depths of 49 metres although there is a scour on both sides of the wreck of around 1 metre deep. The wreck has sunk far into the soft mud seabed and rises no more than a metre above seabed level, the hull is oriented generally north/south. Tidal streams are strong enough to make this a slack water dive, this will also aid laying a shot into an extremely small target. Ironically one of her sisterships, the *Briton I*, lies less than 4 miles to the west in position 55°18.765'N, 005°27.786'W (GPS). Details of the *Briton I* can be found in ***Argyll Shipwrecks***.

HMS SEALION

960dt. Steel submarine.
Built by Cammel Laird & Co Ltd, Birkenhead.
Launched March 1934.

Dimensions 208.7' x 24.0' x 10.5'

The *Sealion* was an 'S' Class Royal Navy submarine. She carried one three inch gun and had a main armament of six torpedo tubes. On 3rd March, 1945 after a short but successful career, she was sunk as an Asdic target two and a half miles south west of Pladda in a general depth of 62 metres.

The wreck lies in position 55°23.389'N, 005°08.288'W (GPS) and rises 7.8 metres from the seabed. She lies approximately 140/320 degrees.

HMS ***Sealion***.

STRATHDEE

169nt. Iron steamship.
Built by Dobson & Charles,Grangemouth.

Dimensions 141.2' x 21.7' x 11.2'

The *Strathdee*, owned by Messrs J & J Hay of Glasgow, was lost in collision with the Allen Line Steamship *Buenos Ayrean* on Tuesday 20th February, 1883.

The small coaster, en route to Dublin with a cargo of coal, sank two minutes after the collision approximately two miles east of Holy Isle. The *Buenos Ayrean* circled the area for over an hour but could only find one survivor from the crew of thirteen which had been aboard the *Strathdee*.

STRATHGARRY

136gt. Iron steamship.
Built by William Hamilton & Co, Port Glasgow.
Launched 1880.
(ex PEARL)

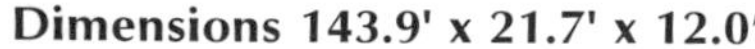
Dimensions 143.9' x 21.7' x 12.0'

The *Strathgarry* was owned by J Manson & Son, Glasgow. On Monday 20th March, 1893 she was inward bound to Glasgow when she encountered thick fog off the south coast of Arran and later ran aground on Torrylin Beach.

The crew took to the lifeboats and landed safely. Despite subsequent attempts to refloat her by the Glasgow and Greenock Shipping Company tug *Admiral*, she became a total wreck. The SS *Marlborough* of London also stranded on the same beach, on the same day, but she was successfully pulled off by the *Admiral* and continued her voyage to Glasgow.

SS ***Tuscan***.

TUSCAN

195gt. Steel motor vessel.
Built by Peter MacGregor, Kirkintilloch.
Launched 1935

Dimensions 65.6′ x 18.4′ x 8.7′

The Clyde puffer *Tuscan* foundered one mile north east of Brodick Pier on Tuesday 6th June, 1955 after being swamped by heavy seas. The crew of three managed to escape in a small dinghy and although it capsized, they were eventually rescued by the British Railway's steamer *Kildonan*, which had been alongside Brodick Pier.

The *Tuscan*, owned by Hay & Company of Troon, had been carrying 90 tons of coal to Brodick as emergency supplies because of a rail strike.

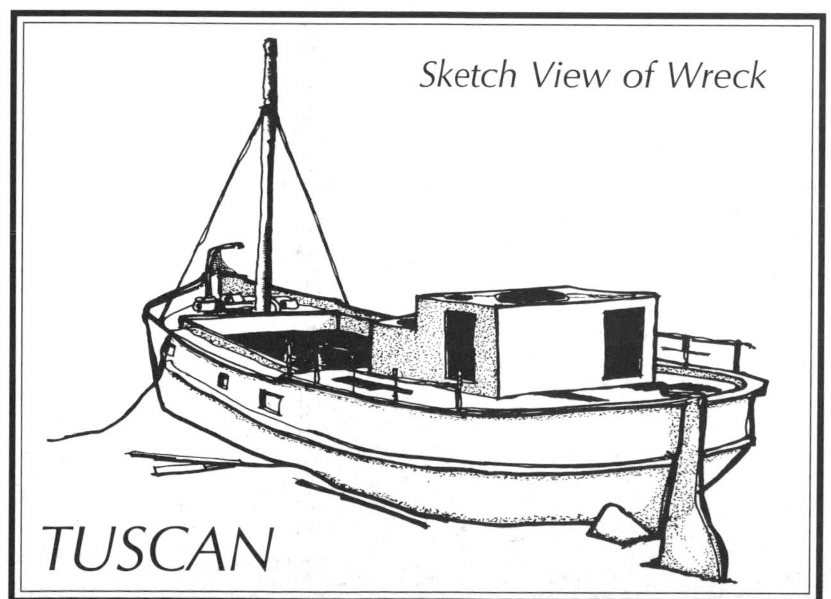

The *Tuscan* lies in position 55°35.116'N, 005°06.783'W (GPS), with general seabed depths around the wreck of 42 metres. She is completely intact, sitting upright on a flat seabed and her raised rear deckhouse is another two or three metres shallower. The bow faces south east. Visibility in the area is generally 5-10 metres. The wreck lies close to the route of the Ardrossan to Brodick ferry so good boat cover is essential. The wreck is owned by a syndicate of four divers, one of whom is resident on the island.

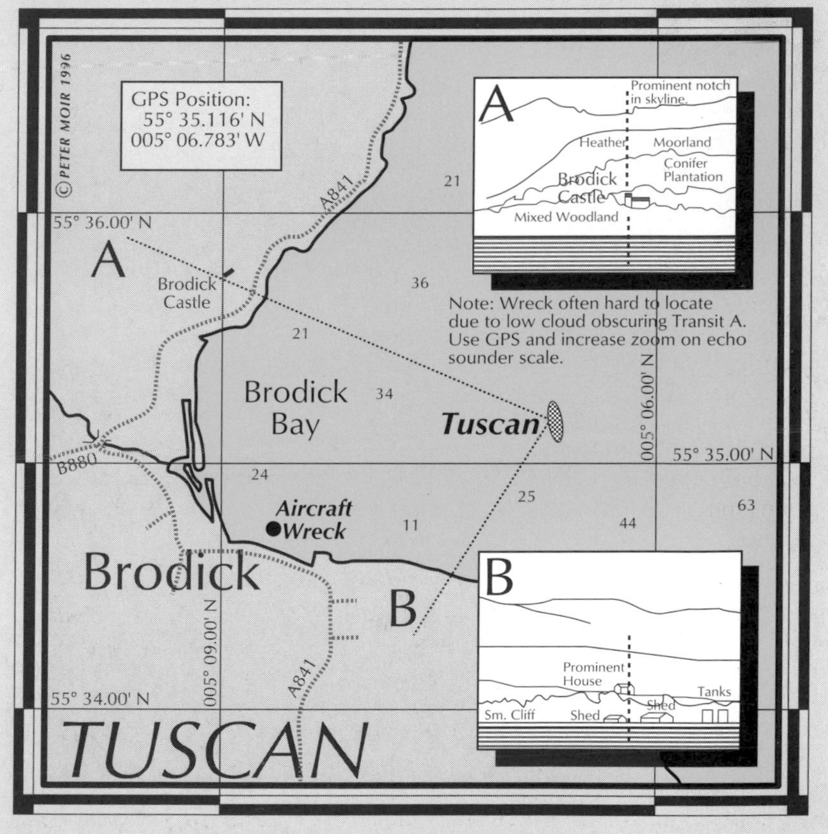

ARRAN

Listed below are a selection of 65 smaller vessels wrecked within this area. This list is included as a basis for further research. Names suffixed by (S) denote extensive salvage work or total removal subsequent to date of loss.

NAME	BUILT	TONNAGE	HULL	TYPE	LOST	CAUSE	LOCATION
Acorn	1857	50nt	W	Sk	03.02.1889	S	Kingscross Point
Annie	1867	153nt	W	Bn	06.12.1877	S	Drumadoon Point
Aura	1865	191nt	W	Bn	29.12.1877	S	S end of Holy Isle
Baltic	1856	93nt	W	Bn	22.02.1876	S	Near Lamlash Bay
Bonawe	1903	223gt	S	SS	08.06.1917	C	Off Corrie
Branch	1858	120nt	W	Sr	25.01.1878	S	Largybeg Point
Brothers	1859	55nt	W	Sr	26.02.1882	S	Pladda
Carnsew	1836	61nt	W	Sr	17.10.1879	F	Off Whiting Bay
Castle Green	1848	47nt	W	Sr	01.09.1888	C	Off Pladda
Dart	1848	26nt	W	Sk	13.03.1879	F	Whiting Bay
Diamond	1816	78bn	W	Bgn	17.01.1845	S	Kildonan
Diana	1862	132nt	W	Bn	13.02.1894	S	Holy Isle
Dundrum	1847	39nt	W	Sl	11.12.1883	S	Holy Isle
Dunvegan(S)		632nt	I	SS	04.12.1936	S	Holy Isle
Eliza	1800	307bn	W	Bk	13.02.1852	F	Off Pladda
Elizabeth McClure	1848	58nt	W	Sr	13.10.1891	S	Hamilton Rock
Elizabeth Wilson	1860	44nt	W	Sr	16.11.1888	S	Holy Isle
Ellen Ann	1822	68nt	W	Sr	11.05.1883	S	Near Dippen Head
Emily	1848	97nt	W	Bn	27.01.1884	S	Holy Isle
Enigma	1845	74bn	W	Sr	17.04.1877	S	East side Holy Isle
Fairy	1850	93nt	W	Sr	21.10.1857	C	Off Dippen Head
Falco	1859	433nt	W	Bk	07.12.1887	S	Kildonan
Fay	1874	34nt	I	SS	27.09.1875	F	Off Pladda
Friends	1855	49gt	W	Sk	06.12.1874	F	3m NE of Pladda
Furness Maid	1863	42nt	W	Sr	07.05.1891	C	2m E of Brodick
Gleaner	1841	62nt	W	Sr	30.11.1890	F	Catacol Bay
Glenlivet	1871	75nt	I	SS	07.05.1891	S	Bennan Head
Harriet Julia	1855	138nt	W	Bn	13.10.1891	S	Clauchlands Point
Henry Holland	1835	161bn	W	Bg	15.03.1853	S	Corrygills

NAME	BUILT	TONNAGE	HULL	TYPE	LOST	CAUSE	LOCATION
Hercules	1878	26nt	I	SS	30.09.1904	S	Whiting Bay
Huntress(S)		132bn	W	Bgn	08.10.1870	S	Lamlash
J M Stevens	1871	142nt	W	Sr	06.03.1884	C	Off Pladda
Janet Kelso	1840	19nt	W	Sk	20.11.1849	S	Off Kildonan
Jeannie Blair		53nt	W	Sr	23.09.1879	S	Pladda
Jules et Celine		53nt	W	Sl	23.10.1879	F	Off Pladda
Kestrel	1841	184nt	W	Bg	04.01.1886	S	Kingscross Point
Lady Mary	1833	76nt	W	Bn	15.12.1880	S	Kingscross Point
Laurel	1827	271bn	W	S	04.02.1851	C	Off Lamlash
Lucy		192nt	W	Bn	01.10.1891	S	Kingscross Point
Maid of Orleans	1855	4nt	W	P.Tug	13.02.1885	F	4m E of Brodick
Margaret McColl	1862	64nt	W	Sr	25.02.1876	S	Bennan Head
Margaret Wemyss	1866	24gt	W	Sk	17.04.1893	S	Brodick Bay
Mary	1817	230bn	W	Bgn	03.11.1821	C/S	Corrygills
Mary Abigail		77nt	W	Bn	01.08.1876	S	Holy Isle
Mary Rowlands	1858	99nt	W	Sr	04.08.1904	C	Off Pladda
Mona		8nt	W	Syt	23.01.1885	S	N end of Whiting Bay
Nancy	1838	65nt	W	Bn	02.10.1885	S	Imachar Point
Neptune	1892	38nt	I	SS	01.11.1897	S	Pladda
Ottawa	1866	137nt	W	Bn	23.01.1884	S	Holy Isle
Pallas	1786	158bn	W	Bgn	00.08.1787	S	Holy Isle
Pearl	1855	44nt	W	Sk	29.09.1863	S	Dougarie
Petrel	1842	70nt	W	Sr	31.10.1884	S	Whiting Bay
Pleiades	1863	90nt	W	Bn	22.12.1894	S	Holy Isle
Prindsesse Lovise	1869	430nt	W	Bg	22.02.1894	C	Off Brodick
Provider		23nt	W	MFV	17.10.1932	S	Brodick Bay
Risk	1848	208nt	W	Bg	03.02.1884	S	Holy Isle
Roscote	1865	587nt	I	Bk	01.01.1885	S	Torrylin
St Barachan(S)			I	SS	12.03.1923	S	Iron Rock Ledges
Sanspareil	1857	132nt	W	Sr	13.10.1891	C	Lamlash Bay
Sprite	1855	121nt	W	Bn	11.02.1880	S	Holy Isle
Success	1871	40gt	W	Sl	25.09.1891	S	Holy Isle
Syren	1857	111nt	W	Bgn	20.12.1876	S	Lamlash
Topaze	1862	49nt	W	Sr	26.02.1902	S	Near Corrie
Waverley(S)	1883	220gt	I	SS	11.12.1883	S	Imachur Point
William	1839	109nt	W	Sr	10.12.1868	S	Near Pladda

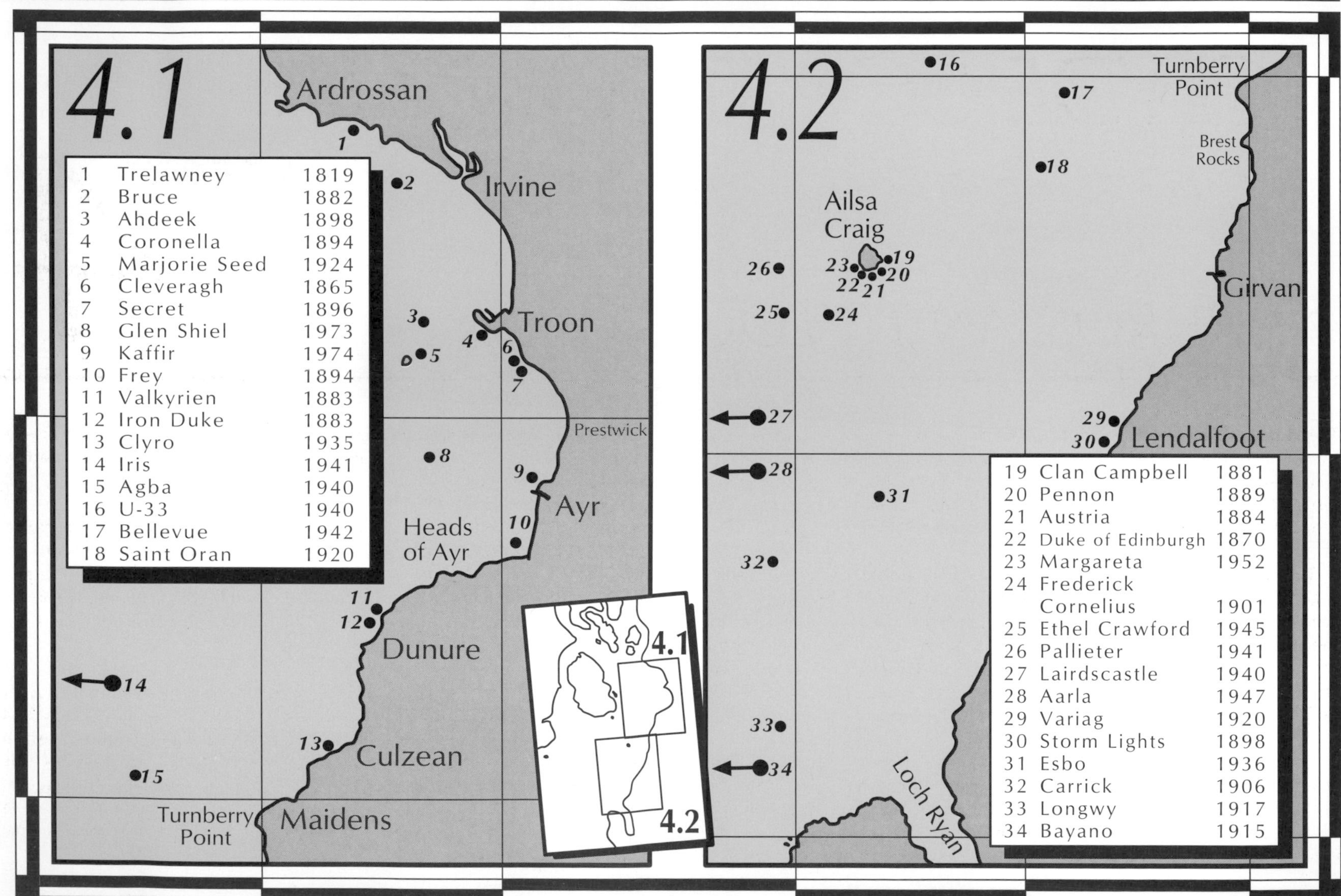
4.1
Ardrossan
Irvine
Troon
Prestwick
Ayr
Heads of Ayr
Dunure
Culzean
Maidens
Turnberry Point
1 Trelawney 1819
2 Bruce 1882
3 Ahdeek 1898
4 Coronella 1894
5 Marjorie Seed 1924
6 Cleveragh 1865
7 Secret 1896
8 Glen Shiel 1973
9 Kaffir 1974
10 Frey 1894
11 Valkyrien 1883
12 Iron Duke 1883
13 Clyro 1935
14 Iris 1941
15 Agba 1940
16 U-33 1940
17 Bellevue 1942
18 Saint Oran 1920
4.2
Turnberry Point
Brest Rocks
Ailsa Craig
Girvan
Lendalfoot
Loch Ryan
19 Clan Campbell 1881
20 Pennon 1889
21 Austria 1884
22 Duke of Edinburgh 1870
23 Margareta 1952
24 Frederick Cornelius 1901
25 Ethel Crawford 1945
26 Pallieter 1941
27 Lairdscastle 1940
28 Aarla 1947
29 Variag 1920
30 Storm Lights 1898
31 Esbo 1936
32 Carrick 1906
33 Longwy 1917
34 Bayano 1915

CLYDE COAST SOUTH

Chapter 4

ARDROSSAN TO LOCH RYAN

The southern reaches of the Firth of Clyde, now over twenty miles wide, extend from Ardrossan to beyond the granite mound of Ailsa Craig. The wrecks here can basically be divided into two categories. Firstly, strandings ashore as a result of storms and poor visibility, and secondly, losses in deep water as a result of war action, collision or foundering in adverse weather.

The mainland coast, south from Ardrossan to Finnarts Point in Wigtownshire, is generally shallow with sandy bays and rocky headlands. This coastline has seen many strandings as vessels were driven ashore only a few miles from the shelter and safety of the Upper Firth. Indeed, many of the wrecks included in this chapter happened in sight of their destinations or ports of departure at Ardrossan, Troon, Irvine and Ayr. Many of these ships were refloated, removed or heavily salvaged and, where wreckage remains, are well broken and difficult to identify.

Offshore the towering, granite cliffs of Ailsa Craig provide home for huge colonies of seabirds. They have seen the tragic end of many vessels over the years. This small island rises from the sea in the middle of the Firth and did not have a lighthouse until 1886. Its position in the middle of the approaches to the Clyde and the lack of a warning light resulted in a sizeable number of ships, both sail and steam powered, running aground on its rocky shores with the loss of many lives. Even after the construction of the lighthouse, ships continued to meet with disaster on and around 'The Craig'.

Many of the wrecks that lie offshore in deep water, between Turnberry, Pladda and west to the North Channel have to a greater degree remained undived. However, over the last 4-5 years divers have turned their attentions to this area and a number have been located and dived for the first time. The list of un-located or unknown wrecks is fast reducing, and this is reflected in the number of new wrecks included in this chapter.

Many are yet to be discovered and could provide very interesting diving for the patient diver willing to apply the necessary time to discovering their exact whereabouts. Recent developments in electronic navigation and location equipment, including Global Positioning System (GPS), are making this exploration more worthwhile and increasing the chances of success. The wrecks, many in the 40 to 60 metres depth range, are pushing or are beyond the limits of safety for sports diving on compressed air and therefore only for the very experienced diver.

The ***Aarla*** laid up at Bowling.

The ***Aarla*** as ***Hecate***.

AARLA

265 nt. Steel motor yacht.
Built by D & W Henderson & Co Ltd, Glasgow.
Launched 1903. (ex HECATE ex AAR)

Dimensions 161.3' x 25.6' x 12.6'

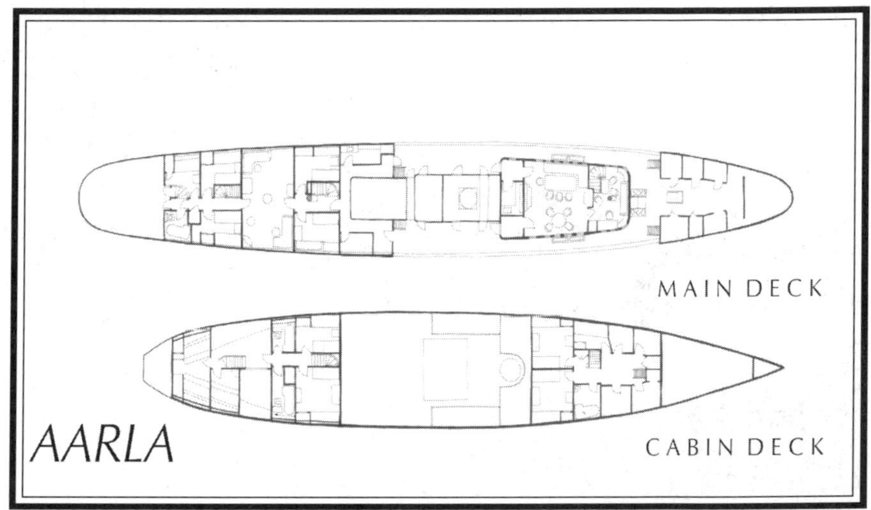

The *Aarla* was designed and built as a private steam yacht in Glasgow in 1903. She passed into German ownership in 1931 and was fitted with twin six cylinder diesel engines by Blohm & Voss of Hamburg before returning to British ownership to continue her career as a pleasure yacht until the outbreak of the Second World War in 1939.

In October 1939 she was purchased by the Admiralty for war service as an anti-submarine patrol vessel. After successful duty in British waters she was transferred to perform the same task based in Freetown and Dakar in West Africa in 1942. By late 1944 the *Aarla* was beginning to show signs of her continual service and she was dry docked in Dakar during December 1944 and January 1945 for extensive repairs to her hull. As the war in Africa was now concluded, on completion of these repairs, the *Aarla* set sail for Britain, leaving Dakar in July 1945. On her voyage to Falmouth she encountered some very heavy weather and had to put into Leixos for temporary repairs to a fractured soil pipe below the water line and to the starboard main engine which had seized.

Despite these difficulties, she eventually reached her final destination on the Clyde on the 17th September, 1945. She had been visually inspected by Lloyds at Falmouth en route and again, by the Sea Transport Inspecting Officer at Greenock, at anchor at Tighnabruaich. These visual surveys, which were the only surveys carried out on the *Aarla* since her last full inspection in 1933, indicated that the owner would need to spend at least £16,000 to return her to pre-war condition.

The *Aarla* lay at her moorings, off Tighnabruaich, under the care and maintenance of Messrs Smith Brothers until June 1947, when she was purchased by the Park Lane Shipping Company of London for £6,000, intended for service as a pleasure cruise ship on the east coast of England. The purchasers apparently took no professional advice on the condition of the *Aarla*, relying on an old picture in Lloyds and an inspection by Captain R D Young, who had been engaged to sail her to the south of England, to decide on the condition of the vessel.

Captain Young declared the *Aarla* fit to sail to the south coast, where she was to undergo an major refit before entering commercial service. On the morning of 26th June, 1947 Captain Young, with eight crew, raised anchor at Tighnabruaich and set sail for Lowestoft, via Ardrossan for fuel, and Torquay. What happened on the voyage has never been established as there were no survivors from the sinking of the *Aarla*, south of Ailsa Craig, in the early hours of the following morning.

Fragments of the story of the disaster can be pieced together from the testimony of the crew of the SS *Lairdsdale* who were en route from Ardrossan to Belfast that same night. At just after 2:30am the *Lairdsdale* was three and a half miles west of Ailsa Craig, steaming into a rough sea whipped up by a force seven south westerly gale. The helmsman reported a flash of light off their starboard bow followed by the flicker of a ship's lights some five miles distant. The captain of the *Lairdsdale* ordered a change of course to head for the other ship to offer assistance, if required. When they were about two miles from the unknown vessel, the lights disappeared. They continued their course and soon began to see signs of wreckage around the area where the ship's lights had been. It was obvious that the ship had sunk. They could hear shouts from the water through the darkness but, despite a desperate search, the shouts stopped before anyone could be rescued. They continued to search but found only more wreckage and one body. The next day the Royal Navy, Royal Air Force and the lifeboat joined the search but, again, no trace of the crew or any indication of the name of the vessel could be found. Over the next few days, bodies from the wreck were washed ashore on Kintyre and Arran and finally the six foot nameplate of the *Aarla* was also discovered on Kintyre, at last revealing the name of the sunken vessel.

The subsequent inquiry into the sinking could not definitively conclude on the cause of the incident. Many believed that the flash of light seen by the crew of the *Lairdsdale* could have been an explosion caused by the *Aarla* colliding with some floating debris from a deep sea dump of war munitions south of Ailsa Craig. This theory is supported by many discoveries of such munitions on the shores of the mainland coast, Kintyre and Arran, over the years. It is further supported by the unexplained loss of another vessel in the same area only a month earlier for apparently the same reason. It is however also certain that the *Aarla* was not in a totally seaworthy condition when she left Tighnabruaich with temporary repairs made on the homeward journey from Africa two years earlier still in place. It is also certain that some, if not all, of the lifesaving equipment on board was not in working order. One lifeboat was known to be unserviceable, while the lifejackets worn by the drowned crewmen should have shown lights when they took to the water. No such lights were seen by the crew of the *Lairdsdale* despite the fact that they reported hearing shouts when they reached the vicinity of the sinking.

The wreck of the *Aarla* lies in deep water somewhere south west of Ailsa Craig and to date has eluded attempts to locate her.

AGBA

193nt. Steel steamship.
Built by Dublin Shipbuilders Ltd., Dublin.
Launched October 1921.
(ex MOYGANNON)

Dimensions 164.9'X 25.7' x 9.5'

The *Agba* was launched in 1921 as the *Moygannon* for the Clanrye Steamship Company to replace their collier the *Retriever* which had been lost during WWI. The *Moygannon* remained in this ownership until 1938 when she was taken over by Fisher's of Newry, renamed Agba, and became part of the Newry and Kilkeel Steamship Company. The *Agba* was built as a general cargo vessel and worked most of her life on the UK coastal trade with occassional trips to European ports.

It was on such a voyage, on Saturday 12th March, 1940 that the *Agba* was lost in collision with a Dutch vessel, the *Mano,* off the Ayrshire coast, fortunately with no loss of live. At the time of the collision the *Agba* was inward bound to Ayr from Newry in ballast and accidentally strayed across the path of an out going convoy.

The wreck of the *Agba* lies approximately 5.5 miles WNW of Turnberry Point in position 55°21.167'N, 004°57.767'W (GPS). The wreck is substantially intact, lying over on its starboard side and is oriented approximately 100/280 degrees with bows pointing towards the Ayrshire coast. Seabed depths around the wreck are generally 54–55 metres with a least depth over the bridge section of 48 metres. There appears to be little or no tide on the wreck even on spring tides, visibility is generally 4-5 metres.

The wreck appears to have fallen away towards the stern, parts maybe below seabed level, this may also suggest where the collision occurred. Nets are also draped across the wreck around midships, this coupled with the depth make the *Agba*, like many wrecks in this part of the Clyde only for those suitably trained and equipped for deep diving.

SS *Agba* as ***Moygannon.***

AHDEEK

998nt. Iron steamship.
Built by Short Bros, Sunderland.
Launched 1881.

Dimensions 245.6' x 34.5' x 18.5'

The cargo steamer *Ahdeek*, owned by Messrs Donald & Taylor of Glasgow, arrived in Ayr Bay around 5pm on Sunday 11th December, 1898. A strong south westerly gale was blowing at the time which prevented her from entering the harbour to discharge her cargo of iron ore. The master of the *Ahdeek*, Captain Moore, decided to ride out the gale in Ayr Bay and anchored his vessel off the Saltpan Patches. However, it was not long before a signal was received from the Harbour Master at Ayr ordering the *Ahdeek* to proceed to Troon and discharge her cargo there.

Shortly after weighing anchor the *Ahdeek* bottomed heavily on outlying reefs puncturing her ballast tanks and damaging her propeller and rudder. She managed to clear the reefs and her distress signals were soon answered by tugs from Ayr and Troon. The Troon tug successfully took her in tow, while the Ayr tug stood by to assist with steering.

As the vessels headed northwards into Prestwick Bay, Captain Moore went below to survey the damage. On his return to the bridge, he gave the order to abandon ship as the *Ahdeek* was taking water in very quickly. The crew left in the ship's lifeboat and were soon picked up by the Ayr tug which returned to her home port.

The Troon tug continued towing the now deserted steamer towards Troon. However, around 10:30pm, the *Ahdeek* suddenly foundered about one mile west of Troon Harbour. The tug's crew, unaware that the *Ahdeek's* crew had safely left their ship and been picked up, circled the area for over an hour searching for survivors. It was not until they returned to Troon that they discovered that the crew were safe.

As dawn broke the next day the only parts of the wreck that were visible were the tops of her masts. She had sunk in ten fathoms of water and at half tide her decks were only seven fathoms below the surface. After inspection by Captain Burns of the Glasgow Salvage Association the *Ahdeek* was written off as a total loss. Due to her position, lying in the main fairway to Troon Harbour, she presented a serious hazard to navigation and as such, later that month, her masts, funnel, and deck structures were removed with explosives.

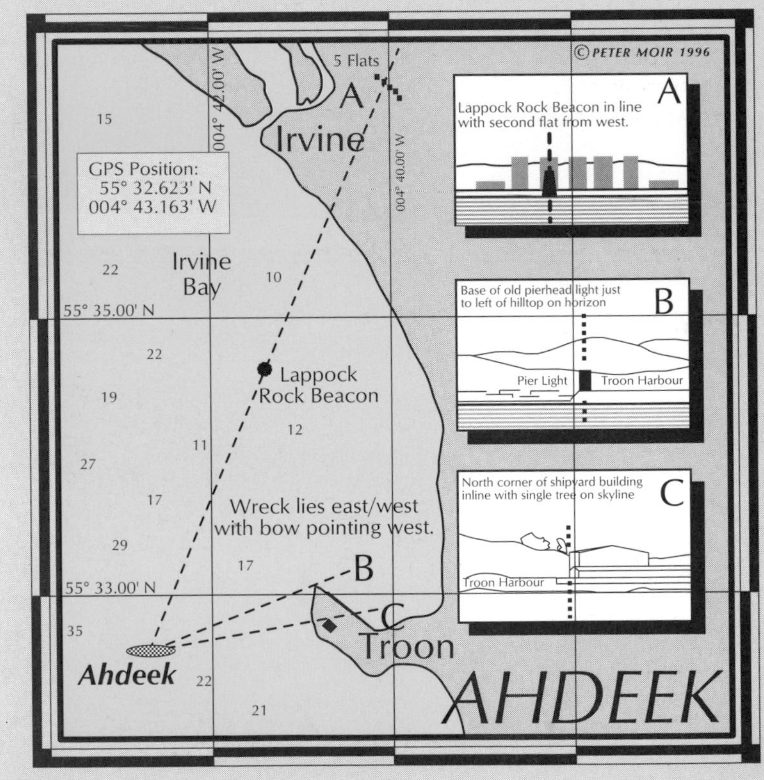

The Wreck Today

The wreck, which lies approximately 1.25 miles west of Troon in position 55°32.623'N, 004°43.163'W (GPS), was, for many years, thought to be the wreck of the *Marjorie Seed*. However in June 1987 a builders plate was found on the wreck which confirmed her builders as Short Brothers of Sunderland and her yard number as 122. After investigation the wreck was finally correctly identified as the *Ahdeek*.

The remains of the *Ahdeek* lie on a flat, sand seabed in 22 metres, oriented approximately 110/290, with her bow pointing in a westerly direction. The hull is slowly collapsing onto the seabed and many parts of the wreckage have already disappeared beneath the sand. The midships section, aft to the stern is the most interesting part of the wreck, and includes engine and boiler rooms and stern accommodation.

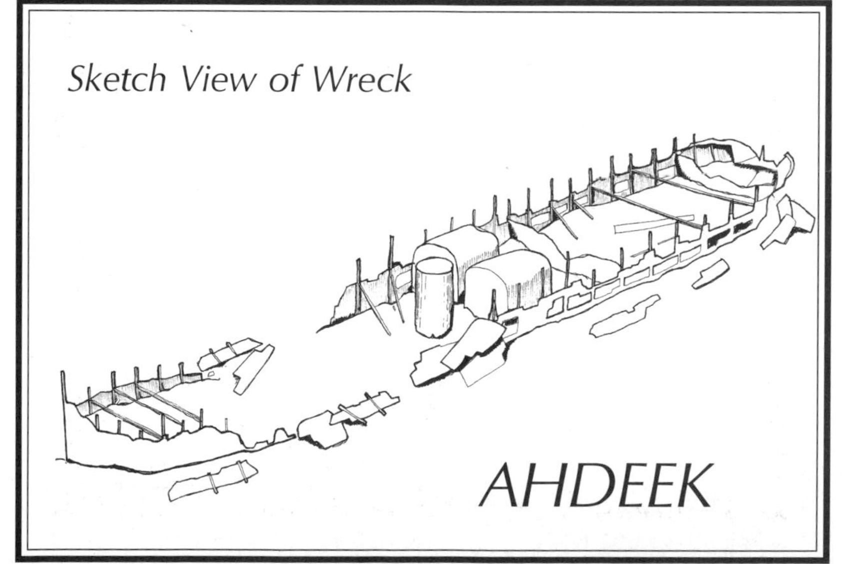

AUSTRIA

1083nt. Iron steamship.
Built in Newcastle.
Launched 1884.

Dimensions 257' x 34' x 18'

Ailsa Craig, like many small islands lying within major shipping fairways, has claimed its fair share of shipwrecks over the centuries. Most of these casualties have been the direct result of poor visibility, a situation which was partially alleviated by the completion of the lighthouse and foghorn in 1886. The need for the lighthouse on the island was highlighted barely two years prior to its completion when the cargo steamer *Austria* ran ashore there on Wednesday 15th October, 1884 and later became a total loss.

The *Austria* had left Fuime in the Adriatic on 28th September with a crew of twenty one, a stowaway and about 1800 tons of general cargo. Just after midnight on 15th October she was abeam of Corsewall Lighthouse, heading north for Glasgow. Her master, Captain Helig, who was in charge of the watch, set a course north east true and retired below, leaving the deck in the charge of the second mate, James Morris. The *Austria* continued on this course for the next two hours when, suddenly, the bow lookout reported land dead ahead. The helm was put "hard-a-starboard" and the engine room telegraphed to reverse full speed but, before either could take effect, she ran aground, seriously damaging her hull plating and holing her bow ballast tanks.

Captain Helig appeared on deck in an extremely disturbed state and gave orders for the lifeboats to be launched. However, the crew remained aboard as the sea was relatively calm and they were in no immediate danger. Around 7pm, the tide having risen, Captain Helig decided to try and back his vessel off the island but the chief engineer refused to obey his order, stating that the vessel would probably founder if she was moved from her present position. After a violent argument between the senior officers and a consultation with the rest of the crew the first officer, Mr Henry, took command of the *Austria* as Captain Helig was thought to be drunk and incapable of performing his duty.

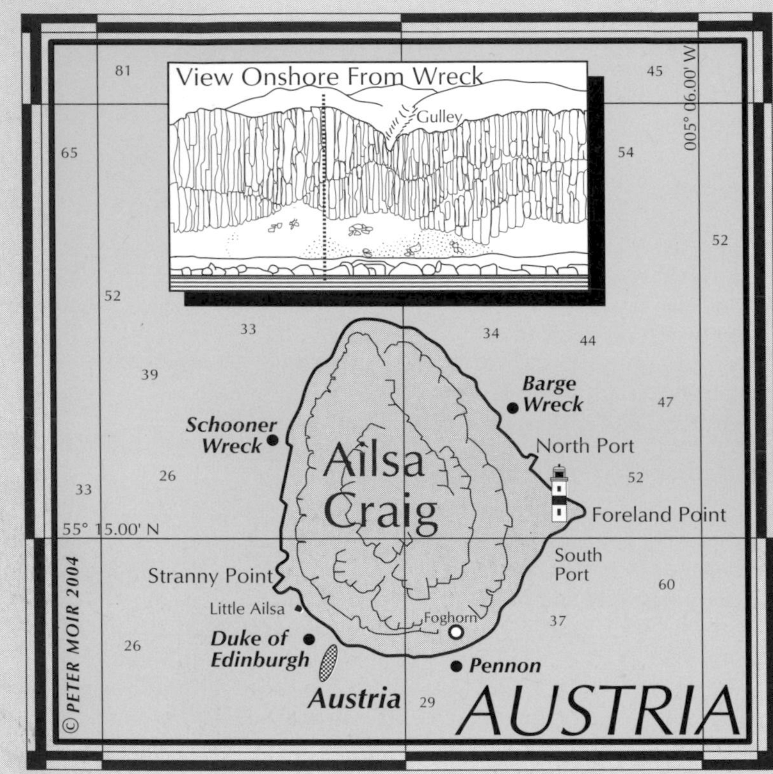

Shortly after daybreak a tug arrived on the scene which took Mr Henry to Ardrossan where he made arrangements for salvage. Two tugs with lighters were dispatched to "the Craig" the following day and succeeded in salvaging a portion of her cargo of flour and rape seed which was sold for £863. Salvage of her cargo and fittings by the Glasgow Salvage Association continued over the next few weeks and realised another £1,491. The wreck itself was eventually sold at auction in Girvan on 4th December for £191, a sad end to a vessel that had only been launched earlier that same year at a cost of £35,000.

At a subsequent enquiry, Captain Helig and second officer James Morris were jointly found responsible for the loss of the *Austria*. Captain Helig was severely censured for having laid a course from Corsewall Point which, at best, would have taken the *Austria* half a mile west of Ailsa Craig. James Morris was criticised for not keeping a proper lookout, especially after stating in his own evidence that his vision had been impaired by smoke from the funnel blowing across the bridge. Both men had their master's certificates suspended for six months. Captain Helig was charged with drunkeness in command of the vessel but this was never fully proven, although in evidence various crew members stated that a good deal of alcohol had been consumed that night.

Although not positively identified as such, the authors are of the opinion that what remains of the *Austria*, after extensive salvage activity, lie off the south coast of Ailsa Craig in approximate position 55°14.783'N, 005°07.250'W (GPS). The wreck located here is of a large steamship heavily broken and scattered among the boulder shingle seabed, lying in general depths of 10 to 20 metres. However, wreckage has also been found in deep water between 30 and 35 metres and again 200 metres west of the reported position in 20 metres. It is not known whether they are all part of the same wreck.

Ailsa Craig lighthouse.

HMS BAYANO

3500nt. Armed merchant cruiser.
Built by A Stephen & Sons Ltd, Glasgow.
Launched 1913.

Dimensions 416.6' x 53.2' x 30.1'

The *Bayano* had powerful six cylinder triple expansion engines and was employed by her owners, Elders & Fyffes Limited, bringing bananas from the Caribbean to Europe.

She was hired by the Royal Navy on 21st November, 1914 along with the *Changuinola, Montague, Patia* and *Patnea*, also from the Elders & Fyffes fleet. They were converted into armed merchant cruisers and used to bolster the Northern Patrol, enforcing the blockade on supplies to Germany in the icy waters between Shetland, Iceland and Norway.

On 11th March, 1915 the *Bayano* was returning to sea and her patrol duties under the command of Captain Carr with a crew of nearly two hundred and fifty men. At 4:45am she was a few miles north of Corsewall Point, Galloway. The night was clear but overcast and very dark and the sea was calm. Two thirds of the crew were asleep, leaving the third watch in charge of the vessel as she steamed through the night. Without warning she was hit by a torpedo from the German submarine *U-27*. The huge explosion flung most of the sleeping men from their hammocks and killed many instantly in and around the engine room where the torpedo actually struck. The initial explosion was quickly followed by a series of further explosions as the ship's magazine detonated, filling the doomed vessel with smoke and steam as water rushed in through the gaping holes in her hull.

The survivors later told many stories of heroism aboard the sinking ship. The wireless operators who remained at their posts broadcasting SOS messages as the ship sank or the sailor who handed out lifejackets to his frightened colleagues as the sea rose around his ankles or the captain who went down with his ship after organising the evacuation of as many of the crew as possible.

Within a few minutes of the initial explosion the *Bayano* sank by the bow, her stern rising dramatically into the air before she finally vanished in a huge cloud of steam and smoke. There was a final explosion as she disappeared beneath the surface. The tremendous suction caused by the huge ship sinking dragged down many of the unfortunate seamen who had jumped into the sea.

Corsewall Lighthouse.

The first vessel to arrive on the scene was the collier SS *Castlereagh* of Belfast. Captain McGarrick described the horrific scene which confronted his ship and crew as a "sea of corpses in lifejackets." He stopped his engines to attempt to pick up survivors but was immediately alerted by the approach of a U-boat, probably the same *U-27* that had sunk the *Bayano* some time earlier. He ordered full steam ahead and set off on a zig-zag course with the submarine in hot pursuit. Thankfully, after a dramatic twenty minute chase, they managed to escape and later safely reached port.

Some hours later the SS *Balermino*, bound for Ayr from Belfast, also arrived at the scene of the sinking. Captain Foster was attracted by survivors waving wildly from the remains of two of the ship's liferafts and an upturned lifeboat. He stopped and picked up twenty four badly injured survivors suffering from exposure and hunger. The *Bayano* had been lost with over two hundred of her crew. The wreck of the *Bayano* lies in deep water a few miles north of Corsewall Point. She has not been identified as there are a number of large wrecks charted in this area.

BELLEVUE

51nt. Steel steam trawler.
Built by Mackie & Thomson, Glasgow.
Launched July 1897.
(ex ESCORT)

Dimensions 104.2' x 21.0' x 10.7'

The story behind the loss of the Granton registered trawler *Bellevue* was never fully publicised at the time, due to wartime reporting restrictions and now only a few scraps of information can be pieced together to form the basis of a story. The *Bellevue* was working the west coast at the beginning of 1942, and left Ayr for the fishing grounds on Saturday 21st February with a crew of eight aboard. The *Bellevue* was never seen again and the first indication that a tragic accident had occurred came the following day when three bodies were washed ashore at Whiting Bay, on the Isle of Arran.

Archives of wartime casualties record the location of the *Bellevue* as being off Turnberry, but give no indication as to the cause of her loss. The authors have found the wreck of a trawler approximately 3.5 miles west of Turnberry Lighthouse lying in 56 metres. The wreck which has a corresponding beam measurement to the *Bellevue* also liberated a navigation lamp some years ago from a Leith maker. This coupled with the *Bellevue* being the only recorded trawler lost in the vicinity makes it a most likely candidate.

The wreck lies in position 55°19.411'N, 004°56.152'W (GPS) with a least depth of 42m at the top of the bow post, with general seabed depths of 54 to 56m. The wreck is visually dramatic especially in good visibility. Lying oriented 130/310 degrees with stern pointing west, the hull rears out of the seabed from the engine room with bows pointing towards the surface, the deck must slope at an angle of at least 45 degrees. This unusal position could suggest that the vessel either hit or trawled up a mine, with the stern section being blown off or certainly badly damaged, before sinking stern first and coming to rest pointing skyward. The wreck is often blessed with good visibility but due to the depth and net across the bridge area and over the port side it is only for the experienced and suitably trained.

BRUCE

80gt. Steel steamship.
Built by Scott & Sons, Bowling.
Launched 1875.

The *Bruce* was employed by her owners, Gilles & Reid of Glasgow, on regular trips between Glasgow, Irvine and the Irish coast. Early in the morning of 27th January, 1882 she left Irvine with a cargo of ninety tons of manganese waste. As she left the River Irvine a strong southerly wind was blowing and when she turned north west about one and a half miles from the bar she heeled over to port in the beam sea and sank. The incident was seen from the pilot house and a tug was sent to the rescue but by the time it reached the scene only Captain Burrows remained alive, clinging to some floating wreckage. There is no record of the wreck, which was reported in fourteen fathoms, ever being found.

CARRICK

195nt. Steel steamship.
Built by D & W Henderson & Co., Glasgow.
Launched 1885.
(ex SALTEES)

Dimensions 186.0' x 28.0' x 14.2'

The *Carrick* was owned by the Ayr Steam Shipping Company and was employed ferrying cargo and passengers between the ports of south west Scotland, north west England and Ireland. In the early hours of the morning of 26th May, 1906 she was returning to her home port with a cargo of cattle under the command of Captain Leadbetter with a crew of eleven. They also had six passengers aboard.

Around 3am they were close to Ailsa Craig when they were enveloped in a dense fog, reducing visibility to around twenty yards. The captain slowed his engines, posted additional lookouts and began sounding his steam whistle. Meanwhile, the SS *Duke of Gordon* reached the same area on her voyage from Greenock to Dublin with about fifty passengers on board. She too was engulfed in the dense fog and Captain Reddin also reduced his speed and crept forward with lookouts posted.

On board the *Carrick* the crew strained nervously to see through the dark foggy night and seemed to be almost out of danger as dawn began to break when the bow lookout reported lights on the port bow immediately followed by lights dead ahead. The helmsman turned hard to port but it was too late. The bow of the *Duke of Gordon* tore into the starboard side of the *Carrick* near the fore rigging. The impact ripped a hole in the hull of the *Carrick* and rolled her over on her beam. The passengers below were plunged into a state of disarray and panic before the ship righted herself, allowing them to recover and make their way on deck. Two of the crew managed to jump onto the bow of the *Duke of Gordon* before the two ships drifted apart and lost sight of each other in the fog. Those remaining on board the *Carrick* quickly launched one of the lifeboats but, before they could all get aboard, she settled down and sank, taking the captain, who refused to leave the bridge, the cabin boy and two of the passengers with her. The passengers and crew in the lifeboat were lucky to escape with their lives as first the suction of the sinking ship, then the panic stricken struggles of the unfortunate cattle fighting for their lives in the sea, threatened to capsize their boat. After rescuing two further exhausted passengers from the water they were picked up by the SS *Mastiff* which had, by now, arrived on the scene. The *Duke of Gordon* meanwhile, although damaged in the collision, searched the area for survivors but, after some time, gave up and resumed her voyage, safely reaching Dublin later in the day.

The Wreck Today

The intact wreck of the *Carrick*, charted in position 55°06.962'N, 005°10.740'W (GPS), has recently been positively identified after the recovery of her ship's bell. The wreck, which sits upright in general depths of 45 metres is heavily entangled with fishing net and, as such, should only be attempted by the experienced diver. The added complexities of a very exposed site and depth make this an advanced dive but still a rewarding one.

CLAN CAMPBELL

729nt. Iron barque.
Built by Bartram Haswell & Co, Sunderland.
Launched March 1875.

Dimensions 185.0' x 31.5' x 18.3'

The *Clan Campbell*, owned by Thomas Dunlop of Glasgow, left Le Havre for Glasgow on 10th January, 1881. By 10pm on 17th January she was abeam of Corsewall Point making five knots in the fresh south easterly wind. About this time the tug *Commodore* of Greenock came alongside and the two masters negotiated a towage rate to Glasgow.

With negotiations complete the *Clan Campbell* continued northwards under sail, closely followed by the tug, as Peter McEwan, master of the *Clan Campbell*, did not wish to pick up the tow until he reached the Cloch Lighthouse at Gourock.

Shortly after midnight Ailsa Craig was sighted about three miles to the north west. The tug's master, aware that the *Clan Campbell* had been making too much leeway across the firth, offered to take the barque in tow. His offer was declined. Around 1am, with Ailsa Craig less than a mile away, the tug's master boarded the *Clan Campbell* and was informed that a hawser was being made ready. However, after three unsuccessful attempts to get the line aboard the tug, the *Clan Campbell* ran ashore on the south east corner of Ailsa Craig and remained fast. The tug offered to tow her off for £200 but this was declined when it was discovered that she was badly holed and filling fast with water. The crew abandoned ship and rowed ashore in the ship's lifeboat.

The *Clan Campbell*, valued at £10,000, was eventually abandoned after being stripped of her spars, rigging, sails and fittings. At a subsequent enquiry, Peter McEwan was found in default for not accepting a tow sooner and for not navigating his vessel with proper care. His master's certificate was suspended for six months during which he was given a mate's certificate.

CLEVERAGH

216nt. Wooden schooner.
Built in Stockholm.
Launched 1851.

Dimensions 105.4' x 26.5' x 13.0′

As the *Cleveragh* sped across the Irish Sea under a favourable wind, her crew could not imagine the disaster that lay ahead. She had sailed from Liverpool on 19th December, 1865 with a cargo of coal for Pernambuco, under the command of Captain Hourigan. However, as she reached Innishtrahull, the wind suddenly increased carrying away her jib boom and she began making water. They struggled on for a few more hours but, as the pumps were now manned constantly and she was very difficult to handle without a jib, Captain Hourigan decided to run for Troon to make repairs.

The wind moderated as they approached the Ayrshire coast and the captain and crew, at last, began to relax. Early in the morning of 27th December they were proceeding north and, on sighting the light at Troon harbour, turned east towards the port entrance. However they had turned too early. As they approached the shore they ran straight onto the Black Rocks which lie just off shore, south of the harbour. For a few moments she refloated and the crew thought they had escaped again, but she was quickly washed back onto the lee shore, despite dropping her anchors in a final attempt to keep her off. The skipper of a passing tug agreed to try to refloat her at high tide but did not return and the *Cleveragh* became a total wreck. Her captain and crew made it safely ashore.

CLYRO

107nt. Steel steam trawler.
Built by Smiths Dockyard, Middlesborough.
Launched 1917.
(ex THOMAS TWINEY)

Dimensions 125.5′x 23.4′x12.8′

Girvan lifeboat and the Ballantrae rocket life-saving brigade were called to assist when the Milford Haven trawler *Clyro* went ashore at Culzean around midnight on Tuesday 13th August, 1935. Fortunately the night was calm and the crew of fourteen were in no immediate danger, although six soaking and tired crew were initially taken ashore by locals from Maidens.

The ***Clyro***.

The following day the remaining crew and Captain Stean left the wreck as her position was becoming increasingly poor with little prospect of refloating her. The *Clyro* had been badly holed and over successive days she developed a list and later broke in two.

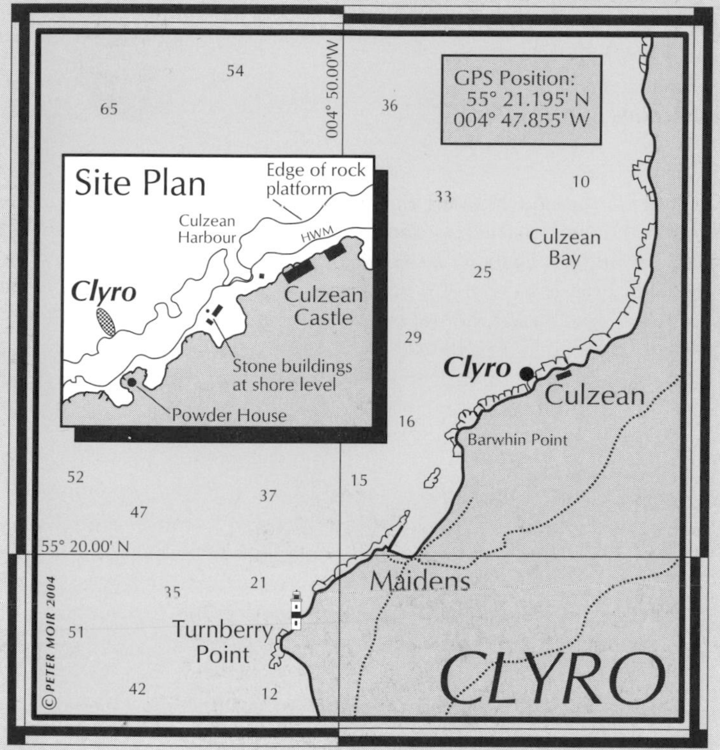

The authors believe that the wreck was later part salvaged in-situ, as a number of steel plate lie well inshore from the wreck, close to steel eye bolts which have been placed in the cliff walls.

The remains of the *Clyro* lie approximately 600 metre south of Culzean Castle, in position 55°21.195'N, 004°47.855'W (GPS). Another aid to

View onshore with boiler in foreground.

location is provided by a small stone structure on the cliff edge, directly inshore known as the Power House., although this is only visible during winter months due to tree foliage. The wreck is completely broken up and may have been subject to some salvage work.

The most recognisable parts are her engine, rudder, propellor and boiler, the latter breaks water at low tide. The seabed here is predominantly rock and boulders, depths range from 0-4 metres. The site is exposed to wind and swell from south west round to north, and can only really be dived by boat.

CORONELLA

108nt. Wooden brigantine.
Built by Miller & Co, Walton, Nova Scotia.
Launched 1862.

Dimensions 91.8' x 24.5' x 10.4′

The *Coronella* left Glasgow on her voyage to Dingle in Ireland with a cargo of three hundred tons of coal on 18th December, 1894. Her crew of six enjoyed a peaceful voyage until they reached the coast of Northern Ireland. As they passed Belfast Lough on 21st December the skies darkened ominously and soon they were fighting their way through the teeth of a howling gale.

The wind continued to increase to hurricane force, tearing her sails and rigging to tatters. She was swept, out of control, northwards towards the Scottish coast as the crew clung for their lives to the remains of the rigging. As the helpless vessel was washed towards the shore at Port Ronald, Troon a number of local men risked their lives by clambering over the rocks to wait for the brigantine to run aground. The instant she grounded they threw a rope to the ship and they helped her terrified and frozen crew to struggle ashore through the swell and spray. The ship's boy, John Hart, fell from the rope into the sea but was rescued and he and all the other five crew members reached shore safely.

The **Coronella** ashore.

DUKE OF EDINBURGH

797gt. Iron paddlesteamer.
Built by R Duncan & Co, Port Glasgow.
Launched 1866.
(ex EARL OF DUBLIN)

Dimensions 279' x 27' x 15′

The *Duke of Edinburgh* was not a lucky ship. Her short career was a catalogue of accidents and disasters which ended on a foggy night in 1870 under the gannet infested cliffs of Ailsa Craig.

Only three years earlier, on her maiden voyage from Glasgow to Dublin, the then *Earl of Dublin* ran aground near Ballyherbert and became a total wreck. The wreck was purchased by Harland & Wolff, who dismantled her where she lay and rebuilt her in their yard in Belfast, adding thirty feet to her length in the process.

If her owners thought that the change of name to *Duke of Edinburgh* would also change her luck they were to be disappointed because, on her sea trials, she ran into a wooden lighthouse in Belfast Lough, almost killing the keeper and his wife. The incidents continued under her new owners, the Dublin & Glasgow Steampacket Company Ltd, when she grounded in the Clyde early in 1870, losing her rudder in the process.

The final chapter in the *Duke of Edinburgh's* eventful history began as she left Dublin on her usual route for Glasgow on 18th January, 1870 with a general cargo, some cattle and thirty passengers. The trip across the North Channel was uncomfortable as the sea pounded on their port quarter and the passengers and crew were relieved to reach the Clyde estuary and the shelter of the Kintyre peninsula from the worst of the Atlantic swell. As they headed north, through the night, the weather became foggy and Captain Byrne ordered engines slowed as they neared the vicinity of Ailsa Craig.

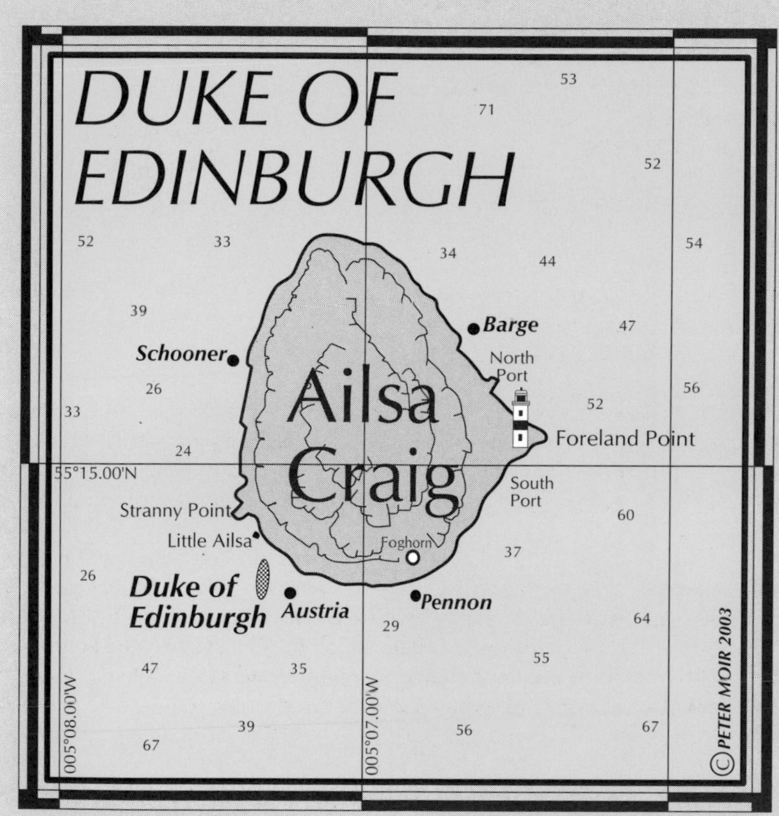

The *Duke of Edinburgh* was still travelling at thirteen knots when the lookout reported a fog bank off the port bow. Captain Byrne took this fog bank to be Ailsa Craig and turned slightly to starboard to pass the island to the east. Almost immediately another fog bank appeared dead ahead but, inexplicably, the *Duke of Edinburgh* steamed straight into this second fog bank which, in fact, was shrouding the treacherous rocky shores of Ailsa.

The *Duke of Edinburgh* ran ashore on the west of the island with such force that more than half the length of the vessel reached above the high water mark. The horrendous crash was heard by a number of other vessels up to two miles off, who rushed to the vessel's assistance.

Meanwhile, on board, the passengers, who had been thrown into a state of total confusion and terror by the impact, were being calmed by the crew who explained that they were in no immediate danger as the vessel was high and dry on the rocks and the sea was fairly calm.

Over the next few hours a number of vessels arrived on the scene in answer to the *Duke of Edinburgh's* distress rockets and soon the passengers, crew and even the cattle were on their way to the mainland. This was followed by the removal of most of the cargo to lighten the ship before attempts were made to refloat her. A number of unsuccessful attempts were made to drag her from the rocks until, on 28th January, the weather broke with a strong south westerly gale. Huge waves crashed over her stern section bumping her already badly damaged hull on the rocky seabed until, on 3rd February, she broke in two amidships and became a total wreck.

The Wreck Today

The wreck, thought to be the remains of the *Duke of Edinburgh,* lies close inshore on the south west coast of Ailsa Craig in approximate position 55°14.833'N, 005°07.317'W (GPS). It is not certain that the wreckage at this site is the *Duke of Edinburgh* as there have been a number of wrecks in this vicinity and nothing has been found, to the authors' knowledge, which positively identifies the name of the wreck.

The wreckage lies between 10 and 20 metres and is mainly the hull plates and ribs of what has obviously been a fairly large vessel. Little else recognisable remains. The shingle seabed in and around the wreck is littered with shards of broken crockery. The site is very exposed and can only be dived in calm conditions.

ESBO

1832nt steamship.
Built by W Pickersgill & Son, Sunderland.
Launched December 1900.
(ex MALIN ex ELENI ex GENESEE ex FINLAND ex CONDYLIS ex AURISTAN)

Dimensions 324.0' x 47.1' x 21.7'

At 5:27am on the morning of 19th October, 1935 the radio at Seaforth Wireless Station crackled into life and a strongly accented voice announced "*Esbo* round Selker Rocks; afraid going ashore." This was the start of a series of events that would eventually lead to the loss of the Finnish steamship off the Ayrshire coast. The *Esbo* did indeed go ashore on the Cumberland coast later that day despite desperate attempts to save her by casting her anchors but both cables gave way before help could reach her. As the voice on the radio announced at 12:41 that the crew were forced to attempt to save themselves by taking to the lifeboats their situation looked bad. The Piel lifeboat, which was en route to the scene, had been forced to return to her station after being damaged by mountainous seas. Thankfully though, the nine crewmen who did leave the vessel in the lifeboat reached the shore safely and the remaining fifteen men were later saved by the Bootle and Whitehaven lifesaving team.

The *Esbo* had been en route to Finland from Preston but had encountered very heavy seas off the mouth of the River Ribble and hurricane force winds had gradually pushed her off course and ashore. She was aground nearly a mile from the shore and in a very difficult situation. She was purchased by Robert Frazer & Sons Ltd of Newcastle and Workington who intended to refloat her and break her for scrap. Over the next few months a number of attempts were made to refloat the ship but to no avail. By March the following year a decision to scrap her where she lay seemed likely but one last attempt, on 26th March, using more powerful pumps, was made and this time the Steel & Bennie tugs *Strongbow* and *Vanguard* succeeded in pulling her off. The ship had been badly damaged during her five months ashore and, after a few rough repairs, it was decided to tow her to Troon to be scrapped.

During the journey north they ran into a strong north easterly gale off the Galloway coast and it was evident that the ship was slowly filling as the pumps were unable to cope with the inflow of water through her damaged hull. By the time they reached Benane Head the situation became hopeless when the pumps finally choked with debris. The crew were taken off and the tow rope cut. Almost immediately the bow rose in the air, revealing a large hole, and she sank stern first about two miles from the shore and only thirty miles from her destination.

The ***Esbo*** ashore near Bootle, Cumberland in October 1935.

The Wreck Today

The wreck of the *Esbo* lies on a sandy seabed in position 55°10.016'N, 005°04.137'W (GPS). She has clearly been well stripped of fittings during her five months ashore and is well broken lying in general depths of 28 metres. The bow is the highest part of the wreck rising 8 metres from the seabed. This is a large wreck with plenty to explore. Her huge engines midships, which have toppled on their side as the wreck disintegrates, are particularly impressive. Surprisingly, visibility is often poor due to the deep silt covering the wreck but it still makes an interesting dive. The wreck is a popular site for local sea anglers making fishing line the most likely hazard although the site is also very exposed to winds from any direction.

ETHEL CRAWFORD

87nt. Steel steam trawler.
Built by Scott & Son, Bowling.
Launched April 1919.
(ex JOHN LANGSHAW)

Dimensions 115.8' x 22.2' x 12.2'

The *Ethel Crawford* was originally launched as the *John Langshaw*, built to the specification of an Admiralty Strath class trawler, but being completed too late for action in World War I she was sold to Fleetwood owners and re-named *Ethel Crawford* (FD 404).

She spent the remainder of her life working as a commercial trawler, changing hands in 1924 and 1932 between Aberdeen owners registered as A36, finally being sold to the Ardrossan Trawling Co Ltd in 1941.

It was under this ownership that found the *Ethel Crawford* and her crew of ten, working south west of Ailsa Craig on 20th April, 1945. Two days previously the German mine layer *U-218* had entered the Clyde and laid a pattern of 13 mines in the channel to the west of the Craig. The exact circumstances are unclear, and we have to assume that she either hit or snagged one of the mines with her nets, resulting in the loss of the vessel and her ten crew.

There is a ironic twist to this story that was to see the *U-218* return to the Clyde shortly after the German surrender. She arrived in early June 1945 where she was interned in Loch Ryan until later that year when she along with around 115 other U-boats were towed off the west coast of Ireland and scuttled as part of 'Operation Deadlight'.

The wreck in position 55°13.058'N, 005°15.057'W (GPS) while not positively identified as the *Ethel Crawford* is indeed the remains of a trawler in a number of sections, the bow being most intact and lying on its starboard side. Seabed depths around the wreck are around 51 metres, the wreck rises around 2-3 metres, a net on the bow rising a further 2 metres.

FREDERIK CORNELIUS

69nt. Iron steam trawler.
Built by Edward Brothers, North Shields.
Launched August 1898.

Dimensions 105.7' x 20.9' x 10.9'

Seven crew were drowned when the Dutch trawler *Frederik Cornelius* was run down by the Clyde Shipping Company's steamer *Aranmore*. The accident happened around 6am on Sunday 31st March, 1901 while the trawler was fishing south of Ailsa Craig with a fleet of 5 or 6 other vessels.

The *Aranmore* was inward bound to Glasgow from Plymouth and collided with the trawler broadside on, at full speed. The impact left the trawlers crew in no doubt as to the severity of the situation and those on deck immediately made attempts to clamber aboard the *Aranmore* while the vessels were together.

Unfortunately, four crew below deck at the time went down with the trawler, and as she disappeared below the surface she took another three including her 26 year old master, Frans Nomekes. The five survivors were taken to Glasgow aboard the *Aranmore* and given shelter in the Sailor's Home on the Broomilaw.

Although no tangible evidence as to the wrecks identity, the authors believe the wreck located in position 55°12.933'N, 005°11.833'W (GPS) is that of the *Frederick Cornelius*. The wreck lies in general seabed depths of 49.5 - 50 metres, with least depth of around 47 metres. The hull would appear to be that of an iron or steel fishing vessel lying approximately 010/190 degrees, with bows pointing south. The visibility on this wreck tends to be very poor, mainly due to the fine silt that covers the wreck. Care should also be taken as a net is draped over the port side, in short this is a dive for only the experienced wreck diver.

FREY

1192nt. Wooden barque.
Built by T J Southard, Richmond, USA.
Launched 1871.
(ex OLIVE S SOUTHARD)

Dimensions 186.2' x 37.1' x 23.6'

December 1894 had been the worst month for shipping casualties in the history of the Clyde. Saturday the 29th found the *Frey* inward bound to Greenock from the USA with a cargo of timber. Mountainous seas whipped up by the storm force winds lashed the barque as she dropped anchor in the lee of Lady Isle, off Troon, and fired her distress rockets. The *Frey's* signals were spotted from Troon but it was impossible to launch the lifeboat there due to the storm. After an urgent telegram, the Irvine lifeboat was launched and it raced to the scene. Due to the heavy swell which was crashing over the anchored vessel, the lifeboat was unable to come alongside the *Frey* and so, one by one, the terrified crew jumped from their ship into the surf to be skilfully picked up by the lifeboat.

Unfortunately, the ordeal for the sixteen crewmen and the thirteen lifeboatmen was not yet over because, as they approached the safety of Troon Harbour, the lifeboat was capsized by a huge wave close to Ballast Bank, throwing everyone on board into the sea. The lifeboat immediately righted herself allowing all but two of those on board to clamber back to safety and reach Troon Harbour.

Meanwhile the abandoned *Frey* had broken from her anchor and eventually came ashore on the rocks off Seafield, near the mouth of the River Doon, south of Ayr. The ship was severely damaged losing all of her masts and rigging. At the time of her loss it was anticipated that, after the removal of her cargo, she would be refloated and removed. The authors have not been able to establish if this was successfully achieved.

The puffers ***Kaffir, Stormlight*** and ***Glen Shiel,*** all destined for a watery grave.

GLEN SHIEL

195gt. Steel cargo vessel.
Built by Livingston & Co, Peterhead.
Launched 1959.

Dimensions 105.8' x 22.4' x 8.9'

The *Glen Shiel*, owned by G & G Hamilton Ltd and on charter to Glenlight Shipping Ltd of Glasgow, left Ayr Harbour around 4am on 29th June, 1973 bound for Shieldhall in Glasgow with a cargo of 215 tons of coal.

As she proceeded north west across Ayr Bay the spray blowing over her port rail and running between her hatch boards, which had not been covered by a tarpaulin, caused a constant flow of seawater into the hold. The vessel developed a list to port which caused her cargo to shift. As the angle of her list steadily increased the flow of water into the hold became a flood and she quickly filled and foundered around 4:30am.

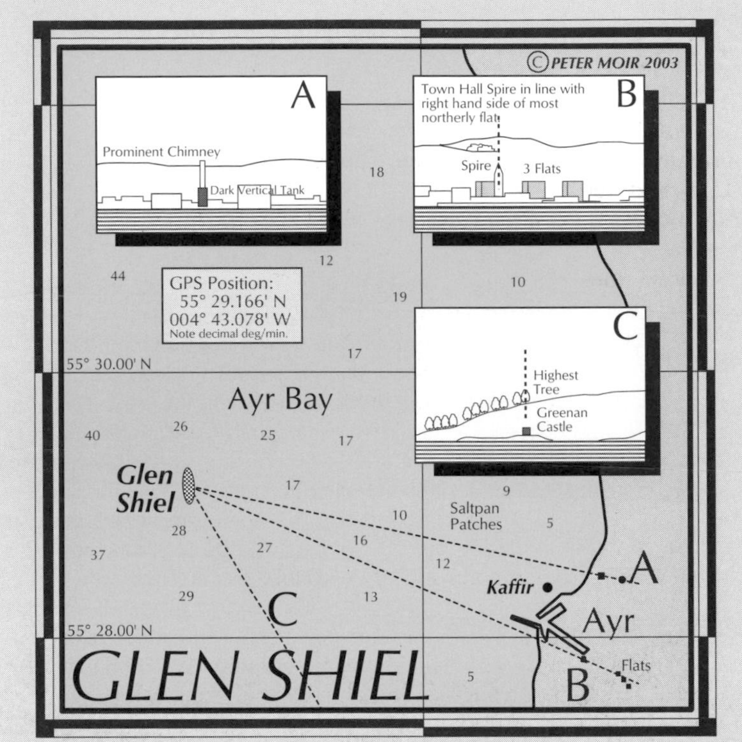

MV ***Glen Sheil.***

The crew were only alerted to the danger shortly before she sank probably due to the gradual build up of water prior to the final deluge. This may well account for the loss of six of the seven crewmen aboard.

The Wreck Today

The wreck of the *Glen Shiel* is located approximately 2.75 miles WNW of Ayr Harbour in position 55°29.166'N, 004°43.078'W (GPS). She lies on her port side oriented 000/180 degrees with her bow pointing south. Seabed depths around the wreck average 25 metres while the least depth over her is 18 metres. The wreck is completely intact except for her mast and propeller which were removed by a commercial diving company in 1977.

IRIS

1181nt. Iron steamship.
Built by E Withy & Co, West Hartlepool.
Launched April 1886.
(ex TORGERD ex GROVEDALE ex THRIFT ex MERCEDES)

Dimensions 275.0' x 37.2' x 19.2'

SS *Iris.*

The ships to form convoy WN53 had gathered at the Tail of the Bank over the preceding two days, and by late evening of the 14th July, 1941 they were all mustered. Shortly before midnight, and one by one, they dropped their moorings and began to move west towards the Cloch in single line, the *Iris* was sixteenth in line, and the convoy numbered twenty one vessels.

The trawler crews manning the submarine boom between the Cloch and Dunoon received signals to open the net shortly after midnight, and the line of ships slipped through at three-minute intervals, each flashing their code signal to the observer's ashore as they passed.

The convoy moved south passed Cumbrae Heads and out into the Firth, hugging the east coast of Arran. The weather was fair, with a light easterly breeze, and the visibility was around three miles. The lighthouse on Holy Isle was passed around 3.25am and the convoy headed on for the turning buoy east of Pladda where they would alter course for the North Channel.

Around 4.00am the ships entered a fog bank and visibility reduced to around 2 cables or less. The *Iris* reduced revolutions to take account of this, although this was generally contrary to navigation instructions for vessels travelling in convoy without specific instructions. Around 4.20am the *Iris* sighted and passed the flashing light of the turning buoy and swung onto a westerly course, signalling her turn with a short blast of her whistle.

A short distance behind was the RFA *Blue Ranger* with her cargo of 1000 tons of fuel oil. Her master was altered by the whistle blast from the *Iris*, and lookouts on the bow of the *Blue Ranger* were alarmed to see the lights of a vessel ahead crossing their bows from port to starboard. The vessels were now very close and while both took avoiding action it did not stop the *Blue Ranger* crashing into the starboard side of the *Iris* at the stern hatch. The bows of the *Blue Ranger* sliced clean through the side of the *Iris* to the hatch cover, and it was not long before the *Iris* began to settle lower in the water. Within ten minutes of the collision the order to abandon ship was given and all her crew were taken aboard the *Blue Ranger*. The *Iris* eventually sank at 4.40am, approximately 3.25miles, 140 degrees from Pladda Lighthouse.

The wreck of the *Iris* lies on a mud seabed in position 55°22.833'N, 005°00.635'W (GPS). This is a deep wreck, with seabed depths of 62 metres, the least depth over the wreck is 48 metres. Visibility is generally in range 3-4 metres at best and we recommend that you dive around high water slack to take benefit of clearer water coming in from the North Channel on the flood tide. Note there is a large net across one end of the wreck. This is an advanced dive and should only be considered by those suitably trained and equipped.

IRON DUKE

32nt. Iron paddle tug.
Launched 1877.

The *Iron Duke* left her home port of Greenock around 11pm on Monday 10th December, 1883 bound for the south end of Arran where her master, Captain McBride, intended to seek towing work from sailing vessels entering the Clyde. Throughout the following day the tug headed south through deteriorating weather and strengthening winds which, by the early evening, had reached hurricane force whipping up mountainous seas and blinding spray.

The *Iron Duke* rode out the storm for several hours, but disaster struck when her engine failed seven miles west of the Heads of Ayr. The north westerly winds quickly pushed the tug towards the Ayrshire coast and she came ashore 700 yards north of Dunure Harbour around 11pm that night. She immediately began to break up. Huge breakers pounded her, quickly destroying her wooden bridge and deckhousing. The six crew members abandoned ship as best they could, struggling through the surf to reach the shore. Five of her crew did manage to get ashore but Captain McBride was washed away, his body being recovered the next day.

By the following morning all that remained of the tug was her iron hull, high on the outlying reefs, with the surrounding shore littered with debris both from the *Iron Duke* and from the barque *Valkyrien* which was also driven ashore nearby that same night.

KAFFIR

98gt. Steel motor coaster.
Built at Kirkintilloch.
Launched 1944.

Dimensions 66.6'x18.3'x8.6'

The *Kaffir*, a small coasting vessel, was owned by the Glenlight Shipping Company of Glasgow. Late in the evening of Monday 23rd September, 1974 she was illegally taken out of Ayr Harbour by her engineer and eventually went ashore 200 metres north of the Monkey Pier. Efforts to refloat the *Kaffir* were made on the next tide but, as her stern gear had been badly damaged, she soon drifted ashore again. Her skipper was injured during the attempt and had to be rescued by helicopter and taken to hospital. The *Kaffir* was eventually written off as a constructive loss in October 1974.

MV ***Kaffir*** discharging cargo at Iona.

The Wreck Today

The remains of the *Kaffir* lie where she stranded in position 55°28.405'N, 004°38.232'W (GPS). She is clearly visible at most states of the tide, although after years of pounding by the sea she is beginning to break up. The wreck now lies in two sections at right angles to the shore, with the stern section closer inshore. Depths around the wreck vary from 4 metres at high water to less than a metre at low water springs. Diving along this section of Ayr beach is not very pleasant due to the proximity of a sewer outfall and silty water from the River Ayr.

LAIRDSCASTLE

1031nt. Steel steamship.
Built by Ardrossan Drydock and Shipbuilding Co.
Launched March 1924.

Dimensions 276.6′ x 37.6′ x 15.3′

The Burns and Laird Line steamer *Lairdscastle* was on her regular run from Glasgow to Belfast when she sank rapidly after a collision in thick fog.

The accident took place on the 4th September, 1940 and occurred somewhere between the Mull of Kintyre and Ailsa Craig. The other vessel involved was the much larger SS *Vernon City* owned by Messrs Reardon Smith, inward bound to Glasgow, the latter although damaged was able to conclude her voyage unassisted.

The 101 passengers and crew managed to abandon ship safely and were later picked up by a Royal Navy vessel in the vacicnity.

The wreck of the *Lairdscastle* is thought to lie in position 55°11.466N, 005°31.367W. The surveyed length appears to match that of the *Lairdscastle*, the wreck in this position sits upright in general seabed depths of 89 metres with a least depth of around 74 metres.

SS *Lairdscastle.*

LONGWY

1323nt. Steel steamship.
Built by Chantiers Nantais de Constructions Maritime, Nantes.
Launched 1903.

Dimensions 282.6' x 40.6' x 19.6′

The *Longwy*, a French general cargo ship was inward bound to the Clyde from Bilbao, with a cargo of iron when she was torpedoed off Corsewall Point on 4th November, 1917. The vessel sank rapidly in relatively shallow water as she had been running a course close to land, to try and avoid the attentions of U-Boats operating in the North Channel. Indeed the wreck was soon located as the top of her masts were visible above water level.

A temporary Notice to Mariners was issued the following day and the Northern Lighthouse Board placed a light buoy on the seaward side of the wreck. The buoy remained in place until October 1919 when it was decided that the wreck was no longer a hazard to navigation.

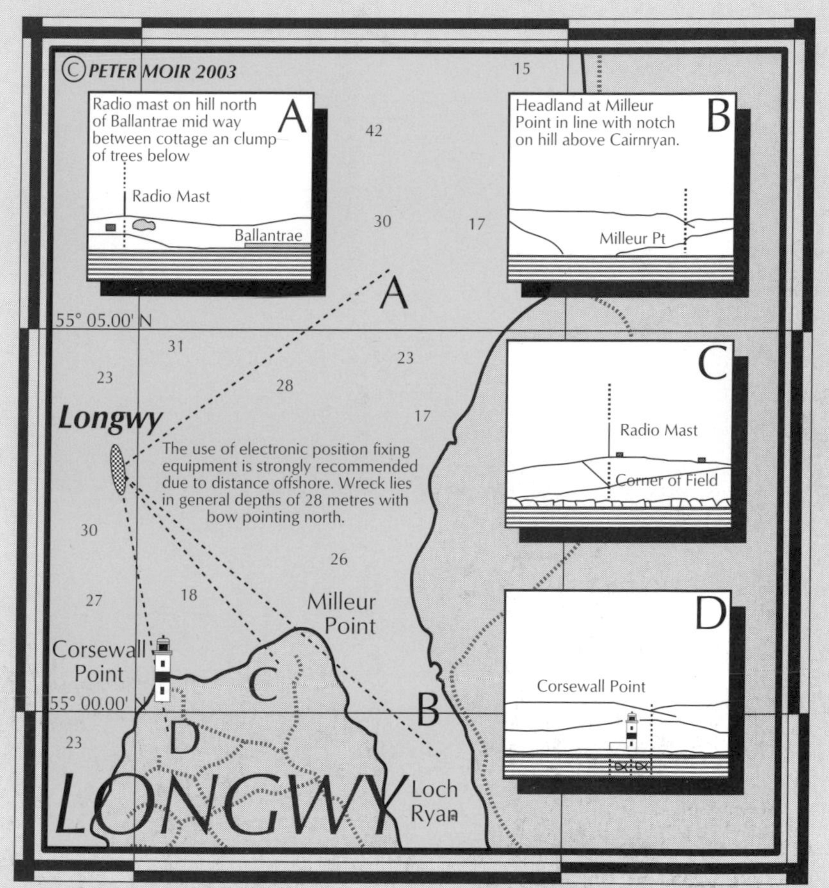

The wreck of the Longwy is marked on Admiralty charts in position 55°03.277'N, 005°10.615'W (GPS), approximately 2.75 miles north of Corsewall Point. The wreck lies in general seabed depths of 28 metres with least depth of 18.5 metres around the midship section. The wreck is oriented 145 / 325 degrees with bow pointing north.

SS ***Margareta*** ashore on Ailsa Craig.- December 1952.

Although the *Longwy* is fairly well broken in parts, the wreck retains much of the size, shape and features of the ship.The most intact part of the wreck is the centre section with engineroom and bridge area.

The site is very exposed to wind from all directions, making access to the site very weather dependent. Also, due to the distance from the shore and the nature of the land nearby, the wreck is difficult to locate using transits opposite. The site is subject to moderate tidal flow at certain states of the tide on springs.

MARGARETA

1694nt. Steel steamship.
Built by J Blumer & Co, Sunderland.
Launched 1904.

Dimensions 323.9' x 46.7' x 20.6'

The Finnish steamship *Margareta*, bound for Glasgow with a cargo of iron ore, ran ashore on the south side of Ailsa Craig on Monday 22nd December, 1952. Lifeboats from Girvan and Campbeltown attended the scene and rescued eleven of her crew who were later landed at Campbeltown. Captain Sundell remained aboard with the rest of the crew to survey damage to her hull however, they too had to be rescued when the *Margareta* began to slip off the rocks in heavy seas.

Three salvage tugs from Metal Industries of Gareloch arrived the following day but continuing bad weather hampered initial salvage attempts. In order to salvage the *Margareta* 700 tons of her cargo had to be jettisoned from her bow hold to allow repair work to be completed. The *Margareta* was refloated on Monday 29th December and towed to Gareloch by the tug *Salveda*, where her cargo was transferred to another vessel. The *Margareta* was later dry docked in January 1953 for repair.

Recovery of the SS ***Margareta*** by the ***Salveda*** on 29th December, 1952.

MARJORIE SEED

1162nt. Steel steamship.
Built by Osborne & Graham, Sunderland.
Launched 1907.
(ex WESTHAMPTON ex ELLI ex WESTHAMPTON ex AMPHION ex BARON CATHCART)

Dimensions 279.3' x 40.1' x 18.1'

In her short seventeen year career the *Marjorie Seed* was renamed five times and had six owners. Her original owners, British Maritime Trust Ltd of West Hartlepool, who launched her as *Westhampton* in 1907, sold her within the year to Furness Withy & Company. They in turn sold her to the Anglo Hellenic Steamship Company Ltd of Greece who named her *Elli* in 1909.

She returned to West Hartlepool, Furness Withy and her original name only a year later. In 1913 she was sold to J Gaff & Company, Glasgow, who sailed her for two years under the name *Amphion*. She then spent nine years from 1915 to 1924 under the ownership of the Kelvin Shipping Company as the *Baron Cathcart* before being sold to her final owners, the Seed Shipping Company of Newcastle, who named her *Marjorie Seed*.

As she left Rothesay Dock, Clydebank for her voyage to Huelva with a cargo of coal and coke on 26th December, 1924 the weather was fair. The weather remained clear as she passed the Cumbraes and headed south towards Ayr. It is therefore a mystery why, a few hours later, she ran aground off the north east tip of Lady Isle. No satisfactory explanations have been given for this serious error in navigation on a clear, calm day but, around 6pm, her radio distress calls were picked up at Troon. Soon a lifeboat and a tug were alongside the half submerged steamer, picking up most of the twenty four crew. Four of the crew remained aboard to inspect the damage and were taken off later to report water four feet deep in the engine room.

At this stage it was still hoped that she could be raised but fate and the unpredictable Scottish winter weather were to take a hand, as the wreck was battered by a severe south west gale for the next week until all hope of successful refloating had vanished. An underwater inspection in early February revealed that the *Marjorie Seed* was badly holed in her port side, her keel buckled and her stern post broken. She was obviously a total wreck. She was extensively salvaged over the ensuing months and years until nothing of any significant value remained on the seabed.

SS ***Marjorie Seed***.

An interesting aspect of the story of the *Marjorie Seed* is that, for many years, she was the unwitting victim of a case of mistaken identity. Nearby lies the wreck of the SS *Ahdeek* which had been known as the *Marjorie Seed* until, in 1987, the two wrecks were positively identified by the discovery of the maker's plate on the *Ahdeek* and a bell bearing the inscription *Westhampton* on the *Marjorie Seed*.

The wreck of the *Marjorie Seed* lies in approximate position 55°31.869'N, 004°43.826'W (GPS) in a general depth of 10 metres. The remains are spread over a wide area of rock and shingle seabed and provide an interesting, if not spectacular, shallow dive over broken plates and girders. The wreckage rises only a metre from the uneven seabed and is therefore undetectable by echo sounder. However, the transits provide an accurate location amid a wide area of wreckage.

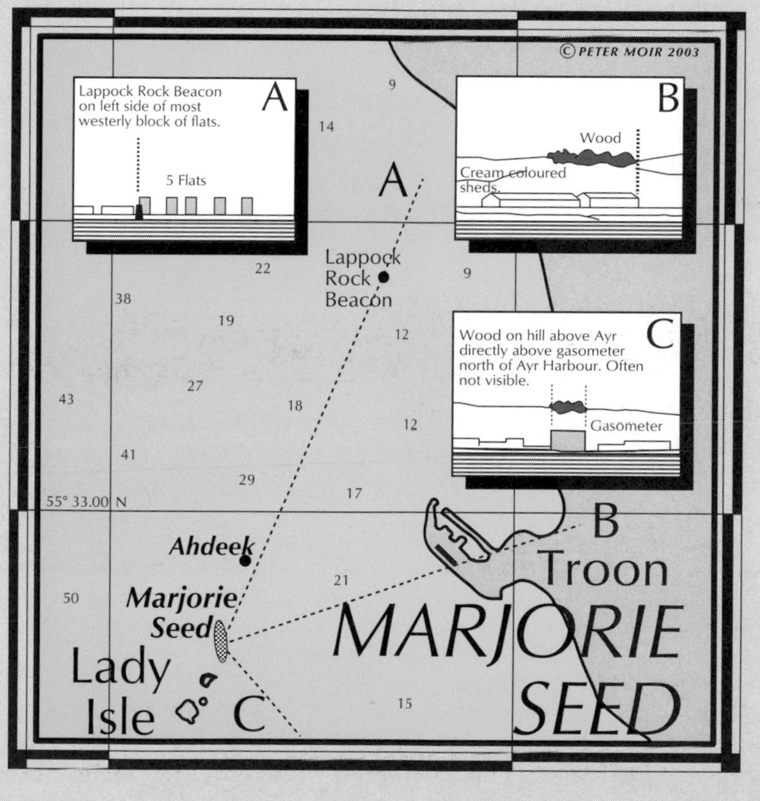

PALLIETER

168gt. Motor vessel.
Built by G. Pattje, Westerbroek.
Launched 1931.
(ex KLAZINA, ex TITIA, ex HERO)

Dimensions 104.2' x 21.0' x 10.7'

The *Palliettter* changed its name no fewer than three times during its short life, the latter reflecting her new Belgium owners, being named after a famous 20th century Flemish literary character. It is extremely likely that due to the hostilities in Europe during WWII, that the *Pallieter* was working around the UK coast carrying general cargos.

As with a number of smaller vessels lost during war years in the Clyde, local censorship barred any mention of shipping losses. This makes it hard to piece together the events leading to their loss. The *Pallieter* was inward bound to Ardrossan from Dublin with a cargo of scrap iron when she sank after colliding with an unknown vessel west of Ailsa Craig on 1st February 1941.

The wreck of the *Pallieter* lies approximately 5 miles west of Ailsa Craig in position 55°14.809'N, 005°15.133'W (GPS). The wreck is substantially intact, lying 170/350 degrees with bows pointing north west. The vessel must have impacted heavily with the seabed, as the top of the focsle is almost level with the surrounding seabed. Moving from the bow the main hold is full and covered with a louvred metal grating, all that can be seen is mud. As you move towards the stern the wreck rises fairly quickly and is approximately 2 metres above the surrounding seabed at the front of the bridge. All the main accommodation and the diesel engine are in the stern section, and by the time you reach the steering quadrant above the rudder stock the deck is around 6-7 metres above the surrounding seabed.

General seabed depths around the wreck are 50-51 metres, a slight tide is noticeable on springs around the stern area. This wreck due to the depth and location is only for experienced and suitably equipped dive teams.

PENNON

94nt. Iron steamship.
Built by T B Seath & Co, Glasgow.
Launched March 1883.

Dimensions 145.0' x 23.1' x 10.6′

The *Pennon*, a small coastal steamer, was owned and registered in Glasgow by a Mr William Russell. On Wednesday 23rd January, 1889 while on a voyage from Duddon to Glasgow with a cargo of iron ore, she ran ashore in thick fog on Ailsa Craig.

The *Pennon* remained ashore for the next week while a salvage team from Glasgow attempted to repair her damaged hull. Their labours were eventually thwarted by a gale and heavy seas on Friday 1st February, which caused considerable damage. Salvage operations were abandoned on 3rd February by which time the wreck was completely submerged at high water. The Glasgow Salvage Company lost two pumps, valued at £750 each, when the *Pennon* finally broke up.

SAINT ORAN

89nt. Steel steamship.
Built by Scott & Son, Bowling
Launched December 1911.

Dimensions 122.0′ x 21.6′ x 9.4′

The *Saint Oran* was a stern engined coaster, owned by J & A Gardner of Glasgow, which that worked between ports in Scotland and Northern Ireland, delivering bulk cargoes such as coal. The *Saint Oran* had loaded a cargo during the afternoon of 29th December 1920, and as she left Troon in the early evening Captain Mitchell noted that visibility in the Firth was poor. The coaster headed south for Turnberry passing the Heads of Ayr and Dunure on the journey south towards Larne.

A few miles south west of Turnberry Lighthouse the lights of an inbound vessel suddenly appeared out of the gloom, unable to alter course in time, both vessels came into collision with the *Saint Oran* being so badly holed that she began to sink almost immediately. Fortunately the other vessel, the Belfast owned steamer *Eveleen* remained afloat and took the crew of the *Saint Oran* aboard, they were later landed safely at Ayr.

The following day a lifeboat containing a lifebelt marked *Saint Oran* – Glasgow, the ship's register, cargo book and official log was found afloat 4 miles south east of Ailsa Craig.

The wreck of the *Saint Oran* lies in position 55°17.667'N, 004°56.654'W (GPS), approximately 4 miles north west of Girvan harbour. The wreck is oriented approximately 010/190 with bow pointing south. Depths on the wreck are between 45-46 metres with general seabed depths of around 48-49 metres.

The hull is substantially intact, with the basic form of fo'c'sle, hold and stern engineroom and accommodation still clearly in place. All deck structures, the funnel and mast have long since collapsed. Due to the depth and distance offshore this dive is for the more experienced dive group, note there is netting draped over the bow section.

SS ***Saint Modan,*** sister ship to the ***Saint Oran***.

SECRET

78nt. Wooden schooner.
Built in 1865.

The *Secret* of St Ives was on a voyage from Hayle in Cornwall to Glasgow with a cargo of eighteen tons of dynamite in six hundred casks under the command of Captain Francis Thomas. As she battled her way northwards on the evening of 11th February, 1896 in gale force winds, her mast snapped as she passed the Heads of Ayr and she was driven, helpless, across Ayr Bay and onto the treacherous Black Rocks off Troon.

The crew of four and the captain immediately took to the ship's boat and after two cold, wet hours reached the shore. Around 8am the next morning, the *Secret* rolled over on the rocks then vanished in a huge explosion as her deadly cargo erupted, scattering wreckage up to a mile from the scene and shattering many nearby windows and doors. As the smoke and the spray cleared the *Secret* had disappeared, leaving only small pieces of wood, rope and sailcloth floating on the surface.

STORM LIGHTS

24nt. Iron paddle tug.
Built by J T Eltringham, South Shields.
Launched 1886.
(ex FLYING SQUIRREL)

Dimensions 108.5' x 18.5' 9.7'

The *Storm Lights* was owned by Mr James Waterson of Belfast. On 23rd November, 1898 while on a voyage from Ardrossan to Belfast under the command of her master, George McGugan, she ran aground on the Carleton Dog Rocks about six miles south of Girvan. The crew landed safely in their own boat as their vessel filled quickly with water. Shortly afterwards, she slipped from the rocks and sank in deep water where she became a total wreck.

The authors have located the wreck of a steam paddle tug in position 55°13.795'N, 005°01.638'W (GPS). The wreck is approximately the same size, vintage and design as the *Storm Lights*, but lies about 5 miles offshore from Lendalfoot. After fruitless attempts to identify the wreck, one possible scenario is that the *Storm Lights* was later refloated but sank while under tow to port. The wreck off Ailsa Craig lies in general seabed depths of 44-45 metres and rises approximately 3 metres off the seabed. A net hangs off the port sponson and rises above the wreck, in recent years this has been used to help locate the wreck but a recent visit in 2003 saw the net lying down on the seabed. The mystery continues.

TRELAWNEY

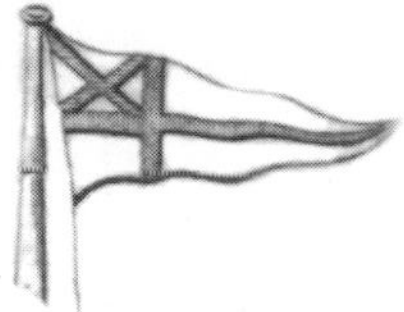

455nt. Wooden sailing ship.
Launched 1809.

On the morning of 22nd January, 1819 the *Trelawney* sailed into the Clyde on the final stage of a voyage from Jamaica to Greenock under the command of her master, David Reid, with a crew of twenty five aboard.

Due to heavy fog they were uncertain of their position and, while believing themselves to be close to the Heads of Ayr, ran aground on the sands between Irvine and Stevenston. They succeeded in getting off but, as the wind increased from the south east, almost immediately went aground again. As the day wore on the wind continued to increase and with it the anxiety of the crewmen aboard the stranded ship. Four of them managed to get ashore in a boat and raise the alarm. After a line from the ship was floated ashore, four local men took a boat into the surf, now pounding on the shore and the *Trelawney*, and succeeded in reaching the ship by pulling themselves along the line. Tragically, on the return trip, all four, plus eleven of the crew they had rescued, were thrown into the sea and drowned as the line broke and the boat capsized.

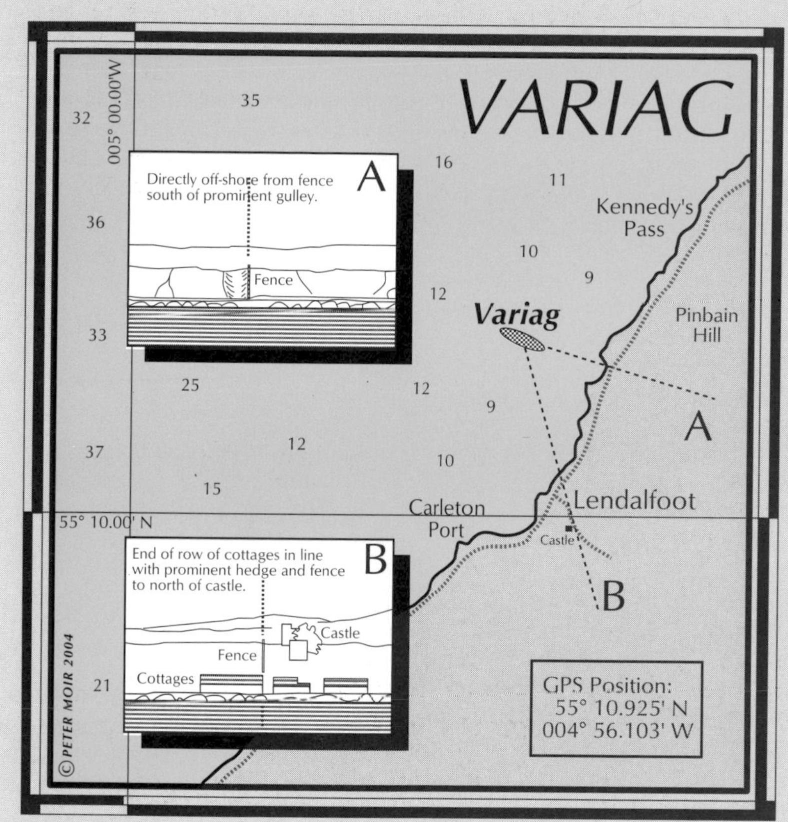

The remains of the *Variag* lie at the north end of Lendalfoot Bay about 400 metres offshore in position 55°10.924'N, 004°56.103'W (GPS). The wreckage, which consists mainly of hull plating and structural members, lies on a flat rock and sand seabed. Debris extends over an area around 4000 square metres in depths of 6 to 10 metres. The wreck only rises one or two metres from the seabed and it is therefore better found by using the transits than by echo sounder. The site is exposed to the prevailing westerly wind and, as such, swell is the major potential problem.

WALRUS

163gt. Steel steamship.
Launched 1892.

The four crew members of the small steamship had a lucky escape when their vessel foundered off Ailsa Craig on Tuesday 15th February 1910. The *Walrus* had left Belfast for Irvine with a cargo of 100 tons of moulding sand earlier in the day, but on reaching Corsewall Point the weather began to worsen. Heavy seas began to wash over the *Walrus*, sending her master crashing to the deck on a number of occasions. The continual deluge eventually got below deck level, and with her pumps unable to cope, her boiler fire was eventually extinguished. Drifting helplessly before the wind and with darkness approaching the crew of the *Walrus* began making frantic signals to passing vessels. Their efforts were finally rewarded when they were spotted by the Burn's steamer *Hound*, which managed to get alongside and the crew jumped aboard shortly before the *Walrus* foundered.

There is a rather sad but also amusing aside to this story which involved the body of the mate, Duncan Galbraith, who had fallen into Belfast Harbour the preceding Saturday and drowned. He was being brought back to Scotland for burial, in a wooden coffin as deck cargo. Unable to transfer the body to the *Hound* before the *Walrus* foundered the crew assumed the body had sunk with vessel. Amazingly the coffin and body was found the following day on Croy shore. This remarkable story does not end here, as the carriage taking the coffin up Croy Brae broke down and involved further adventures over land to Ayr.

The *Walrus* was reported to have foundered 3 miles north of Ailsa Craig, which corresponds with the location of a small steel wreck in 56 metres in position 55°19.615'N, 005°04.211'W. The wreck lies approximately 120/300 degrees with stern to north and rises approximately 2 metres above the seabed. We have dived the wreck on a number of occasions and as yet we have been unable to positively identify the wreck as the *Walrus*, although it is definitely a small rear engined coaster. Visibility is generally poor, certainly no more that 2 metres, the tide is always a factor as well. This is an advanced dive, well into the main shipping lanes used by the fast ferries from Northern Ireland, good boat cover, delayed SMB's are essential.

CLYDE COAST SOUTH

Listed below are a selection of 65 smaller vessels wrecked within this area. This list is included as a basis for further research. Names suffixed by (S) denote extensive salvage work or total removal subsequent to date of loss.

NAME	BUILT	TONNAGE	HULL	TYPE	LOST	CAUSE	LOCATION
Aimwell	1844	40nt	W	Sr	12.12.1883	S	Near Ballantrae
Ann	1847	105bn	W	Bgn	10.09.1865	S	Black Rock, Troon
Annie & Jane	1862	85nt	W	Sr	14.11.1877	S	1m N of Turnberry Lt.Ho
Appia	1873	453nt	W	Bn	08.12.1897	S	Heads of Ayr
Aurora	1819	145nt	W	Bg	23.01.1877	S	Ballantrae
Ayr	1878	13nt	I	P.Tug	11.12.1890	C	Off Ayr
Beta	1856	39nt	W	K	15.07.1910	S	Ailsa Craig
Bonvilston	1893	1815nt	I	SS	07.10.1918	T	9.5m NW Corsewall Point
Briton	1847	214gt	I	PS	31.01.1855	S	Ballantrae
Buffalo	1866	286gt	I	SS	03.09.1918	T	8m NW of Corsewall Point
Caroline	1848	165nt	W	Bkn	26.02.1894	S	North of Irvine Bar
Caros	1848	122nt	W	Bg	08.11.1880	S	Lady Isle
Christina Dawn(S)		300gt	I	SS	14.04.1949	S	Irvine
Culzean Castle	1843	244nt	W	S	11.01.1847	S	Lady Isle
Dispatch			W	Sr	03.02.1854	S	Lady Isle
Doddington	1830	60gt	I	SS	06.03.1869	S	St Nicholas Rock, Ayr
Donna Henrietta	1869	6nt	W	Syt	22.07.1904	S	Lady Isle
Dreamland	1878	99nt	I	Sr	13.07.1878	F	Off Ailsa Craig
Earl Mulgrave	1838	99nt	W	Sr	21.04.1903	C	Off Ailsa Craig
East	1859	1153nt	I	Bk	12.12.1883	S	2.5m S of Girvan
Eliza	1792	100nt	W	Bg	26.10.1892	C	Off Ailsa Craig
Ella		243nt	W	Bn	05.01.1867	S	Near Ballantrae
Emeline	1864	134nt	W	Bgn	27.07.1885	F	Off Turnberry
Equinox			S	MFV	26.05.1996	F	NE of Heads of Ayr
Fanny	1842	106nt	W	Bg	31.10.1880	S	Ayr
Harald Haarfager		146nt	W	Sr	04.11.1879	S	Irvine Bar
Hildred	1878	244nt	W	Bn	26.03.1916	S	Black Rocks, Troon
Irvine	1871	19nt	I	SS	20.12.1882	S	Irvine Bar
Ithuriel		135nt	W	Bn	08.11.1869	S	Port Ballantrae

NAME	BUILT	TONNAGE	HULL	TYPE	LOST	CAUSE	LOCATION
James	1807	79nt	W	Bn	07.12.1877	S	S of Ayr Pier
Jubilee	1836	253nt	W	Bg	06.02.1850	S	Near Girvan
Karl Martins	1875	124nt	W	Sr	26.10.1884	S	Culzean Bay
Lady Montgomerie	1803	77bn	W	Bgn	09.11.1831	F	Off Saltcoats
Leader	1873	78nt	W	Sr	03.08.1909	F	12m NW Corsewall Point
Leonora			W	S	14.01.1827	S	Troon
Liberty	1862	85nt	W	Sr	13.10.1873	C	4m S Pladda
Lincoln	1880	163nt	W	Bn	13.12.1888	C	Off Maidens
Lizzie Gardner	1873	45nt	I	SS	30.01.1881	S	6m S of Girvan
Lucy Emma	1876	24nt	W	K	15.08.1907	S	Turnberry Lighthouse
Madcap	1863	42nt	W	Sr	03.08.1876	C	Off Ballantrae
Maggie Sinclair	1878	15nt	W	Sk	17.08.1898	S	Ailsa Craig
Maria A Hinde(S)	1883	521nt	I	SS	17.03.1885	S	Troon
Mary		134nt	W	Bgn	12.10.1871	F	N of Ailsa Craig
Merrick(S)	1878	223nt	I	SS	29.12.1908	S	2m S of Girvan
Niagra			W	S	00.00.1873	S	Ayr Bay
Nith	1859	141nt	I	SS	19.11.1879	S	Ailsa Craig
Nugget(S)	1910	405gt	S	SS	04.03.1926	S	Ayr Bay
Nyanza	1897	2642nt	S	SS	29.09.1918	T	10m NW Corsewall Point
Ocean	1808	114nt	W	Bgn	07.12.1834	S	Near Culzean
Panaghia Cassianni		375nt	W	Bg	06.03.1858	S	Ayr Bay
Pilgrim		90nt	W	Sr	01.04.1953	F	Off Ballantrae
Protector	1858	196bn	W	Bq	26.10.1887	S	Troon
Queen of the Isles(S)		156gt	I	SS	16.02.1870	S	Brest Rocks, Turnberry
Roecliff	1860	149nt	W	Bg	01.11.1889	S	Troon
Royal Adelaide		405bn	I	Bq	12.01.1840	S	Lendalfoot
St Fillan	1840	41bn	W	Bgn	22.11.1881	C & F	off Saltcoats
Setter	1906	422nt	I	SS	13.09.1918	T	6m NW of Corsewall Point
Splendid	1838	59nt	W	Sr	25.10.1884	S	Ayr
Stars	1902	235nt	I	Sr	27.12.1912	C	2m SW Ailsa Craig
Stokers	1859	60nt	W	PS	00.00.1863	F	Off Ardrossan
Success		75nt	W	Bn	27.01.1860	S	Irvine Bar
Susan	1812	44nt	W	Sr	08.02.1884	S	Black Rocks, Troon
Swift	1838	62nt	W	Sr	29.11.1885	S	Irvine Bar
William Hill	1829	79nt	W	Bg	19.12.1880	S	Ayr Bay
Windsworth	1843	79nt	W	Sr	28.12.1894	S	Ballast Bank, Troon

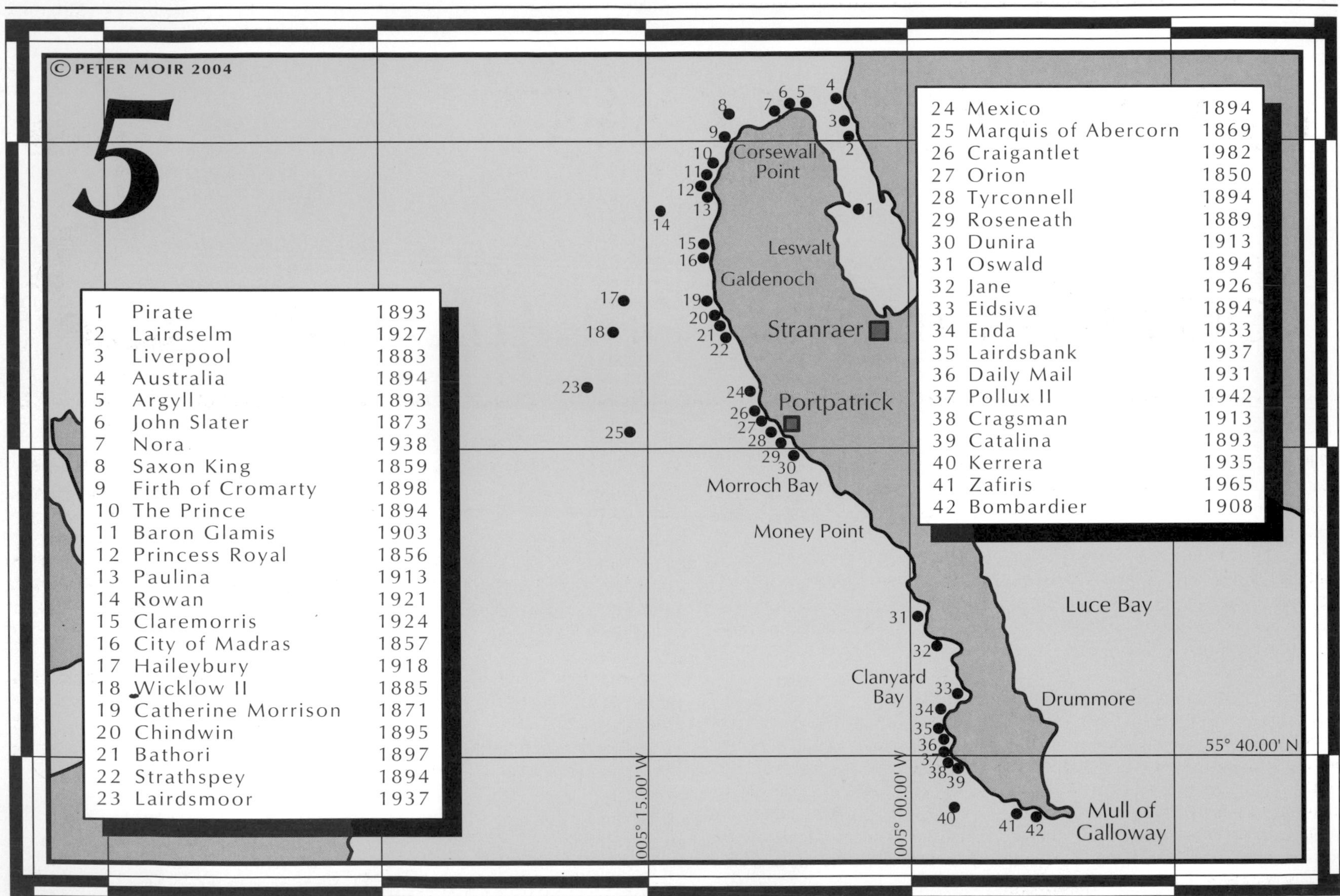
© PETER MOIR 2004
5
1 Pirate 1893
2 Lairdselm 1927
3 Liverpool 1883
4 Australia 1894
5 Argyll 1893
6 John Slater 1873
7 Nora 1938
8 Saxon King 1859
9 Firth of Cromarty 1898
10 The Prince 1894
11 Baron Glamis 1903
12 Princess Royal 1856
13 Paulina 1913
14 Rowan 1921
15 Claremorris 1924
16 City of Madras 1857
17 Haileybury 1918
18 Wicklow II 1885
19 Catherine Morrison 1871
20 Chindwin 1895
21 Bathori 1897
22 Strathspey 1894
23 Lairdsmoor 1937
24 Mexico 1894
25 Marquis of Abercorn 1869
26 Craigantlet 1982
27 Orion 1850
28 Tyrconnell 1894
29 Roseneath 1889
30 Dunira 1913
31 Oswald 1894
32 Jane 1926
33 Eidsiva 1894
34 Enda 1933
35 Lairdsbank 1937
36 Daily Mail 1931
37 Pollux II 1942
38 Cragsman 1913
39 Catalina 1893
40 Kerrera 1935
41 Zafiris 1965
42 Bombardier 1908
Corsewall Point
Leswalt
Galdenoch
Stranraer
Portpatrick
Morroch Bay
Money Point
Luce Bay
Clanyard Bay
Drummore
Mull of Galloway
55° 40.00' N
005° 15.00' W
005° 00.00' W

GALLOWAY COAST

Chapter 5

LOCH RYAN TO MULL OF GALLOWAY

While not included in the area traditionally defined as the Firth of Clyde, the treacherous coast of Galloway, from Corsewall Point in the north to the rocky buttress of the Mull of Galloway in the south, is included in our story because of the number of Clyde bound or based vessels that have been lost on or near its shores. The lighthouse at Corsewall Point often gave ship captains their first landmark and bearing as they entered the Firth or their last sight of Scotland as they sailed south into the Irish Sea. The deep North Channel, which lies to the west of the Galloway peninsula, provides access from the Atlantic to the major ports of Liverpool and Glasgow.

The geographical position of Galloway, to the east of this busy seaway and the prevailing onshore, south west wind, have resulted in the wrecking of dozens of ships on its rocky shores. Galloway itself was the base for a hectic sea traffic between Portpatrick, Stranraer and the ports of Northern Ireland. Some of these local vessels too were to meet with disaster, swept by violent storms to be smashed to pieces among the rocks and inlets of this coastline. Finally, the North Channel provided a happy hunting ground for German U-boats during both wars and many Allied ships, plus some of the submarines themselves, lie in deep water close to the Scottish shoreline.

Diving in Galloway area has to be given a good deal of respect and planning due to the exposed nature of the coastline and the strong tidal movement along the coastline. If the wind is from the west or south and blowing with any strength, diving on the wrecks close inshore is impossible. Even after the wind has abated, visibility can be reduced to virtually zero for days until the sand and silt settles to the seabed. Conditions are further hampered by the strong tidal streams which run parallel to the shore and are a significant hazard to the unwary diver or boatman.

Boat access is limited with best launching facilities in Loch Ryan, although it is possible to launch boats at Portpatrick, Port Logan and Maryport with the assistance of a 4x4 vehicle. Despite these difficulties, in good weather and with proper planning the diving can be excellent, with clear water and colourful sealife on the wrecks located offshore.

ARGYLL

34nt. Iron steamship.
Built by R Duncan & Co, Port Glasgow.
Launched May 1886.

Dimensions 139.9' x 23.1' x 9.4'

The small coastal steamer *Argyll* ran aground on Milleur Point around 3am on 17th September, 1893 while on a voyage from Glasgow to Campbeltown and Stranraer. She was badly holed on the rocks and sank shortly after going ashore.

News of the accident quickly reached Stranraer and the schooner *Scotia* set out for the head of Loch Ryan to render assistance. The crew of the *Argyll* succeeded in off-loading 35 tons of her cargo into the *Scotia* leaving the remainder, which was waterlogged, in the hold.

Efforts to raise the wreck were made by the Glasgow Salvage Association over the next ten days and she was finally raised late on 27th September. Unfortunately, the makeshift concrete repairs to her hull did not hold under pressure and she quickly sank again in four fathoms close to where she had originally stranded. A further attempt to refloat the *Argyll* the following day proved unsuccessful and she was finally abandoned.

The wreck of the *Argyll* was sold at auction on 6th October for £74 with materials and fittings salved realising a further £60. The mate, who had been on watch at the time, was blamed for the accident at the subsequent enquiry. The remains of the *Argyll*, which was substantially salved at a later date, lie scattered among the rocks between 3 and 5 metres in approximate position 55°01.150'N, 005°05.950'W, off Milleur Point.

The ***Argyll*** off Cloch Point.

AUSTRALIA

696nt. Wooden barque.
Built by J Lof, Jacobstad, Finland.
Launched 1865.

Dimensions 158.3' x 36.4' x 18.5'

The *Australia* was en route from Fleetwood to Norway on 22nd December, 1894 under the command of Captain Christophersen. That day was to go down in history as one of the worst storms ever to hit the south west coast of Scotland. Many ships were lost as the howling winds and mountainous seas lashed the coast. The *Australia* was driven ashore near Finnart Point and instantly smashed to pieces with the loss of four of her eleven crew.

The barque ***Australia***.

BARON GLAMIS

1566nt. Steel steamship.
Built by A Rodger & Co, Port Glasgow.
Launched July 1894.

Dimensions 301.2' x 40.6' x 16.7'

It is often said that history never repeats itself but, in this case, it is certainly not true. Forty seven years before the loss of the *Baron Glamis* the *Princess Royal* had run aground on precisely the same spot at Laggan Beacon, off the Galloway coast, in a very similar morning fog.

The *Baron Glamis*, which belonged to the Hogarth Shipping Company of Ardrossan, left Glasgow on 20th January, 1903 bound for Buenos Aires with a general cargo of coal, wood and bricks. She was under the command of Captain E Manning who was making his first voyage down the Clyde in command of a steamship, although he was an experienced sailing ship master. As the *Baron Glamis* approached Corsewall Point, Galloway around 3am on 21st January on a south westerly course, the weather was very foggy. Shortly after passing the Point she ran aground near Laggan Beacon and stuck fast on the rocks.

Although she settled down by the bow, as the water rushed in through a gaping hole in her hull, the crew were in no immediate danger in the calm weather. The rocket brigade and then the Portpatrick lifeboat soon arrived on the scene. However, as the crew prepared to go ashore, the wind increased and by the time they were taken aboard the lifeboat the weather had deteriorated considerably. Shortly before they left, the engine room bulkhead gave way and the sea water flooded the mid section of the stranded vessel which, until this time, had been afloat from midships aft.

The weather continued unsettled for the next two days frustrating the salvage teams who were already standing by at the scene of the wreck. Early in the morning of 24th January she parted amidships and became a total wreck, leaving her cargo and parts of the wreckage floating northwards in the strong tidal current.

Craig Laggan Beacon with Corsewall Lighthouse to the north.

The wreck of the *Baron Glamis* lies in position 54°58.580'N, 005°11.233'W (GPS), north east of Laggan Beacon, in a general depth of 18 metres with least depths of around 12 - 13 metres. She is well broken with the stern section the most intact, lying on a rock and sand seabed. The site is very exposed to the prevailing winds and swell and is also subject to strong tidal streams which run between the reef and the mainland coast, so care is essential when diving this wreck. The authors strongly recommend the use of delayed surface marker buoys when diving this and other wrecks lying in areas of strong tidal movement.

BATHORI

1383nt. Steel steamship.
Built by Wigham Richardson & Co, Newcastle.
Launched 1892.

Dimensions 285.0' 38.2' x 23.1'

One of the more fortunate vessels to go ashore on the Galloway coast was the cargo steamer *Bathori*. Owned by the Royal Hungarian Sea Navigation Company, she stranded in Larbrax Bay on Sunday 5th November, 1897 while heading for Glasgow with a general cargo from her home port of Fiume.

The *Bathori* remained ashore for three months, during which time she was battered by frequent gales, while part of her cargo was removed. This work was undertaken by the Glasgow Salvage Association and much of the cargo, which included flour, almonds, dried fruit and sulphur, was taken to Glasgow by the steamers *Polarlight, Acolight* and *Pirate*.

The *Bathori* was eventually refloated on 8th March, 1898 and moored alongside the Railway Pier at Stranraer while temporary repairs were made. She finally arrived in Glasgow on 11th March where the remainder of her cargo was discharged and she was dry docked for repairs.

SS ***Bombardier*** ashore in West Tarbet Bay.

BOMBARDIER

70nt. Steel steamship.
Built by Ardrossan Dry Dock & S B Co Ltd.
Launched November 1903.

Dimensions 115.1' x 22.1' x 8.5'

The *Bombardier* was registered in Glasgow and owned by Messrs Purdie, Glen & Miller. She ran ashore in fog in West Tarbet Bay on Tuesday 5th May, 1908 while on a voyage from Belfast to Workington in ballast. The crew easily made it ashore in the ship's boat.

From the outset Lloyds agent in Stranraer did not hold much hope of refloating the vessel as she was badly holed. The British Marine Salvage Company commenced work on 6th May. Prospects of salving the *Bombardier* increased over the next few days as weather conditions remained good and repair work proceeded favourably. However, the constant strain of tidal movement was taking its toll on her hull and, on 9th May, her stern post broke. Salvage of the *Bombardier* again became doubtful.

The salvage steamer *McDuff* arrived from Glasgow on 14th May with powerful steam pumps and the temporary repair work continued throughout the next week. An attempt to refloat the *Bombardier* on 22nd May proved unsuccessful due to lack of water. However she was eventually floated off late the following day and towed to Loch Ryan where she was beached. The subsequent damage repair report produced by Lloyds surveyor did not bode well for the *Bombardier*, noting the need for repair of propeller, sternpost and 74 hull plates and renewal of 47 hull plates and her rudder. Finally, and more importantly, it was noted that her hull was badly indented between midships and stern which would require the removal of engine and boiler to effect repairs.

The *Bombardier* was written off as a constructive total loss as the repairs required were found to be uneconomical and she was broken up later that year.

CATALINA

482nt. Iron barque.
Built by Wm Doxford, Sunderland.
Launched November 1868.

Dimensions 151.1' x 28.1' x 16.8'

The German barque *Catalina* left Bowling in ballast on Friday 10th February, 1893 bound for Cardiff, where she was to load cargo. By the morning of Tuesday 14th February she was close to the Maiden Isles off the Irish coast in a freshening south westerly wind. The wind strength steadily increased during the morning and by early afternoon had reached hurricane force. Her sails had been continually reefed as the weather deteriorated and she gradually became uncontrollable in the violent conditions.

The barque **Catalina**.

The *Catalina* was pushed towards the Galloway coast throughout the rest of the day and was eventually driven ashore shortly before midnight near Stockmill Farm just north of Crammag Head. The huge waves slammed her against the rocks. Each time she hit, men jumped for their lives before the swell pulled her off shore again. Finally she wedged on submerged rocks and quickly capsized throwing the remaining men into the sea. Only four of the twelve man crew aboard managed to reach the safety of the rocks through the heavy surf.

The remains of the *Catalina* lie in shallow water beneath Stockmill Farm in position 55°40.034'N, 004°57.945'W (GPS). The wreckage, which is well broken, is scattered and intermingled with the wreckage of the *SS Mazeppa* which sank at the same spot in 1847.

CATHERINE MORRISON

272gt. Wooden brig.

The *Catherine Morrison* was en route from Ardrossan to Odessa with a cargo of coal. In the early hours of the morning of Sunday 1st January, 1871 she encountered a violent storm off Corsewall Point and was driven ashore at Port Beg, Galdenoch Bay where she became a total wreck.

Her crew of nine were drowned as the vessel's wooden hull was smashed to pieces on the rocks.

CHINDWIN

59nt. Iron steam trawler.
Built by Cook Welton & Gemmell, Hull.
Launched 1887.

Dimensions 100.0' x 20.1' x 10.3'

One of the more dramatic stories of shipwreck along this section of coastline concerns the loss of the trawler *Chindwin* and the subsequent efforts of her crew to reach safety.

On Wednesday 6th February, 1895 while returning from the fishing grounds off Colonsay, the *Chindwin* encountered atrocious weather conditions in the North Channel. Gale force winds and heavy snow reduced visibility to such an extent that she became totally lost and eventually stranded in Pan Bay, six miles south of Corsewall Point, around 12:30am the following morning.

The *Chindwin* was hard aground and resisted all attempts to refloat her by going 'full astern'. After firing distress rockets, the crew climbed into the rigging to escape the waves which were breaking over most of the vessel. They remained aloft till daybreak but, with no sign of rescue and numbed by the wind and sub zero temperatures, they decided to try to reach the shore. A large rope with a knotted end was floated ashore and successfully snagged between two pinnacles of rock. The steward, being the youngest and lightest of the crew, volunteered to shin across the ninety foot gap to the shore. Watched by his crew mates, he reached safety and refastened the rope in a more secure location. Slowly the rest of the crew pulled themselves to the shore, drenched and frozen by the stinging spray.

Once ashore, the crew were confronted by sheer cliffs covered with snow and ice. Tired and exhausted, they struggled upwards and finally reached the cliff top and the open expanse of Galdenoch Moor. Already suffering from cold and frostbite, they staggered and crawled through the deep snow for five hours trying to find shelter and assistance. In desperation, they dug a large hole in the snow where they sheltered for some time. Realising that they might die of exposure the crew set off again in search of help.

Around 4am on the Friday morning they came across a large manure heap and managed to light a fire with stalks of straw. As they huddled round trying to absorb the heat, one of the crew, the second engineer, was so numbed by the frostbite that he did not realise his right foot was in the fire and, when it was pulled out, two of his toes were found to be completely charred.

The crew were eventually found shortly after daybreak by a local shepherd and guided to Miekle Galdenoch Farm where they were given dry clothes and warm food. All the roads in the surrounding district were impassable due to the heavy snow and the survivors had to wait till the following day before they could be transported to Stranraer to receive badly needed medical attention.

The wreck of the *Chindwin* was later purchased by a Mr Garscadden of Glasgow who had also recently purchased the wreck of the *Strathspey*, wrecked close by in December 1894. The authors have been unable to establish the extent or success of the salvage operations.

CITY OF MADRAS

914 bn. Iron ship.
Built in Glasgow.
Launched 1855.

Dimensions 184.3' x 27.5' x 11.5'

The full rigged ship *City of Madras* left Glasgow for Calcutta on Friday 27th February 1857. The ship was under the command of Captain James Stobbo and she had aboard a valuable general cargo. By the following Sunday, the 1st March, the *City of Madras* had left the narrow channels of the Upper Clyde far behind and the Maiden's Light off the Antrim coast was sighted around 6.30pm.

Around this time, the captain went below leaving the first mate, Matthew Reed on watch. The weather conditions at the time were fair with variable winds and cloud, it was therefore strange why the *City of Madras* should run aground on the Galloway coast shortly before midnight. The crew managed to safely abandon ship and all got ashore near to Mark Farm, some 3 miles south of Dally Bay, but the vessel was almost fully waterlogged.

The *City of Madras* remained ashore and over the following two weeks began to break up, until on the 16th March, Lloyd's List reported that she had completely broken up. The wreck was sold on the 14th June at an auction in Stranraer, it is not know how successful the new owners were at recovering any of the cargo or ships fittings.

As to the cause of the stranding, a subsequent Board of Trade Inquiry at Stranraer found the mate to blame for not properly taking soundings when navigating close to shore, nor of making any allowance for the strong tides, that run along this stretch of coastline. Matthew Reed had his certificate suspended for six months.

CLAREMORRIS

238nt. Steel steamship.
Built by Scott & Sons, Bowling.
Launched 1917.

Dimensions 179.6' x 28.6' x 10.9'

The *Claremorris* was employed by her owner, John Kelly of Belfast, on regular trips from Northern Ireland to south west Scotland and northern England. On the morning of Tuesday 23rd December, 1924 she was en route from Dundalk to Ardrossan when she went ashore in rough weather, a few miles south of Corsewall Point.

The *Claremorris* was jammed between two large rocks close to the shore at March Point. The lamp trimmer, James Thomson, volunteered to attempt to reach the shore and summon help. As the sea crashed on the rocks around him he scrambled down a ladder onto the rocks and headed towards safety.

SS ***Claremorris***.

Meanwhile, the continuous sounding of the ship's horn had alerted a local farmer and he, with some other local inhabitants, arrived on the scene and succeeded in getting a rope to the wreck. The crew of ten then safely struggled ashore. James Thomson's body was eventually washed ashore some days later.

The Wreck Today

The wreck of the *Claremorris* lies in Redstone Cove in position 54°56.035'N, 005°11.175'W (GPS) and can be located to the north of the prominent rocky outcrop with the aid of the photograph below. The wreck is very broken up and concreted into the surrounding rock and boulder seabed which can be covered with thick kelp during the summer months. Depths across the site range from 3 to 8 metres at high water, and parts of the wreck almost break surface at low water.

SS ***Claremorris*** ashore.

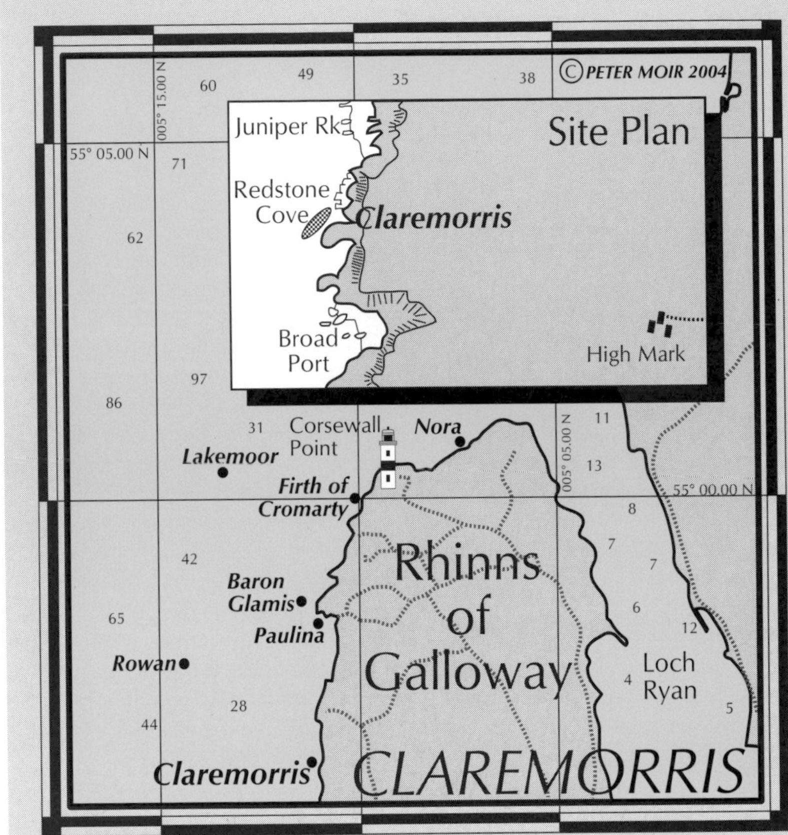

The wrecks layout is very much as the photograph suggests, with engine room and stern to the seaward and bow section in the shallows further into the small bay. The site is very exposed to the prevailing wind, tidal streams are noticeable offshore but not on the wreck itself. Like many of the wreck sites along this section of coastline the *Claremorris* is only accessible by boat and can be used as a second dive after visiting either the *Haileybury* or *Rowan* further offshore.

CRAGSMAN

68nt. Steel steamship.
Built by Irvine S B & Eng Co Ltd.
Launched 1903.

Dimensions 110.4' x 20.3' x 8.2'

The coastal steamer *Cragsman* drifted ashore and stranded on a rock called Norway Craig 700 yards north of Crammag Head around 8pm on Saturday 15th November, 1913. At the time she was on a voyage from Glasgow to

Liverpool with a cargo of granite sets for her owners J Kennedy & Sons, when she sprang a leak off Portpatrick around 6pm. The pumps were unable to cope with the steady influx of water and her boiler fire was eventually extinguished. Out of control and drifting rapidly towards the coast in stormy conditions, the eight crew decided to abandon ship and rowed south for West Tarbet Bay where they landed around 11pm.

The *Cragsman* lay partially submerged with only her bows visible at the base of the cliffs for the remainder of that month and eventually became a constructive total loss after a series of westerly gales.

The wreck of the *Cragsman* lies in position 54°40.179'N, 004°57.964'W (GPS) to the west side of a small islet which must be Norway Craig. The remains lie scattered down a shelving rock and boulder slope inhabited by many colourful crustaceans and fish. The wreck extends from about 8 metres where the bow section and winch can be found to around 14.5 metres where the remains of the boiler lie upright. A large pile of granite setts can be found in the 11.5-13 metre mark although smaller quantities are strewn all about the area. This is a very scenic dive site and with the tide running south you can drift towards Crammag Head and across the remains of the barque *Catalina* and the steamship *Mazeppa*.

CRAIGANTLET

440nt. Steel motor vessel.
Built 1972.

Dimensions 77.98m x 13.29m x 4.16m

Eleven crewmen from the Cypriot registered container ship *Craigantlet* had to be airlifted to safety when their vessel ran aground below Killantringan Lighthouse during a storm shortly before 4am on Friday 26th February, 1982. The Coastguard Centre at Ramsey, Isle of Man, coordinated the rescue and, while Portpatrick lifeboat and cliff rescue teams stood by, the crew were shuttled to safety by a Royal Navy Sea King helicopter from HMS Gannet at Prestwick.

The *Craigantlet* had left Belfast the previous evening en route to Liverpool with a containerised cargo stowed above deck and below deck level. Some of the containers held dangerous chemical waste products and the area around Portmaggie was soon cordoned off by police. As stormy conditions continued throughout the following week, most of the deck cargo was washed overboard and toxic waste from fractured containers began to contaminate the surrounding beaches. An extensive and costly clean up operation had to be mounted and the area remained closed to the public for over a month. A few local residents, including the lighthouse keepers, were evacuated until operations were completed. The lighthouse was, in the meantime, marked by an emergency beacon.

MV ***Craigantlet*** ashore below Killantringan Lighthouse.

The Wreck Today

The *Craigantlet* broke her back shortly after going ashore and with continuing bad weather and the effects of the recovery operations she eventually broke in two. Since her loss the continual pounding by storms has taken its toll on the wreck. A visit to the site in 1996 proved suprising in that only one section of the bow was breaking the surface, the remainder lay in shallow water a jumble of steel plating and deck fittings.

Today sections of the wreck still remain visible at low water, as can be seen from the photograph below. The remains of the *Craigantlet* lie in position 54°51.622'N, 005°08.796'W (GPS), in no more that 3-4 metres of water. As noted for other wrecks in the area, visibility underwater can often be virtually nil after high winds, spring tides and heavy rain, or any combination of these. The site is sheltered from the tidal movement north/south along this coast but open to the the prevailing wind and sea.

Parts of the ***Craigantlet*** still break surface in Portamaggie, south of the lighthouse. July 2003.

DAILY MAIL

42nt. Steel steamtrawler.
Launched 1930.

Dimensions 125.5' x 23.5' x 12.7'

The newly built trawler *Daily Mail* was returning to her home port of Fleetwood with a full hold of fish when she ran aground on Crammag Head. The accident happened just before midnight on Sunday 10th May, 1931 and fortunately the vessel remained fast on the rocks.

Unsure of their exact location and the extent of the damage the skipper, Albert Heywood, immediately radioed an SOS. Their call was answered by another Fleetwood trawler, the *Tranquil*, which came to her assistance and rescued the fourrteen crew from the *Daily Mail*. Before abandoning their stricken vessel the skipper went below to try and determine the full extent of any damage, and confirmed that many of the compartments were awash. The *Tranquil* stayed close by until first light, by which time the *Daily Mail* had floated off the rocks and drifted north, eventually stranding on the north shore of Barncorkie Bay (aka Portencorkie).

A salvage officer was summoned and on inspection found the vessel listing to port, and sitting on large boulders in around 3 metres, parallel to the shore. The condition of the wreck was obviously considered salvable and by the 16th May the salvage vessel *Trover* and divers were on site. Salvage work continued for the next week and the vessel was successfully moved on 22nd in prepration to repair the most damaged section of the hull , the port bilge. However, a patch of bad weather over the following week, caused further damage, to the rudder and the propshaft, the engine and boiler were also noted as being 'set up'. A further inspection on the 29th May confirmed that it was no longer economically viable to refloat the *Daily Mail* and the salvage team returned to Liverpool.

The remains of the *Daily Mail* lie in 2.5-4 metres of water on the north side of the bay, in position 54°40.609'N, 004°57.941'W (GPS). The debris lies between large rocks and boulders, little remains that is recognisable.

DUNIRA

150gt. Iron steamship.
Built by Bow McLachlan & Co Ltd, Paisley.
Launched 1901.

Dimensions 90.0' x 20.2' x 8.1'

The *Dunira* was managed by J & G Frew of Glasgow for her owners, the Home Trade Steam Carrying Co, and was under tow by the SS *Dunsmore* from Ramsey to Greenock after her engines had failed. As they approached Portpatrick the tow line snapped and the *Dunira* was swept towards the rocky coast in a freshening westerly breeze.

The crew's distress rockets were quickly answered by the Portpatrick lifeboat which succeeded in taking off two of the crew while the *Dunira* held at anchor a few hundred yards from the shore. Before the lifeboat could rescue the remaining three crewmen the anchor line parted and the *Dunira* was again swept towards the shore. Coxswain Smith succeeded in snatching the three men from the pitching, rolling ship, sustaining considerable damage to the lifeboat in the process, before the *Dunira* was finally washed ashore at South Wick Rock three quarters of a mile south of Portpatrick harbour where she became a total wreck.

Unable to regain contact with the tug, Captain Obsen decided to head south to try to reach the comparative shelter of Luce Bay. Unfortunately the conditions were more than a match for the *Eidsiva* and she was driven ashore around 5pm.

The Port Logan Rocket Brigade, who had been following the route of the barque, set up their apparatus and had a line aboard the wreck within twenty minutes of their arrival in the bay. First ashore was the mate with Captain Obsen's two year old son, closely followed by his wife and within thirty minutes all eleven aboard were safely ashore. The survivors were initially looked after by local families where they received dry clothes and food before proceeding to the Shipwrecked Mariners' Home in Drummore.

The wreck of the *Eidsiva* was eventually abandoned after being stripped of her spars, rigging, sails and fittings.

EIDSIVA

454nt. Wooden barque.
Built by R V Haeren, Drammen, Norway.
Launched 1876.

Dimensions 136.9' x 29.5' x 16.4'

The Norwegian barque *Eidsiva* was wrecked in Clanyard Bay six miles north of the Mull of Galloway on Thursday 1st March, 1894 during stormy conditions.

The barque had left Barrow the previous afternoon, under tow by the Fleetwood tug *Flyde*, bound for Ayr where she was to load a cargo of coal for the West Indies. During the height of the storm, around 4am on Thursday morning, the tow rope broke while the vessels were off Portpatrick.

The barque ***Eidsiva***.

ENDA

256nt. Iron steamship.
Built by D & W Henderson & Co, Glasgow.
Launched September 1882.
(ex BRIER ex LAIRDSOAK)

Dimensions 209.8' x 30.2' x 15.3'

SS ***Enda*** ashore near Gounie Point.

The Burns & Laird cargo passenger steamer *Enda* ran ashore near Gounie Point, south of Clanyard Bay, on Saturday 25th February, 1933. She had left Londonderry the previous afternoon, bound for Heysham, with a cargo of linen, dairy products and 150 head of livestock. While crossing the North Channel she encountered gale force winds accompanied by blinding snow and eventually ran aground around 5am.

Although distress rockets were immediately fired they failed to attract attention, and the twenty three crew members and a young mother and child climbed down onto the rocks. At daybreak some of the crew returned to the *Enda* and set off more flares. These were answered by the ICI steamer *Sodium* which had been at anchor in Clanyard Bay nearby. A lifeboat was sent inshore and picked up five of the crew and the young mother and child who were later landed at Stranraer.

Shortly after, the Drummore Lifesaving Crew arrived on the scene after struggling through deep snow. Relieved that their services were not required, they escorted the remainder of the crew back to the Shipwrecked Mariners' Home in Drummore where they received hot food and dry clothes.

An interesting aside to this story concerns the early days of marine radio communications. Ships in distress could broadcast their SOS messages on the BBC Home Service frequency and so be heard on a normal domestic radio. Such a message was transmitted from the *Enda* that morning and simply stated 'ship ashore at Port Logan - will anybody in the vicinity inform coastguard and lifeboat.' Among the listeners was the wife of coxswain of the Donaghadee lifeboat who immediately informed her husband. The lifeboat was quickly launched and battled into the easterly gale for three and a half hours across the North Channel. When the lifeboat arrived at the scene they found the *Enda* deserted, except for the livestock. They later returned to the Irish coast after receiving news that the crew were safe.

The *Enda* remained ashore for the next two weeks. A Dundee based salvage company succeeded in saving a portion of the cargo but abandoned their attempts to refloat the ship when she broke up during bad weather at the beginning of March.

The Wreck Today

The remains of the *Enda* lie in position 54°41.444'N, 004°58.263'W (GPS), close to the shore and 200 metres north east of Gounie point. The wreck can only be approached from the sea and boats can be launched at Port Logan. Tidal streams in the area can be strong even close inshore over the wreck. Good boat cover is essential.

FIRTH OF CROMARTY

1398nt. Iron barque.
Built by Russell & Co, Port Glasgow.
Launched 1888.

Dimensions 244.7' x 37.5' x 21.4'

The ***Firth of Cromarty*** ashore south of Corsewall Lighthouse.

The *Firth of Cromarty* left her home port of Glasgow on Saturday 26th August, 1898 bound for Sydney and Newcastle, New South Wales with around 2250 tons of general cargo. She was towed as far as Rothesay by the tug *Defender* where she dropped anchor around midnight. Shortly after 6am the following morning the two vessels left Rothesay and by 8pm were passing Ailsa Craig where, with a favourable wind, the barque dropped her tow and set sail.

She headed south for the Irish Sea, sighting Corsewall Lighthouse around 9pm. Two hours later she was close inshore, off Corsewall Point, with her crew on deck ready to 'wear ship' when the strong north westerly wind suddenly veered round to the south west. Her sails flapped uselessly in the wind and, as the crew struggled to regain control and steerage, her stern grounded on the rocks at Bloody Point and she held fast. The barque shuddered several times as the large breakers bounced her on the rocks before she swung round, beam on to the sea, and canted over on her starboard side. Parts of the rigging and spars rained down on the crew as they ran to find shelter from the waves breaking over the main deck. The only shelter available was the forecastle and poop decks, where the crew remained, cold and wet, throughout the night.

By daybreak the weather had greatly improved. The crew managed to launch the port lifeboat and, with ten men aboard, headed off to find help. The lifeboat, under the charge of the first mate, John McMillan, eventually landed in Loch Ryan where they were looked after by a local farmer. The remainder of the crew were rescued by Portpatrick Rocket Brigade later that morning.

The wreck was soon visited by both the Glasgow and Liverpool Salvage Associations but, owing to bad weather, they were unable to board the wreck until 31st August. They soon discovered that the *Firth of Cromarty* had become a total wreck the night of her loss when she had broken her back. In the intervening period her decks had burst open and large quantities of her gear and cargo, which included whisky, beer, iron, crockery, haberdashery and preserves, were washed ashore along the adjacent coastline. Salvage work commenced on 1st September with the arrival of the steamers *Stormlight* and *Sealight* and, over the next four weeks, a substantial portion of her cargo was saved and shipped to Glasgow. The wreck was eventually abandoned at the end of September, 1898 and soon disappeared, pounded by yet another storm on this exposed coastline.

At a subsequent enquiry her master, James Nelson, was found in default for the loss of the barque and his master's certificate was suspended for six months.

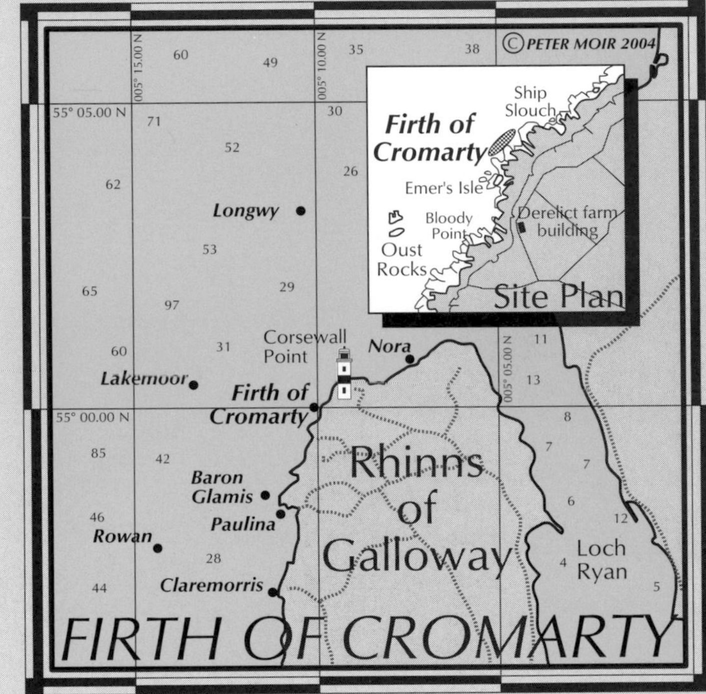

The wreck of the *Firth of Cromarty* lies in approximate position 55°00.025'N, 005°10.242'W (GPS), 500 metres north east of Oust Rocks. The remains are scattered among gullies and at the base of the rock shelf in 8 to 10 metres. Sections of hull and mast can be seen but nothing remains in any shiplike form. Parts of her cargo can be found surrounding the wreckage welded into clumps or sometimes lying loose in corners. The wreck is best approached by sea from launch sites in Loch Ryan or Dally Bay, two miles south, although launching here is across a sandy beach via a narrow winding track from the main road. Strong tidal streams can be expected in this area on spring tides.

JANE

87nt. Steel steamship.
Built by Scott & Son, Bowling.
Launched 1903.

100.4′ x 23.2′ x 10.6′

The small steam coaster *Jane* ran aground at the north end of Port Logan Bay on 15th February, 1926 during bad weather. She had been en route from Liverpool to Glasgow at the time for her owners Monroe Shipping.

Although damaged during the stranding, she was refloated a month later and returned to her coasting trade.

HAILEYBURY

1809nt. Steel steamship.
Built by Wm. Pickersgill & Son, Sunderland.
Launched 1902.

Dimensions 324.0′ x 47.1′ x 21.7′

The London registered steamship *Haileybury* sank off the Galloway Coast on 22nd February, 1918 after being torpedoed by the German submarine *U-91*. The vessel took many hours to sink, which allowed the crew plenty of time to abandon ship, unfortunately the master and one crew member were killed as a result of the attack.

U-91 made here escape and went on to sink a total of 40 ships with a recorded tonnage of 96,250. The submarine was later broken up in France in July 1921.

The wreck of the *Haileybury* lies approximately 5 miles south west of Corsewall Lighthouse, in position 54°55.183'N, 005°16.041'W (GPS). General seabed depths around the wreck are 44 metres with shallowest depth on the wreck of 34 metres. The hull is oriented 080/260 degrees with stern towards the Galloway coast.

One of the most striking features of this wreck is the prominent sterncastle, with gun still in place, pointing towards the shore. The gun and counter stern section is a blaze of colour with anenomes and soft corals, of special not are the crimson jewel anenomes which have colonised the gun and pedestal. The wreck is substantial in size, and will take at least a full dive to explore. The *Haileybury* was the sistership of the *Esbo,* which lies approximately 16 miles to the north off Bennane Head, a picture can be found on page 135.

A word of caution, the wreck is swept by strong tides on both ebb and flood and can only be dived at slack water, while this should be checked locally the authors have found this to be around 1.5 hours before HW/LW Greenock. This will vary on phase of tide as will period of slack water.

JOHN SLATER

176nt. Wooden brigantine.
Built by Bartram & Co, Sunderland.
Launched April 1862.

Dimensions 97.0' x 23.0' x 12.8'

The gallant rescue of the crew of the *John Slater* illustrates well the lengths that men will go to to save the lives of their fellow mariners in distress.

On Thursday 16th December, 1873 the steamer *Garland* left Stranraer around 11am for the Irish coast. As she headed west into rough seas off Corsewall Point, a dismasted sailing vessel was sighted ahead flying distress signals. Captain Campbell immediately headed the *Garland* for the vessel which turned out to be the Barrow brigantine *John Slater* with seven men aboard. Due to the weather conditions, attempts to pass a line aboard the *John Slater* were unsuccessful forcing Captain Campbell to ask for volunteers to row across with the rope. Five men immediately agreed to try and, after nearly capsizing on two occasions, managed to get the tow rope aboard the *John Slater*. As soon as the men were back on board the *Garland*, the slack was taken up and the two vessels headed for Loch Ryan. They had not travelled far when the tow rope, stretched and strained by the heaving of the two ships in the swell, snapped with a loud crack leaving the *John Slater*, once again, helpless and wallowing and drifting towards the shore. For the next two hours the crew of the *Garland* repeatedly tried to get another rope aboard the *John Slater* but without success.

Meanwhile, the vessels drifted ever closer to the rocks at Milleur Point and finally Captain Campbell shouted for the crew of the *John Slater* to abandon ship. Four men immediately left the *John Slater* in a small boat and were picked up by the *Garland* just before their boat was smashed to pieces against the side of the steamer. When no more than 500 yards offshore, the *Garland's* lifeboat again set off for the *John Slater* and the remaining crew were rescued only minutes before she ran ashore. Almost immediately the brigantine started to break up.

The ordeal was not yet over for the men in the lifeboat. Seeing that they were not making any headway offshore, Captain Campbell took the *Garland* close inshore and positioned her up wind of the lifeboat. This provided some shelter till they rounded Milleur Point and entered the calmer waters of Loch Ryan. The men in the lifeboat were then taken on board the *Garland* which returned to Stranraer, where they were looked after at the local Mariner's Home.

KERRERA

85gt. Iron steamship.
Built by J & J Hay, Kirkintilloch.
Launched 1894.

Dimensions 65.8' x 17.9' x 8.4'

The *Kerrera*, a typical Clyde puffer was lost off the Galloway coast on Sunday 27th October, 1935. She had been enroute to Glasgow with a cargo of cement in bags, when she hit bad weather off Crammag Head and sank as a result of engine failure and having shipped a large amount of water. Fortunately the crew were rescued by a passing trawler, and landed safely ashore.

The wreck of the *Kerrera* lies in position 54°38.142'N, 004°57.587'W (GPS), and is clearly identifiable by the 2 metre high mass of bag shaped cement blocks, neatly stacked in the hold. The wreck lies generally north/south on a rock and stone seabed in depths of 51-52 metres. The stern section of the wreck which lies to the north is most intact and rises approximately 4 metres off the seabed, the engine, boiler and propellor are still in place.

This dive is only for the most experienced, backed up by reliable boat cover and all divers must carry delayed surface marker buoys. The slack water window on this wreck is very short and the tidal flow picks up extremely quickly to a rate where you can neither swim or even haul yourself into the tide. This coupled with the exposed nature of the site make this wreck potentially hazardous for the inexperienced and perhaps the experienced alike!

LAIRDSBANK

316nt. Steel steamship.
Built by Harland & Wolff Ltd, Belfast.
Launched 1936.

229.0′ x 37.2′ x 11.5′

The Burns and Laird steamer *Lairdsbank* had a lucky escape when she ran aground on the Galloway coast on Tuesday 6th April, 1937.

She had been enroute from Londonderry to Heysham with a cargo of livestock when she encountered thick fog in the North Channel. Her speed was immediately reduced as she inched through the inky darkness of early morning but eventually ran ashore on Laggantalluch Head.

Help was immediately requested and a tug, the *Flying Falcon* was sent from Greenock and succeeded in pulling her off on high water, some 18 hours after her accident. Fortunately the sea conditions were calm at the time or she may well have joined other members of the Burns fleet lost along this coastline. Most notable of these was the *Lairdsmoor*, which sank after a collision with the motorship *Taranaki* off Portpatrick two days later.

LAIRDSELM

280nt. Steel steamship.
Built by A & J Inglis Ltd, Glasgow.
Launched 1911.
(ex SABLE)

Dimensions 195.2' x 31.1' x 13.0'

The Glasgow steamer *Lairdselm*, owned by the Burns & Laird Line, sank near the mouth of Loch Ryan on Sunday 22nd December, 1929.

She had sailed from Glasgow the previous day around 5pm with a cargo of 200 tons of diesel engine sections for Messrs Harland & Wolff of Belfast. As she headed south, the captain had problems with the trim of his vessel when the cargo began to shift and he decided to head for Loch Ryan. The *Lairdselm* arrived in Loch Ryan around 2am and anchored off the south end of Finnarts Bay. Precisely what happened during the night is not known but, around 9:30am the next morning, the crew were roused by cries of 'All hands on deck - take to the boats'. They quickly abandoned ship and rowed south for Cairnryan Lighthouse where they were helped ashore and provided with food by the local inhabitants.

SS ***Lairdselm***.

The *Lairdselm* had developed a discernible list while at anchor which increased steadily until she finally heeled over and sank shortly after the crew had abandoned ship. The wreck lay close to the main shipping fairway in six fathoms and, as she only just broke the surface at low water, a buoy was positioned over the wreck by the Northern Lighthouse Board's steamer *Hesperus* the following day.

The authors have been unable to establish the exact fate of the *Lairdselm* apart from the fact that she was written off as a total loss and that a salvage contract was placed with Mr James Gush of Greenock in February 1930 for the removal of the wreck. However it is thought that, after a certain amount of salvage of both the wreck and her cargo, the remainder was dispersed. Although not positively identified as such, the authors are of the opinion that the foul ground noted by the Admiralty in position 55°00.300'N, 005°03.600'W marks the remains of the *Lairdselm* as it cross refers exactly with the reported position of her sinking.

LAIRDSMOOR

668nt. Steel steamship.
Built by A & J Inglis Ltd, Glasgow.
Launched 1919.
(ex MOORFOWL)

Dimensions 265.0' x 36.1' x 15.9'

The *Lairdsmoor* was owned by the Burns & Laird Line and was en route from Dublin to Greenock on 7th April, 1937. Aboard were thirty three crew and six passengers and she was carrying a general cargo.

Around 3:20am the *Lairdsmoor* came into collision with the MV *Taranaki* in dense fog, a few miles west of Black Head. The *Lairdsmoor* was badly holed in the collision and immediately began to sink. Assistance was called for and the Donaghadee lifeboat was launched within 8 minutes of the call. The *Lairdsmoor* had been mortally damaged in the collision and was slowly sinking. Maroons were fired and all the passengers and crew transfered to the *Taranaki* which was also severely damaged but remaining afloat. The master of the *Lairdsmoor,* Captain John Campbell stayed aboard until the last passenger was safely transferred. Tragically he was lost when the *Lairdsmoor* sank along with a fireman Mr Richard McBride.

SS ***Lairdsmoor***.

The *Lairdsmoor* sank approximately 5 miles west of Black Head and may well be the wreck charted in position 54°51.748'N, 005°21.869'W.

LIVERPOOL

1455gt. Iron barque.
Built in Quebec.
Launched 1855.

Dimensions 217.7' x 40.1' x 22.9'

The *Liverpool* was owned by John Hall of Newcastle and had sailed for Quebec from Sunderland on 24th August, 1883 with a cargo of coal. Her return journey to Greenock, with a cargo of timber, was uneventful for her twenty one crew until they reached the Clyde on the evening of 11th December.

Around 8pm the winds increased to gale force and Captain Davidson ordered sails set to race for shelter in Loch Ryan. Before long, mountainous seas were breaking over his vessel carrying away companionways, the binnacle and most of her loose deck fittings. Her fate was sealed when her rudder chains broke leaving her helpless to be driven towards the rocky coast. Despite attempts to save her by casting her anchors, the *Liverpool* was dashed against the shore at Garry Point in Loch Ryan and quickly smashed to pieces. Nineteen of the crew were lost.

The wreck of the *Liverpool* was sold for £800 in May 1884 and subsequently extensively salvaged.

MARQUIS OF ABERCORN

100gt. Iron paddlesteamer.
Launched 1862.
(ex GREAT NORTHERN)

The *Marquis of Abercorn* was owned by Lewis Potter and was employed on the Glasgow/Dublin route. In the early hours of the morning of Tuesday 18th May, 1869 she sank after a collision with the steamer *Lord Gough*, also owned by Lewis Potter and Company. Her crew and passengers were rescued by the *Lord Gough* but the *Marquis of Abercorn* sank around forty five minutes after the collision with the loss of her valuable cargo and two hundred cattle.

The reason why the collision took place on a clear night in calm weather eight miles west of Portpatrick remains uncertain. The testimony of the passengers only relates that they were awakened by the crash as the bow of the *Lord Gough* struck the *Marquis of Abercorn* at her port gangway. She immediately began to sink by the bow but, despite the panic of the passengers, the crew managed to safely launch two of the ship's lifeboats. By the time the passengers and the crew were aboard the lifeboats the bow of the *Marquis of Abercorn* was submerged and, soon after they boarded the *Lord Gough*, her stern lifted high into the air and she slipped beneath the surface with a loud explosion.

MEXICO

642gt. Wooden brig.
Built in Stockholm, Sweden.
Launched 1865.

Dimensions 143.2' x 31.8' x 18.5'

As is the case in many of these incidents, the wreck of the brig *Mexico*, in Knock Bay, Galloway on 12th February, 1894 showed the courage and determination of the rescue services in saving the unfortunate victims of disaster at sea.

The *Mexico* was bound for Kristiansen, Norway from Ardrossan with a cargo of coal. Captain Neilson and his ten crewmen had battled the elements for many days before she was finally driven ashore. The rocket brigade had been alerted by the *Mexico's* distress rockets as she was swept northwards, out of control, past the entrance to Portpatrick Harbour. The lifeboat was also launched, but huge seas made it impossible for her to leave the harbour. Meanwhile the rocket brigade crew fought their way through driving snow and sleet to find the *Mexico* aground, some distance from the shore, in Knock Bay.

As they reached the shoreline wreckage was already washing ashore from the wreck which, by now, had lost all of her masts, rigging and sails and it was clear that time was running out for a rescue. They quickly set up their gear in the spray at the water's edge and fired a series of rockets towards the *Mexico*. The fifth shot found its target and soon the exhausted crew were being pulled to safety. All the crew were safely brought to shore although one died of natural causes later that day.

NORA

89nt. Steel steamship.
Built by Scott & Sons, Bowling.
Launched 1907.

Dimensions 100.2' x 23.1' x 10.7'

The *Nora*, a small rear engined coastal steamer owned by Kyle Shipping Company, stranded at Caspin one and a half miles east of Corsewall Lighthouse around 2pm on Wednesday 23rd November, 1938.

She had left Girvan in ballast at 10pm the previous evening bound for Creetown where she was to load a cargo of granite sets. As she headed south she encountered heavy rain and poor visibility off Corsewall Point and eventually ran aground, ripping a large hole in her hull. The sea at the time was calm with an offshore wind so Captain Soutar and his crew remained aboard with the intention of trying to refloat her. However the *Nora* was hard aground and, with a falling tide, resisted all attempts to move her off the rocks.

Around 4am they set off distress rockets which were seen by the lighthouse keeper at Corsewall who notified Portpatrick Coastguard. The Portpatrick lifeboat and Rocket Brigade were quickly mustered and set off for the wreck, the rocket crew arriving at 6am, closely followed by the lifeboat.

The *Nora* was well up on the rocks and the Coastguards were able to board her by ladder. They were met by the *Nora's* captain and informed that the crew were still attempting to refloat the vessel but were having little success.

The weather meanwhile was deteriorating. The wind swung round to the west and increased exposing the *Nora* to a heavy swell. Shortly after 10am the lifeboat moved inshore and took off four of the crew members as waves were beginning to break over the wreck. The lifeboat made one final attempt to refloat the *Nora* but she remained hard aground. With worsening weather conditions the lifeboat headed back for Portpatrick where she arrived at 1:30pm. The *Nora's* crew were provided with a hot meal in the Devonshire Arms Hotel, courtesy of the Shipwrecked Mariners' Aid Society. The *Nora* became a total wreck later that day as a result of the bad weather and later broke up. The remains of the *Nora* lie close inshore in position 55°00.869'N, 005°07.274'W (GPS), and consist of sections of metal and hull scattered among rocks in shallow water no deeper than 5 metres.

SS *Nora*.

PS *Orion*.

ORION

899gt. Iron paddlesteamer.
Built by Caird & Co, Greenock.
Launched December 1846.

Dimensions 210.0' x 27.1' x 18.0'

In January 1839 the outer lighthouse on the South Pier at Portpatrick was damaged in a storm and it was decided that, as the inner light was still in operation and clearly visible from the sea, the outer light should not be repaired. The decision seemed perfectly reasonable at the time but nobody could have anticipated its tragic consequences.

Eleven years later, on 17th June, 1850 the J & G Burns steamer *Orion* left Liverpool for Glasgow on a calm, clear sunny afternoon under the command of Captain Henderson. She was fully laden and most of her one hundred and ten passengers strolled around the decks or chatted cheerfully in the sunshine as she moved out into the Mersey and reached full steaming speed. By the early hours of the following morning most of her passengers were below decks asleep as she reached the Scottish coast. Captain Henderson slowed his ship, carefully feeling his way through a thick sea mist which had reduced visibility to less than two hundred yards. He spotted Portpatrick Light off his starboard bow but wrongly identified it as the damaged outer light. It was in fact the inner light.

This error resulted in the *Orion* steaming much closer to the shore than the captain had intended. She struck a submerged rock just north of the entrance to Portpatrick harbour and began to sink immediately. The rock had torn a hole in the ship's watertight compartments and smashed a bulkhead - she was doomed.

The passengers who had been asleep in their cabins as the *Orion* struck rushed, panic stricken, onto the decks of the sinking ship, most still in their nightclothes, and screamed for help into the darkness. Three of the ship's lifeboats were launched but before the first one could leave for the shore it was swamped by the rush of more than twenty desperate passengers. The boat overturned plunging the occupants into the sea leaving the horrified people aboard the *Orion* to watch helplessly as they all gradually sank beneath the dark surface and drowned. The other two boats managed to take ten people each safely to the shore. There was much controversy later as it seems that most of her crew and even the captain himself did little to help the evacuation of the passengers preferring instead to try to save their own lives. Meanwhile, a number of boats had been launched from the shore and were heading for the *Orion* to assist in the rescue. The confusion aboard ship was compounded further when the rising seawater reached the boilers and a huge explosion ripped through the dying ship.

Tragically, before the rescuers could reach the wreck, the *Orion* lurched to starboard, flinging many of the passengers on deck into the sea, and then quickly sank by the bow. The suction of the huge ship sinking beneath the waves pulled down many of the people struggling in the sea and huge rolling waves swamped many more. The boats from Portpatrick picked their way between the wreckage and the floating bodies to save as many of the passengers and crew as they could. Some of the survivors managed to swim the short distance to the shore where they were greeted by the many locals who had gathered to assist. The exact death toll was never established but it is certain that at least sixty people lost their lives in one of the worst accidents to occur in the long history of Clyde shipping. The wreck, which lay in around forty feet of water, was sold at auction, as she lay, on 24th July, 1850 to be followed by the sale of her fittings, including her bell and ship's furniture, on the 26th. She was extensively salvaged over the ensuing months and years.

The wreck of the *Orion* is reported to be 80 metres north west of the west end of Portpatrick's north pier in approximate position 54°50.566'N, 005°07.482'W. The depth is around 10 metres. The wreckage here is very broken with only a few girders to be found. There have been a number of wrecks in this area over the years so it is impossible to be certain that the wreckage in this position is the *Orion*.

OSWALD

1157nt. Iron steamship.
Built by Turnbull & Son, Whitby.
Launched 1890.

Dimensions 258.5' x 37.2' x 18.1'

Throughout the history of Clyde navigation few storms have been more destructive than the hurricane which swept across southern Scotland during the early hours of Saturday 22nd December, 1894. Many vessels were wrecked along the Clyde coast with eleven being recorded in the Galloway region alone.

The most disastrous casualty to occur along this stretch of coastline was the loss of the Whitby registered steamer *Oswald*, with her crew of nineteen, while on a voyage from Londonderry to Cardiff. The *Oswald* was driven ashore sometime after midnight on 22nd December and, due to the intensity of the storm, only part of her boiler remained above water level when the wreck was discovered near Port Gill around 9am the next morning. The surrounding coastline was strewn with debris and it was not until pieces of wreckage were found bearing her name that the identity of the lost ship was established.

Her loss was the subject of a Board of Trade enquiry which concluded that, as she was travelling in ballast, her draught was substantially reduced and as a result her propeller and rudder would have had little effect in the prevailing weather conditions and, as such, she would have been totally out of control.

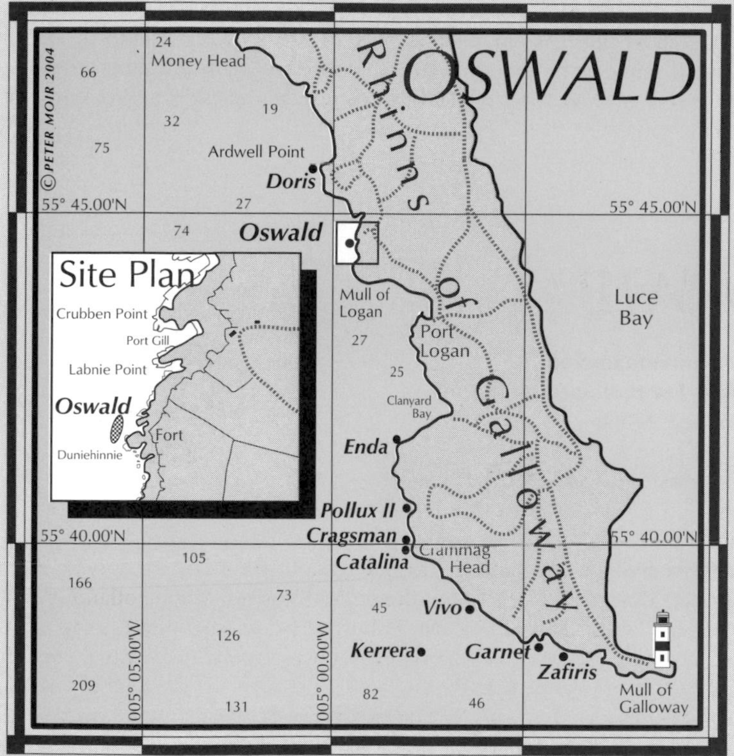

The remains of the *Oswald* are reported to lie in shallow water south of Port Gill in approximate position 54°44.500'N, 004°59.483'W (GPS). Boats can be launched at Port Logan 1 1/2 miles south of the site. However, it should be noted that overfalls and strong tidal streams can occur at certain states of the tide off Logan Head.

PAULINA

1387nt. Steel steamship.
Built by Sir Raylton Dixon & Co Ltd, Middlesborough.
Launched June 1909.

Dimensions 293.0' x 47.2' x 20.0'

One of the largest vessels to be lost on the Galloway coast was the Spanish steamer *Paulina* while on a voyage from Santander to Troon with a cargo of iron ore.

Shortly before midnight on 10th February, 1913, as she neared the Scottish coast, she ran into dense fog off Black Head and Corsewall Light, her main navigational fix. She continued north sounding her siren but ran ashore at the north end of Dally Bay around 12:30am the following morning. The twenty seven crew aboard left the stranded vessel around 2am in two lifeboats, one commanded by the first mate, the other by the master of the *Paulina*, Captain Rosales. The mate's lifeboat reached the shore around 7am, as daylight broke, and the thirteen men aboard landed at Dally Bay. The captain's lifeboat drifted for eight hours before they were picked up by the Glasgow bound steamer *Cairo*.

SS ***Paulina*** ashore in Dally Bay.

Regular reports were received by Lloyds of London during the following week from their agent in Stranraer, noting a gradual deterioration in the condition of the wreck. By 22nd February the agent's telegram reported substantial buckling and corrugation of her hull with the bow section listing slightly to starboard. Here the reports end and it can only be surmised that she was abandoned as a total wreck. However, it would seem reasonable to suggest that a wreck of this size would have been salvaged in some form at a later date.

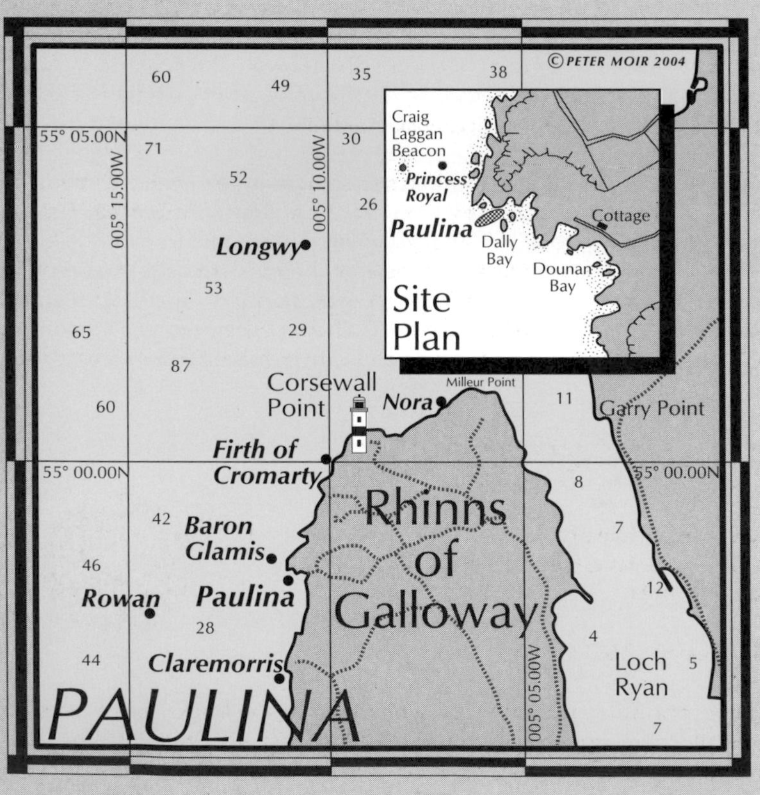

The Wreck Today

The remains of the *Paulina* lie south west of the north point of Dally Bay between 8 and 14 metres in position 54°58.436'N, 005°11.134'W (GPS). The wreckage is visible, close to the rocky shore, above the surface at certain states of the tide. It is heavily broken as would be expected in this exposed location and is scattered among rocks and sand along the north shore of the bay. The main items of interest are the engine and boilers which stand proud of the seabed. Boats can be launched in Dally Bay however the track down to the shore is very narrow with frequent bends and launching is across sand.

PIRATE

69nt. Iron steamship.
Built by Scott & Sons, Bowling.
Launched 1884.

Dimensions 130.0' x 21.1' x 9.9'

The small cargo passenger steamer *Pirate* was purchased by the Argyll & Wigtown Steamship Company in 1893 to replace the SS *Argyll* which had been wrecked on Milleur Point in September, 1893.

On Friday 6th August, 1909 the *Pirate* anchored off the Scar in Loch Ryan, waiting for thick fog to clear. Around mid morning the steamer *Princess Maud*, of the Larne and Stranraer Steamship Joint Committee, left the Railway Pier in Stranraer for the Irish coast. As she headed up Loch Ryan the poor visibility obscured the *Pirate*, which had unwisely been anchored in the main fairway, and, as a result, the *Princess Maud* ran directly into the *Pirate*, leaving a large hole on the starboard bow of the stationary vessel. The four passengers and crew were immediately transferred to the *Princess Maud*, as the *Pirate* rapidly began to sink, and were later landed at Stranraer.

SS **Pirate** sunk in Loch Ryan.

The *Pirate* had sunk, bow first, in four fathoms although her stern remained afloat at certain stages of the tide. Captain Burns of the Glasgow Salvage Association visited the wreck on 10th August and took charge of the salvage operation. The steamlighters *Starlight* and *Sealight* soon arrived from Greenock with salvage equipment and work was completed three days later when the *Pirate* was successfully raised and beached at Stranraer. After temporary repairs she left for Glasgow, under her own steam, on 19th August, returning to service in September.

As an interesting footnote, the *Pirate*, having escaped destruction in this incident, was finally totally lost in October 1913 when she ran aground in fog on the Kintyre coast.

POLLUX II

526 nt. Steel steamship.
Built by Howaldstwerke, Keil, Germany.
Launched 1890.

Dimensions 205.8' x 30.7' x 13.8'

The *Pollux II* was an Estonian registered cargo ship which was on charter to the Ministry of War. On Boxing Day, 1942 she was inward bound from Newport, USA to Londonderry with a cargo of 375 tons of tobacco, medical supplies and metal when she caught fire off the Mull of Galloway. The crew were forced to abandon ship and, out of control, *Pollux II* drifted ashore on the south side of Portencorkie Bay, south of Laggantalluch Head.

She was still burning fiercely when she came ashore but the inflow of water gradually extinguished the flames leaving a blackened hulk stranded on the rocks. The wreck quickly became the centre of intense activity as the local population took the opportunity to supplement their wartime rations. The wreck, which lies close to the shore in a general depth of 5 metres in position 54°40.450'N, 004°58.110'W (GPS), was salvaged in the 1960's but some wreckage is still visible including some non ferrous bits and pieces remaining from her cargo.

PRINCESS ROYAL

447gt. Iron paddlesteamer.
Built by Tod & McGregor, Partick, Glasgow.
Launched 1841.

Dimensions 195' x 28' x 17'

The *Princess Royal* ran aground in fog on Craig Laggan Rocks, two miles south of Corsewall Point around 3:30am on Wednesday 28th May, 1856. The 120 passengers and her crew, who were travelling to Greenock, were safely landed on a beach under the supervision of her master, Captain McChlery.

PS ***Princess Royal*** on the Ebbstone Reef.

The survivors did not have to wait long to be rescued as a passing steamer, the *Herald*, en route to Greenock, came inshore and took them on board.

The *Princess Royal* had recently undergone a complete refit, including the installation of a new boiler, at a cost of £6,000. Her owners were therefore anxious to get salvage operations underway as soon as possible, while the weather remained favourable. A salvage team left Greenock later the same day and subsequently succeeded in removing most of her valuable general cargo which was landed at Stranraer. Efforts to refloat the *Princess Royal* herself were less successful. Her hull was badly damaged and, during bad weather the following week, she broke in two and became a total wreck.

The remains of the *Princess Royal*, which include parts of the paddle box frames, are reported to lie on the east side of Craig Laggan Rocks (Ebbstone) in approximate position 54°58.517'N, 005°11.283'W (GPS), between 4 and 10 metres. The rocks are marked by a prominent cylindrical concrete beacon to the north of Dally Bay, where small boats can be launched across a sandy beach. Good boat cover is essential around this area due to strong tidal streams around the rocks.

ROSENEATH

735nt. Iron barque.
Built in Glasgow.
Launched 1857.

Dimensions 187.0' x 31.7' x 19.3'

Six lives were lost when the *Roseneath* ran ashore 400 yards south of Portpatrick harbour on Saturday 2nd February, 1889.

The *Roseneath*, which was loaded with 150 tons of rubbish ballast, had left Dublin for Glasgow the previous morning under tow of the Greenock tug *Defiance*. Around 2am on Saturday morning the two vessels encountered bad weather off the Copeland Islands which resulted in the tug's towing eye giving way. Strenuous efforts were made by the crew of the *Defiance* to get a line aboard the *Roseneath* but, due to the weather conditions and the darkness, they were unsuccessful.

As daylight broke it soon became clear to Captain Robert Browne of the *Roseneath* that his vessel was being rapidly driven towards the Galloway coast. Due to the hurricane force winds he was unable to set any sail and his vessel was out of control. In desperation he decided to head for the narrow entrance to Portpatrick harbour where, at worst, he could run the barque ashore in relative shelter. His plan nearly worked - had it not been for a series of squalls which lashed the *Roseneath* within a mile of the coast and pushed her south of the harbour entrance. Unable to head upwind she was eventually driven ashore around 8:30am north of Castle Point. As the *Roseneath* heeled over onto her side exposing her deck to the full force of the sea, the eleven people aboard struggled to climb into the rigging. However, six people including the mate, his wife and child, were washed overboard and drowned. The remainder of the crew were rescued by the Portpatrick Rocket Brigade.

The *Roseneath* eventually broke up later that day and became a total wreck.

ROWAN

1493gt. Steel steamship.
Built by D & W Henderson & Co Ltd, Glasgow.
Launched 1909.

Dimensions 280.8' x 38.1' x 16.5'

The audience at the Lyric Theatre, Glasgow on the afternoon of 8th October, 1921 could not have imagined the catastrophic effect of their cries for an encore by the Southern Syncopated Orchestra. The resultant delay to the departure of the orchestra set in motion a series of events which was to lead to the tragic sinking of the Laird Lines steamer *Rowan* in the early hours of the following morning in one of the most unusual incidents in the history of Clyde shipping.

The orchestra had booked passage on the *Rowan* to Dublin for their next engagement and were due to meet the ship at Greenock that evening. If Captain Brown on the *Rowan* had not chosen to wait for almost an hour to meet the orchestra from the train at Greenock his ship would have passed the place of its fatal collision without incident. The *Rowan* finally left Greenock at around 7pm on Saturday 8th October and sailed south towards Ailsa Craig and Galloway.

Five hours later, after an uneventful voyage down the Firth, she reached the Galloway coast where the visibility was dramatically reduced by banks of thick fog rolling across the North Channel. Captain Brown slowed the *Rowan* to around half her normal steaming speed and continued southwards on his journey. At about 12:10am the American steamer *West Camak* suddenly appeared out of the fog and, despite efforts by both captains, collided with the stern of the *Rowan*. Although damage to the *Rowan* was not severe Captain Brown ordered all the passengers on deck and the ship's lifesaving equipment made ready. This precaution was to save many lives.

Just as the passengers were beginning to recover from the collision with the *West Camak* the SS *Clan Malcolm*, en route from Glasgow to Birkenhead, appeared and crashed into the *Rowan* on her starboard side amidships, almost cutting her in two. The passengers and crew were sent sprawling across the decks and many were thrown overboard into the sea. The *Rowan* sank almost immediately leaving the *West Camak*, the *Clan Malcolm* and the destroyer HMS *Wrestler*, which had answered the *West Camak's* distress call, to rescue around one hundred passengers and crew.

Despite the darkness, poor visibility and rough seas, they were successful in picking up seventy seven cold and frightened survivors who had been clinging to liferafts or wreckage from the *Rowan*. Almost all of them had been wearing lifebelts or lifejackets at the time of the second collision and it is certain that, if Captain Brown had not been so cautious, more lives would have been lost. As it was, around twenty people, including the captain himself, lost their lives in the disaster. Many of the survivors were landed a few hours later at Princes Pier, Greenock where large crowds had gathered to hear the story of this strange, double collision and listen to the terrifying experience of the survivors.

The Wreck Today

The wreck of the *Rowan* lies approximately 2 miles offshore from Dally Bay in position 54°57.912'N, 005°14.411'W (GPS). Seabed depth in the area is approximately 49 metres with a least depth over the wreck of 42 metres. Strong tides run up and down this section of coastline which are accentuated over wrecks like the *Rowan* sitting upright on the seabed. In short, this is a slack water dive and only for the experienced diver.

SAXON KING

453gt. Wooden barque.
Built in Sunderland.
Launched 1854.

The long voyage from Samarang in Java to Cork had been difficult for Captain Deans of the *Saxon King* but the final leg of his journey to Port Glasgow with his cargo of sugar was to prove disastrous. Soon after leaving Cork a bitter dispute, between himself and the mate, resulted in the mate refusing to carry out any further duties. Captain Deans was left as the only officer aboard capable of keeping watch.

He had been on watch for twenty six hours, without a break, when his ship ran aground on the South Reef Rock near Belfast Lough. Although the *Saxon King* was refloated by throwing a portion of her cargo overboard, she was seriously damaged with her hull leaking and waterlogged. Captain Deans' bad luck continued as his vessel was battered by a gale as he sailed across the North Channel and by the time he reached the Galloway coast most of his sails had been torn to shreds.

On the evening of Tuesday 11th January, 1859 he anchored north of Corsewall Point near the entrance to Loch Ryan, to avoid his vessel being swept ashore. The crew immediately abandoned ship leaving only the captain and two fishermen aboard.

The next morning the steamer *Albion*, on her regular trip from Stranraer to Glasgow, came alongside and offered assistance. A plan to take the *Saxon King* in tow was abandoned after attempts to raise her anchor failed so the *Albion* continued on its journey leaving Captain Deans on the *Saxon King* to await the arrival of two tugs which, by this time, were on their way to the scene. Unfortunately, before they arrived the *Saxon King* sank in a reported depth of nine fathoms. At the subsequent enquiry Captain Deans' master certificate was suspended for three months.

STRATHSPEY

992nt. Iron steamship.
Built by Burrell & Son, Dumbarton.
Launched 1883.
(ex DEAK)

Dimensions 240.0' x 34.1' x 22.6'

The *Strathspey* left Ghent for Glasgow on 28th November, 1894 in ballast. She was commanded by Captain Daniel Dunn and had a crew of twenty one aboard. By the evening of 2nd December she had steamed northwards, through the Irish Sea, and was approaching the Galloway coast.

As darkness fell, the visibility was seriously reduced as the *Strathspey* was enveloped in a dense fog, making navigation extremely difficult. Captain Dunn, an experienced skipper, was not alarmed by their situation but, nonetheless, ordered a depth sounding to be made. The nervous crew were relieved to learn that the depth was seventy eight fathoms.

They continued north at normal steaming speed and, although the captain posted a lookout at the bow, the crew returned to their normal duties. An hour later another sounding was taken showing that the depth had decreased to twenty five fathoms but the captain maintained his speed, anxious to make good time for his voyage.

At around 7:30pm the Portpatrick Light was sighted on their starboard beam. Inexplicably, the captain took no further soundings and continued his course northwards. He made two small adjustments to this course before running aground on the offshore rocks in Saltpan Bay, north of Portpatrick, just after 8pm. Despite efforts to pull themselves off by reversing engines, the *Strathspey* was stuck fast and soon the water rushing in through a hole in her hull, extinguished the boiler fires.

The crew fired distress rockets but these were not spotted due to the density of the fog and help did not arrive until next morning. However, the crew were in no danger as the weather was very calm and the Portpatrick Lifeboat took them off safely the next day. At first it was hoped that the *Strathspey* could be refloated, but she was eventually sold as scrap to a Mr Garscadden of Glasgow for £93.11s.

There is an interesting postscript to the story of the *Strathspey* when, on 22nd December, the SS *Seamew* arrived at Portpatrick to begin the salvage work. The *Seamew* was wrecked in Portpatrick harbour in the hurricane which swept the Scottish coast that night. The *Strathspey* was smashed to pieces in the same violent storm.

The Wreck Today

The wreck lies in shallow water in Saltpan Bay approximately 150 metres from the shore. She lies in around 4 to 5 metres of water and is in two major pieces although wreckage is spread over a considerable area. The site is very exposed to the prevailing south west winds.

THE PRINCE

142nt. Iron steamship.
Built by J Fullerton & Co, Paisley.
Launched 1890.

Dimensions: 142.0′ x 25.1′ x10.8′

The Prince being dismantled at South Cairn.

The Glasgow registered steamer *The Prince*, owned by Messrs. J & J Hay, was another casualty of the great storm of December 1894. The small steamship stranded at South Cairn, about a mile and a half south of Corsewall Lighthouse on 22nd December with the loss of 2 of her 11 crew.

The Prince had been en route to North Wales from Sligo in ballast but became unmanageable in the atrocious weather conditions. Fortunately the vessel was pushed high on the rocks when she stranded, and as the tide ebbed, the crew were able to reach the safety of dry land.

The wreck was later sold at auction in 1895 and as can be seen from the photographs, was dismantled in-situ.

TYRCONNEL

74nt. Steel steamship.
Built by J Fullerton & Co, Paisley.
Launched March 1892.

Dimensions 130.2″ x 22.1″ x 9.6′

SS *Tyrconnel* ashore in Ward Bay, Portpatrick.

Another casualty of the great storm of 22nd December, 1894 was the Belfast owned coaster *Tyrconnel*. She had left Dundalk the previous evening en route to Belfast with 135 tons of general cargo, and although the weather at the time was noted as boisterous, her skipper, Captain Rogers decided to make passage and hug the north east coastline for shelter.

Just after midnight the wind increased to hurricane force and the small steamer was pushed further offshore and eventually had to run with the mountainous seas towards the Galloway coast. Out of control she was eventually driven ashore in Ward Bay, just north of the harbour entrance at Portpatrick.

As can be seen from the photograph, the *Tyrconnel* stranded well up the beach, this and the quick action of the local rocket brigade enabled all the crew to get ashore safely, but no doubt soaked to the skin.

The *Tyrconnel* was eventually refloated in April 1895, after surviving a number of storms during her short stay ashore. Other vessels lost in the storm along this section of coastline such as the *Oswald*, *Seamew* and *The Prince* were less fortunate, and all became total wrecks.

WICKLOW II

524nt. Iron steamship.
Built by R Steele & Co, Greenock.
Launched January 1882.

Dimensions 225.4' x 31.1' x 15.4'

The cargo passenger steamer *Wicklow II*, owned by the Clyde Shipping Company, was lost in collision with the steamer *Amphion* off Corsewall Point on Friday 27th March, 1885 while on a voyage from Glasgow to Waterford and Southampton.

The *Wicklow II* was badly holed on her starboard side amidships and immediately began to sink. The forty one passengers and crew abandoned ship in four lifeboats and were later rescued by the Glasgow bound Burns steamer *Bear*. The *Wicklow II* remained afloat for three hours before she eventually sank approximately seven miles south west of Corsewall Point.

The *Amphion*, the other vessel involved, immediately returned to Stranraer where she was beached with her bow hold full of water. She was soon repaired and returned to her usual run between Stranraer and the Irish coast.

Coastguards rescue survivors from the ***Zafiris***.

SS ***Zafiris*** ashore on Old Mill Head.

ZAFARIS

3000gt. Greek motor vessel.
Built 1945

The *Zafaris* was wrecked on Old Mill Point approximately one and a half miles west north west of the Mull of Galloway around 5am on Friday 17th December, 1965. She had been on a voyage from Rouen to Belfast with a cargo of grain when she ran ashore in heavy weather and poor visibility.

Flares were immediately fired but fell unseen. An SOS message was intercepted by the Isle of Man Coastguard but was unclear and was misinterpreted to the effect that the vessel was in difficulties off the Isle of Man. Lifeboats spent several fruitless hours searching for the *Zafaris* until the true location was discovered by a local farmer, Mr William McCulloch of Cardrain Farm, Drummore, who alerted the Coastguard.

The Portpatrick Lifeboat was called out and the Drummore Lifesaving Team were summoned to the scene of the wreck. On their arrival the coastguards lowered a rope ladder down the 200 foot cliff face and one of their members, Magnus Scollay, descended to the base.

While waiting to be rescued the Greek crew had succeeded in getting a line ashore and organised a shuttle service in a small rubber dinghy from the *Zafaris* to the shore. The crew were then individually assisted up the rope ladder to the top of the cliff and safety. After being examined by a local doctor four of the crew were taken to hospital in Stranraer as three were suffering from exposure and one had received burns from setting off the flares.

It was later discovered that a member of the crew had taken to a liferaft shortly after the vessel stranded but unfortunately only the raft was found after an extensive search by air and sea. The *Zafaris* had been extensively holed as she went ashore and her holds soon flooded. Later that month during stormy conditions she broke her back and became a total loss. Various sources suggest that salvage was carried out at a later date.

The Wreck Today

However, remains of the wreck still lie in approximate position 54°38.383'N, 004°54.113'W (GPS) between 8 and 12 metres on a rocky seabed. The tides in the area can be very strong making care and good boat cover essential while diving the site.

GALLOWAY

Listed below are a selection of 65 smaller vessels wrecked within this area. This list is included as a basis for further research. Names suffixed by (S) denote extensive salvage work or total removal subsequent to date of loss.

NAME	BUILT	TONNAGE	HULL	TYPE	LOST	CAUSE	LOCATION
Aber	1857		I	PS	28.08.1871	C	Off Portpatrick
Agnes	1833	37nt	W	Sr	02.10.1900	F	Off Corsewall Point
Agnes Anderson	1855	1088nt	W	S	03.10.1860	S	Near Portpatrick
Albion	1838	88nt	W	Bg	27.03.1858	F	Off Mull of Galloway
Alina	1874	160nt	W	Bn	27.02.1885	S	Near Corsewall Point
Belle Adventure	1855	98nt	W	Sr	22.11.1881	S	Port Gill
Brilliant	1848	124nt	W	Sr	12.02.1894	S	Cairnryan
Calypso	1791	79bn	W	Bgn	25.01.1794	S	Bernhills, Portpatrick
Camlough(S)	1920	540gt	S	SS	14.01.1932	S	Monreith Bay
Celine		135nt	W	Bg	17.01.1872	S	Morroch Bay
Clyde(S)			W	SS	15.06.1833	S	Near Port Logan
Clydesdale	1826	145gt	W	PS	15.05.1828	S	Corsewall Point
Daisy		93nt	W	Bn	24.03.1886	S	Laggan Point
Dasher	1821	130nt	W	PS	19.12.1830	S	Portpatrick
Douro	1867	195nt	W	Bn	10.02.1872	F	Corsewall Point
Eugine	1844	150nt	W	Bg	06.02.1856	S	Near Portpatrick
Eunomia	1857	446bn	W	Bk	04.11.1883	S	2m NW Mull of Galloway
Falcon	1864	302nt	W	Bkn	19.02.1883	Fr	Cairnryan
Friends	1798	112bn	W	Bgn	30.12.1844	S	Dally Bay
Garnet	1889	485gt	S	SS	02.04.1890	S	Cardrain
General Cathcart	1855	45nt	W	Sr	15.08.1890	S	Portpatrick
Glenwillliam	1880	255nt	I	SS	15.06.1887	C	Off Portpatrick
Gulnare		271bn	W	Bk	06.05.1867	S	Dunman, Crammag Head
Hayburn	1882	149gt	I	SS	17.07.1889	S	Broadsea Bay
Hinda	1839	289bn	W	Bk	12.05.1850	S	0.5m South of Corsewall Pt
Hope		96nt	W	Bg	03.03.1879	C	Off Corsewall Point
Intrepid	1853	59nt	W	Sr	06.10.1879	S	Corsewall Point
Jane	1856	154gt	W	Bgn	29.10.1863	S	West Tarbet Bay
Jura	1861	87gt	I	SS	30.09.1863	S	Cardrain

NAME	BUILT	TONNAGE	HULL	TYPE	LOST	CAUSE	LOCATION
Kitty Clyde	1899	101nt	W	Bkn	07.02.1895	S	Money Point
Lakemoor	1917	2045gt	I	SS	11.04.1918	T	Off Corsewall Point
LCV 789			S	LCV	24.09.1942	S	Near Corsewall Point
Lion			I	S	01.02.1835	S	Portpatrick
Lurcher(S)			I	SS	22.05.1920	S	Morroch Bay
Macrae	1893	45nt	I	SS	07.12.1895	S	Clanyard Bay
Margarets	1849	52nt	W	Sr	17.01.1865	S	Corsewall Point
Maria		121bn	W	Bgn	08.02.1867	S	Laggan Point
Marianne	1897	560nt	W	Bk	06.02.1905	S	Galdenoch
Matty	1774	152bn	W	Bgn	02.09.1806	S	Near Stanraer
Mauritius	1864	334nt	W	Bk	06.11.1872	F	Off Portpatrick
Mocking Bird	1870	115nt	W	Sr	07.02.1890	S	Entrance to Loch Ryan
Morag Glen		46nt	I	SS	29.11.1898	F	Off Corsewall Point
Mount Carmel(S)		315bn	W	Bk	29.10.1863	S	Mull of Galloway
Nevis(S)		58nt	I	SS	12.12.1898	S	Labrax Bay
Nora	1867	214nt	W	Bkn	20.09.1896	S	Near Portpatrick
Nora Caine	1877	93nt	W	Sr	13.02.1895	S	Gregory Point
Norseman	1875	155nt	I	SS	27.12.1879	F	Off Portpatrick
Nouva Fortuna	1845	292nt	W	Bk	27.12.1852	S	Port Logan
Orange Field		100bn	W	Bg	20.07.1790	S	N of Portpatrick
Oronoko	1787	105bn	W	Bgn	11.01.1810	S	Portpatrick
Peruvian	1845	64nt	W	Sr	01.11.1878	F	Off Galdenoch
Rio Verde	1901	4025gt	S	SS	21.02.1918	T	4m W of Crammag Head
Rockcliffe	1906	89nt	S	SS	11.11.1907	S	Portobello Bay
Rosanna	1852	153nt	W	Bg	13.04.1869	S	3m N Mull of Galloway
Sandhurst	1897	3034gt	S	SS	06.05.1918	T	6m NW Corsewall Point
Seamew (S)	1863	28nt	I	SS	22.12.1894	S	Portpatrick
Socrates	1906	110nt	S	SS	07.01.1913	S	Clanyard Bay
Solway Queen	1883	307nt	I	SS	02.04.1918	T	7m W of Black Head
Stag	1821	103bn	W	Bgn	05.12.1825	S	Laggan Point
Timandra	1865	105nt	W	Bn	02.04.1890	C	Off Mull of Galloway
Ulabrand	1899	2011gt	I	SS	22.02.1918	T	2m W of Crammag Head
Victoire	1861	97nt	W	Bn	11.12.1883	S	Near Cairnryan
Vivo(S)	1910	103nt	S	Str	21.08.1910	S	3.5m N of Mull of Galloway
William		244nt	W	S	13.07.1847	S	Near Portpatrick
William Castle	1917	223gt	S	Str	19.10.1928	S	Salt Pan Bay
William Penn		848t	W	S	29.10.1854	C	Off Mull of Galloway

HMS ULYSSES

1090 dt. U Class Destroyer.
Built by William Doxford & Sons, Sunderland.
Launched March 1917.

Dimensions 270' x 27.0' x 10.7'

The *Ulysses* sank after being in collision with the steamship *Ellerie* on 29th October 1918 with no loss of life. The *Ulysses* was later salved.

WARTIME LOSSES

Chapter 6

THE CLYDE

The River Clyde was used as one of the major ports and anchorages for Allied forces during both World Wars. As a result it was one of the most valuable targets for raiding enemy aircraft and U-Boats, either directly, using bombs and torpedoes, or indirectly, by placing mines in the busy shipping channels.

There were, therefore, many casualties on the river during both wars. Many have already been mentioned in previous chapters but, due to the inevitable censorship in place during wartime, there are many ships known to be lost 'in the Clyde' but their exact or even approximate whereabouts are unknown.

This chapter lists details of a few wrecks in this category which could be worthy of further research.

SS ***Warrior*** - sank on 15th March 1941 after striking a mine.

K-13

2650dt. Steel submarine.
Built by Fairfield S B & E Co Ltd, Glasgow.
Launched 1916.

It is strange that out of the 6 submarines to have sunk in the Firth of Clyde only one was lost through conflict, two by planned action, and three by accident. It was the latter cause that resulted in the loss of the *K-13* on 29th January 1917 while she was undergoing her acceptance trials in the Gareloch. Fortunately she passed her initial diving trial to 80 feet and some of the certifying Naval staff disembarked prior to a further dive.

It was during the second dive that things went horribly wrong. The submarine went into a uncontrolled descent coming to rest 64 feet below on the bed of the loch. 80 people had remained on board and they were now entombed with all attempts to raise the vessel proving unsuccessful.

Seawater was pouring into the submarine and orders to close the watertight doors were given. Meanwhile fumes emanating from electrical equipment created further problems throughout most parts of the vessel. Of the original 80 aboard, only 48 managed to gain the relative safety of the control room, 32 drowned or were poisoned by fumes in other sections of the submarine. The remaining crew could only wait for rescue and, as oxygen levels reduced, they became more and more tired and confused.

Fortunately the surface party had guessed that something had gone wrong. Divers were soon sent down to the vessel and an air line connected to provide fresh air. Connections were also made to the submarines air bank which after replenishment was successfully used to blow the forward ballast tanks and the bow eventually broke surface. Holes were immediately cut in the hull and the survivors finally resurfaced after being underwater for over 50 hours.

As to the cause, human error would appear to be to blame. *K-13* was part of the 17 strong 'K' Class fleet submarine, powered by 10,000hp geared turbine steam power plant for surface propulsion. It would appear that a number of air vents to the boiler room had not been shut properly during the dive, allowing seawater to flood into the hull.As to her fate. *K-13* was raised and re-commissioned as *K-22*. She was later to attain notoriety in January 1918, after being involved in the infamous 'Battle of May Island', ...but that's another story.

TOPAZE

421 nt. Admiralty Hired Trawler.
Built by Smiths Dockyard Co, Middlesborough.
Launched 1935.

Dimensions 157' x 26.2' x 12.0'

The *Topaze* was hired for anti-submarine duties in 1935 and was lost in collision with the battleship HMS *Rodney* on 20th April 1941. The collision occurred a few miles south of Little Cumbrae Island, and the wreck of the *Topaze* can be found in position 55°40.756'N, 004°59.156'W (GPS), in general depths of 74-75 metres rising up to a least depth of 62 metres. The wreck is substantially intact.

The ***Topaze***.

TRYGON

289 nt. Admiralty Hired Trawler.
Built by Cook Welton & Gemmell, Hull.
Launched 1908.

Dimensions 130.0' x 23.0' x 12.2'

The Fleetwood trawler *Trygon* (FD221) was hired for minesweping duties in 1914 and was sunk off Whiting Bay after a collision with an unknown vessel on Tuesday 30th March, 1915.

The wreck has been dived and is located on the east side of a shelving bank off Whiting Bay in position 55°29.783'N, 005°02.767'W (GPS) in depths ranging from 54 to 61 metres.

VANDAL

540 nt. V Class Coastal Submarine.
Built by Vickers Armstrong, Barrow.
Launched November 1942.

Dimensions 197' x 16' x 12.7'

The *Vandal* was launched in November 1942 and completed her acceptance trials by mid February 1942. On the 20th February she joined the 3rd submarine Flottila based at Holy Loch on the Clyde.

The *Vandal* commenced a 3 day familiarisation exercise off the north end of Arran on the 22nd February, under the command of Lt James S Bridger with a compliment of 19 aboard. The first two days of trials passed without event and the *Vandal* moored up in the safe anchorage of Lochranza on the evening of 23rd February. The following morning she was seen departing the loch around 8.30am. This was the last time she was to be seen for over 50years.

Submarine P-64 HMS ***Vandal***.

The loss of the *Vandal* has been one of the more intriguing mysteries in Royal Naval history. At the time of her loss various reports suggested that the submarine lay off Lochranza, north of Inchmarnock or even in the Holy Loch. It was not until 1995 that a remote vehicle was sent down to inspect an obstruction in 98-101 metres off the north end of Arran that the *Vandal* was finally located. In 2003 a team of experienced mixed gas divers visted the wreck and shot both still and video footage of the wreck, and confirmed its identity by filming the name *Vandal* along the side of the conning tower.

The wreck of the *Vandal* is located approximately mid way between Lochranza and the Clonnaig ferry slip on Kintyre, she lies in general depths of 100 metres on a gently sloping seabed. May she and her crew rest in peace.

BIBLIOGRAPHY

BOOKS

Blake	Clyde Lighthouses	Jackson, Son & Co 1956
College	Ships of the Royal Navy - Vol.1	Greenhill 1987
College	Ships of the Royal Navy - Vol.2	Greenhill 1987
Cunningham	Portpatrick and its Lifeboats	Wigtown Free Press
Drummond	A River Runs to War	Allen 1960
Duckworth & Langmuir	Clyde and Other Coastal Steamers	Brown 1939
Duckworth & Langmuir	Clyde River and Other Steamers	Brown 1937
Duckworth & Langmuir	Railway & Other Steamers	Shipping Histories 1948
Hocking	Dictionary of Disasters at Sea	London Stamp Exchange 1989
HMSO	British Vessels Lost at Sea 1914-18	Stephens 1977
HMSO	British Vessels Lost at Sea 1939-45	Stephens 1983
Johnston	Arran Shipwrecks	Johnstone Marine 1994
Larn Shipwreck Index of GB - Vol. 4		Lloyds Register
Larn Shipwrecks of GB & Ireland		David & Charles 1981
MacHaffie	Short Sea Route	Stephenson 1975
McDonald	The Clyde Puffer	David and Charles 1977
McQueen	Echoes of Old Paddlewheels	Gowans & Gray 1924
McQueen	Clyde River Steamers of the Last Fifty Years	Gowans & Gray 1923
Munro	Scottish Lighthouses	Thule Press 1979
National Maritime Museum	Shipbuilding Monograph 48	N M M 1980
Paterson	Golden Years of Clyde Steamers	David & Charles 1969
Paterson	Victorian Summer on the Clyde	David & Charles 1972
Paterson	The Light in the Glens	House of Lochar 1996
Tennant	British Merchant Ships Sunk by U-Boat	Starling Press 1990
Thomas	British Steam Tugs	Waine Research 1983
Thompson	Cook, Welton & Gemmell	Hutton Press 1999
Williamson	Clyde Passenger Steamers	Maclehose 1904
Whittaker	Off Scotland	C-ANNE Publishing 1998
Young	Britain's Sea War	Stephens 1989
Zanelli	Shipwrecks Around Britain	Kaye & Ward 1978
Zanelli	Unknown Shipwrecks Around Britain	Kaye & Ward 1974

NEWSPAPERS

Ayrshire Post
Ardrossan & Saltcoats Hearld
Daily Record
Dunoon Observer & Argyllshire Standard
Galloway Gazette
Glasgow Herald
Glasgow Evening News
Greenock Advertiser
Greenock Telegraph
Lloyds Shipping Gazette
Wigtown Free Press

PERIODICALS

Diver Magazine
Scottish Diver
Scots Magazine
Sea Breezes
The Engineer
Marine Engineer
9>90 Magazine

ARCHIVE MATERIAL AND OTHER SOURCES

Board of Trade Enquiry Reports
Glasgow Chamber of Commerce Archives
House of Commons: British Session Papers Wreck Returns
Hyrdographic Department, Royal Navy
Janes Fighting Ships
Lloyds Register of Shipping
Lloyds Register of Yachts
Northern Lighthouse Board
Royal National Lifeboat Institute
British Sub Aqua Club Wreck Registers

sub
Clyde